MIGHTY MIDGETS AT WAR

The Saga of the LCS(L) Ships from Iwo Jima to Vietnam

by

Robin L. Rielly

Hellgate Press
Central Point, OR

Hellgate Press
a division of PSI Research
P.O. Box 3727
Central Point, OR 97502-0032

(541) 245-6502
(541) 245-6505 fax
info@psi-research.com *e-mail*

Editor: Kathy Marshbank
Book design: Robin L. Rielly and Laurence Brauer, Wordsworth
Cover design: Steven Eliot Burns

The cover painting, by noted marine artist Richard W. DeRossett, depicts the incident which occurred on 27 May, 1945 off Okinawa. *LCS(L) 52* had been damaged by a Japanese bomb while on patrol at Radar Picket Station 15. She was being escorted back to the Hagushi anchorage by *LCS(L) 61* when the ships came under attack. The *Betty* bomber narrowly missed crashing into the *61*, which swerved at the last minute to avoid the *kamikaze's* attack.

Rielly, Robin L.
    Might midgets at war: the saga of the LCS(L) ships from Iwo Jima to Vietnam / Robin L. Rielly. —1st ed.
        p. cm.
    Includes bibliographical references and index.
    ISBN 1-55571-522-2 (pbk.)
    1. World War, 1939-45—Amphibious operations. 2. Landing craft—United States—History—20th century.   3. United States. Navy—Amphibious operations. 4. United States—History, Naval—20th century. I. Title
D769.45 R45 2000
940.54'1—dc21   00-023977

Dedicated to My Father

Robert F. Rielly

Who served as Quartermaster of the *LCS(L)(3) 61*

TABLE OF CONTENTS

FOREWORD

It was a long time ago when thousands of us, most in our early 20s, found ourselves assigned to U.S. Navy ships so small and so little known that we had never heard of them. We headed for the thick of World War II, not in airplanes, submarines, battle wagons and destroyers, but on LCS(L)s as part of the amphibious forces. We were soon under fire in dangerous waters, and were called upon to hew to our training and mission to prevail. We hoped to survive, however, not all of us made it home and many were badly wounded.

In recent years, LCS veterans have been having annual reunions, at which those momentous days are relived with some amazement. Every man on my ship, the *122*, has a different recollection of the events of the two days, June 10-11, 1945, when we were stretched to our limits. Eleven of my crew perished at that time. We survivors, most of us in our 70s (and not our early 70s either) have gradually pieced our memories together to make a coherent whole. That is what Robin L. Rielly has done in this book, put lots of pieces together to make a complete record.

We LCS veterans are very proud of our record in World War II. The role we played was much larger than were our individual ships. It is important that this account is now being made available to a wide audience as part of the history of the United States Navy. Robin L. Rielly has done us, the Navy and history a great service in writing this book, and we salute him.

Richard M. McCool
Captain — USN, Retired

INTRODUCTION

Over the years we have been fascinated by the exploits of our Navy ships of war. The *Bonhomme Richard, Constitution* and *Missouri* have long been household names and few would fail to recognize them. Alongside these important ships of war, however, have sailed and steamed numerous others whose names are not so famous and are not so easily recognized. This volume is intended to shed light on the exploits of one class of ships little-known to most Americans, but which rendered important service in the U.S. Navy in the latter part of World War II, the LCS(L)(3)s.

In the middle of the war, as the American troops began to take island after island in the Pacific Theater, it became obvious that improvements in close fire support were needed in order to protect them as they landed. Landing Craft Infantry (Large) ships that were used to deliver them to the beaches were fitted with additional weapons so that they might serve in that capacity. This proved to be successful and plans were developed for a full modification of the LCI(L) superstructure and below deck compartments, resulting in an entirely new ship, the Landing Craft Support Large Mark 3. Designed specifically as fire support ships, the LCS(L)(3)s mounted a tremendous amount of firepower on their diminutive hulls.

They were first used to support the landings at San Antonio and Subic Bay in the Philippines. From that point on, in numerous island landings in the Philippines, Borneo, Iwo Jima and Okinawa, they served as close fire support vessels. After supporting the landings at Okinawa, they accompanied the destroyers on radar picket duty and intercepted *kamikaze* aircraft that were sent to attack the landing site at Hagushi. Their record in the Okinawa campaign was impressive, with praise directed at them by their accompanying destroyers and from the command structure. With the ending of the war, they assisted in the occupation of Japan, Korea and China, as well as helping in the clearing of numerous mine fields throughout the Far East.

Although their activity in the war was limited to the last year, they were soon back in action again as part of our allies' navies. In that capacity, they were warships once again during the Vietnam conflict and served there for 25 years. The main focus here is their activity in World War II, with a final chapter on their service under foreign flags.

This work is based on many primary sources, particularly LCS(L) action reports and ship logs. Both of these sources are housed in the National Archives in College Park, Maryland. In that facility, I was fortunate in gaining the assistance of two specialists in the area of Naval History, Barry Zerby and Vernon Smith. Their efforts on my behalf resulted in uncovering many of the primary materials needed to complete this work.

The Navy Historical Center at the Washington Navy Yard in Washington, D.C. houses the Operational Archives Branch. One of the features of that branch is the L. Richard Rhame Collection which holds material devoted to the history of the LCS(L) ships. Archivist Judy Short, working with former National Association of U.S.S. LCS(L)(3) 1-130 Historian/Archivist Ray Baumler, has built a collection that is unique and valuable. Ms. Short has been most supportive of this work and has made a great contribution to it. Mike Walker, also of the Operational Archives, was instrumental in finding U. S. Navy records for Vietnam which were used in the last chapter. The same building contains the Navy Library. Numerous volumes of primary source material exist there as well, and Cathy Lloyd and Jane Hort proved most helpful with my searches. Of particular value were the official French Naval records, *Le Marine Francais En Indochine de 1939 a 1955*, and the complete set of *La Revue Maritime*. Both of these sources detailed the French activities in Vietnam on a daily basis and showed the activities of the LCS(L)s under their flag.

Veterans of the naval service are also a great resource. Numerous men who served on the LCS(L)(3) ships generously volunteered their time in interviews, correspondence and the loan of personal memorabilia, much of which has been included in this work. In that regard, I am indebted to: Frank L. Barnby, Earl A. Blakley, Robert Blyth, Ray Brosky, Harold H. Burgess, John H. Cardwell, James Clark, Joe Columbus, Jack Cox, Franklin Davis, Edgar DeCoursey, Nisi L. Dionis, Albert P. Jensen, Lawrence S. Katz, Harold Kaup, James W. Kelley, Walter Longhurst, William Mason, Richard M. McCool, Jr., Clifford Montgomery, Franklin Moulton, Phillip E. Peterson, Powell Pierpoint, Robert F. Rielly, Ed Robinson, William Scrom, Allen R. Selfridge, Mark V. Sellis, Joseph Staigar, Charles R. Thomas, Norman H. Wackenhut and Robert V. Weisser.

Although these are exhaustive resources, they are not complete. Numerous action reports and ship logs are available, some have been lost or misplaced over time. As a result, it is not possible to document the exact day by day activities of each and every ship in the fleet of 130. This volume includes the major actions of the majority of the ships along with their most important operations.

In many cases, the ships had similar experiences, particularly those relating to training and the mundane affairs of shipboard life. I thought it best to follow the activities of one ship that would prove representative. In that regard, I used the story of the *LCS(L) 61* as she went through her shakedown cruises, early training and her return home. The experiences of the men on board the *61* were shared by many in the LCS(L) fleet.

In the course of conducting research, one makes many acquaintances and, along the way, a few new friends. Kenneth R. Krayer, author of *On a Ship With No Name: The U.S.S. LCS(L)(3) 28 in World War Two,* was kind enough to share his knowledge of LCS(L)(3) operations in the Philippines and Borneo, as well as lending photos of the ships in action. In addition, he proofread the chapter dealing with those areas and made valuable suggestions.

Ron MacKay, Jr. is currently researching Landing Ship Medium (Rockets) history. Since LSM(R)s were frequently in the company of the LCS(L) ships at Okinawa, he has amassed a great deal of material, much of it relevant to my research. His gracious loan of LSM(R) Action Reports and photos is greatly appreciated.

Although this work is primarily about the experiences of United States Navy men in World War II, there is another facet of the ships' history that is relatively unknown. During the course of the Vietnam War, LCS(L) ships served there in combat roles for many years. They were the first real warships transferred to the Vietnamese Navy, beginning in 1954. A total of eight of the ships were engaged in combat there for up to 20 years. My efforts to locate former Vietnamese navy officers was facilitated by Quang Ta, who maintains a website for the Association of Former Vietnamese Navy Officers who graduated from OCS, Newport, Rhode Island. Through his efforts, I was able to communicate with a number of former Vietnamese Navy officers, many of whom commanded LSSLs (Landing Ship Support Large). They were most gracious with their assistance and in the support of this work. For information relating to the activities of the ships in the Vietnamese Navy, I am indebted to Hai Tran, Ngoc Nguyen, Quyen Ngoc Nguyen, Sinh The Nguyen and Le Van Rang.

Commander Huu San Vu, who served as Deputy Chief of the Vietnamese Navy Headquarters N3 and Commodore of the Offshore Task Division, hosts an extensive web-site devoted to the history of Vietnam and its navy. He was most generous with his help and proofread the section dealing with the Vietnamese Navy, making many valuable corrections to the text and supplying additional information.

Captain Kiem Do, former Deputy Chief of Staff for Operations in the Vietnamese Navy and the co-author of *Counterpart: A South Vietnamese Naval*

Officer's War, was a most valuable resource. He was able to provide detailed information about changes in LSSL armament and armor, as well as their use in various battles in the Mekong Delta.

Finally, I must give credit to my mentor in this project, Raymond A. Baumler. It was my good fortune to make his acquaintance at the outset, and his energetic support of my work has been most helpful. Ray has served as the Historian and the Archivist for the National Association of U.S.S. LCS(L)(3) 1-130 for many years and his groundbreaking study of the LCS(L)s, entitled *Ten Thousand Men and One Hundred Thirty "Mighty Midget" Ships: The U.S.S. LCS(L)s in World War II*, was a direct outgrowth of his interest in the ship on which he served. For my purposes, it was an invaluable resource. Throughout the project, he unselfishly shared his materials and pointed me in the direction of others. At the end, he proofread the manuscript and made numerous suggestions for its improvement and accuracy. I am greatly indebted to him for his support, assistance and friendship.

One cannot continue projects of this sort without support from family. My wife, Lucille M. Rielly, has continuously encouraged my efforts and served as a final proofreader, making valuable suggestions for the improvement of the work.

It is my desire that I have told the story of the LCS(L)(3) ships accurately. To those who went in "harm's way" in small ships and who met and defeated a fanatical enemy bent on their destruction, we owe a debt of gratitude. It is my hope that in the telling of their story, future generations will recognize their important contribution to our victory in World War II.

In spite of the great support and assistance of those mentioned above, the final responsibility for accuracy and completeness rests with the author.

Robin L. Rielly — 1999

LIST OF ILLUSTRATIONS

LIST OF MAPS

CHAPTER I

THE NEW AMPHIBIOUS WARFARE

It was the year AD 1260 and the monk Nichiren wandered the countryside in Eastern Japan preaching his brand of nationalistic Buddhism known as the *Hokke* (Lotus) Sect. Long a proponent of things Japanese and wary of the outside influences of China, he warned of a coming storm from the East, one that would land the Mongol hordes of Kublai Khan on the shores of his native Japan. According to Nichiren, the invasion would come because the inwardly turned Buddhist sects already influencing Japan had robbed the nation of its vitality and caused widespread corruption in the government, thereby inviting disaster. Soon Kublai Khan assembled a large expedition and set out to add Japan to his list of conquests. His invasion was aimed at southern Japan, specifically the northwest area of the island of Kyushu.

The Mongols had spread their influence from Europe to China and were convinced that Japan should be included in their empire. Mongol success was made possible by their great skill on horseback. Their massed cavalry tactics were superior to all they encountered and they won victory after victory. They felt that the Japanese would fall as well. Desiring a tributary relationship with the Japanese, the great Khan sent his envoys to the Kamakura court only to find his offer rejected. Since the Japanese refused to recognize his authority, he sent his first invasion force against Japan in 1274. It attacked several offshore islands and then moved into Hakata Bay in Northern Kyushu. After several days of fighting, the Mongols were unable to land in force and threatening weather caused their withdrawal with many casualties.

Several years went by, during which time the great Khan sent new envoys to Japan to demand the submission of the nation to Mongol rule. As a response, the Japanese twice sent back their heads. Determined to conquer the Japanese, Kublai

Khan assembled an even larger force of 140,000 men and set off to attack Japan again in 1281.

As the ships of the great Khan approached Hakata Bay, they were faced with obstacles built by the Japanese, which slowed their landing. The Japanese, utilizing their skill in individual combat, were able to keep the Mongols from disembarking and successfully deploying their cavalry forces. Two months went by and the invaders were unable to land *en masse*. Finally, the Japanese were saved by the intervention of a great typhoon. Referred to as a *kamikaze* or "Divine Wind," the typhoon destroyed much of the fleet at anchorage and forced its withdrawal. Of the 140,000 men who set out to conquer Japan, only about half made it back to China. The skill of fighting on land was a significant attribute of the Mongols, but their inability to place their troops ashore led to their downfall. This early event demonstrated the importance of skilled amphibious invasions. Had the Mongols been able to land and assemble, they might have met with success.

Amphibious warfare has been carried on throughout the course of history. Whenever nations sought to conquer one another, they found it necessary to cross rivers, channels and seas in order to land their troops on opposing soil. The Vikings were notorious for their landings on European soil prior to the expeditions of Kublai Khan against Japan. Success or failure during these ventures was frequently dependent upon the ability of the invaded nation to prevent the landing of troops. In those earlier times, the advantage seemed to lay with the attackers, if they could land unnoticed. In cases where they could not, as in the attempted Mongol invasions of Japan, the advantage was held by the defenders who could slaughter the attackers before they landed and deployed. As technology progressed and cannons became a standard weapon on board ship, the transports and their escorts could bombard the beaches and slow down the defenders to allow their troops to disembark. By the late nineteenth century, modern weapons of war had been developed that made this strategy more efficient.

The European experiences in World War I had not necessitated the development of new types of amphibious water craft. During that war, troops were easily landed in France, since the beaches were not held by the Germans. Accordingly, there was little pressure to develop amphibious warfare techniques or new types of ships. However Admiral Robert E. Coontz, Commander in Chief of the United States Fleet, wrote in 1925:

> In connection with landing operations, the Commander in Chief offers the following comments and suggestions:
> a. That the use of the regular ships' boats for the purpose of transporting landing parties ashore, when opposition is to be encountered, is a hazardous

undertaking and little likely to succeed. He considers it of utmost importance that experiments be continued with a view to determine what type of boat is best for this purpose.

b. Consideration of the necessity that ships detailed to cover and support landing operations be equipped with guns permitting high angle fire. This he believes is necessary in order that the Landing Force will not be denied artillery support at a time it is most essential.

c. That a landing operation is likely to result in disaster if the officers in charge of the boats are not experienced with their duties (Dyer Naval 51).

As the world situation developed in the two decades after World War I, it became apparent to England and the United States that the expansionist policies of Japan and possibly Italy and Germany might require the development of new ships that could land troops on foreign soil. Pressure from the U.S. Marine Corps for landing craft that would make their amphibious assaults possible grew, and during the early to mid-1930s, the Fleet Marine Force began to develop doctrines that would be the basis for their amphibious tactics in the next war. An overview of the world's situation at that time seemed to indicate that the major uses for these amphibious assault forces would be in capturing advanced enemy bases for use by the United States Navy. In the early 1940s, it became apparent to the British and the Americans as well, that the *blitzkrieg* type of warfare practiced by the Germans might leave them in control of the European continent, making amphibious assaults on the European coast a distinct possibility.

By 1936 the Navy had begun to experiment with various designs, finding earlier ones to be unacceptable and so "the Bureau of Construction & Repair began the development of a Diesel-powered landing boat, to be approximately 30 feet long" (Pittsburgh Papers 284). Continuous experimentation took place for the next several years with input from both the British and United States Navies. Increased military activity on the part of the Japanese was an ominous sign and the need to develop new types of craft became urgent. Japanese naval forces had already developed landing craft with a hinged ramp in the bow. They had been used extensively in 1937 against the Chinese at Tientsin (Barbey 16). In January of that same year, "the Secretary of the Navy established the Continuing Board in the Navy Department for the Development of Landing Boats for Training Operations" (Pittsburgh Papers 284). Members of this board included representatives from the Bureau of Construction and Repair, the Office of the Chief of Naval Operations, the Marine Corps and the Bureau of Engineering. Based on their recommendations, a five-year, Special Boat Plan was devised and civilian shipyards designed and produced 18 different landing craft prototypes. These were tested by the Navy in 1939 and a number were rejected. Two designs developed by the Higgins Ship Building Company in New Orleans were among the first to be adopted.

Andrew J. Higgins had developed a lighter for use by South American countries that he updated and redesigned with a bow ramp. Higgins boats were used throughout the war. The first of his designs to be adopted was 36 feet long with a ten and one half foot beam. Powered by a single 225 horsepower diesel, it could carry 36 troops or a three ton vehicle. Alternately, a cargo of up to 8,100 pounds might be carried. Designated as LCVP (Landing Craft Vehicle, Personnel) the small craft had 1/4" armor plating on its sides and ramp and was armed with two .30 caliber machine guns. The LCM (Landing Craft, Mechanized), which began with the Mark 1 version at 45 feet, was ultimately developed into several variations which stretched its length to 56 feet. In its final Mark 6 version, it could carry either 60 troops, a 30-ton tank or 60,000 pounds of cargo. As Landing Craft (LC) they were designed to be beached. Since they were less than 150 feet they were not considered ocean going vessels, although many did perform that task.

New developments in the European theater made it obvious that bigger ships, capable of landing large amounts of men and cargo, would have to be developed. American tanks had to be delivered to Great Britain and ultimately would have to be landed on the coast of Europe. Existing ships would simply not do the job, therefore three new types were developed: the LST (Landing Ship Tank), the LCT (Landing Craft Tank) and the LSD (Landing Ship Dock). As the war progressed, these ships and craft would develop many variations according to the demands of the war zone and its requirements. The original Higgins design that carried up to 36 men could not deliver enough manpower to the beach. Although they were useful, they had to be supplemented by the development of a larger landing craft. This need gave rise to the development of the LCI(L) (Landing Craft Infantry (Large)). LCI(L)s were 158' 5 1/2" overall, and eventually underwent a number of changes. Experiences in the Pacific theater demonstrated that additional firepower on these ships was desirable for close in-shore support of troops as they landed. The LCI(L)s were given additional guns, rockets and mortars and new designations as LCI(D), LCI(G), LCI(R), LCI(M) and LCI(FF). Eventually a new superstructure was designed that made this vessel a true gunboat. It became the LCS(L) (3) and it would be nicknamed the *Mighty Midget*.

Landing Ships (LS) and Landing Craft (LC) were designed to traverse the oceans and had to be seaworthy. Since they also had to be beached, numerous studies were conducted on hull shapes to determine the correct ratio-of-slope that would prove useful. This was found to be a ratio of 1:50, with the bow having a shallower draft than the stern (Pittsburgh Papers 285). Landing Vehicles (LV) were designed to be carried on ships and operate on both land and water, making it possible for them to land small amounts of supplies and troops. In spite of the seeming necessity for these types of craft, the outset of World War II found the United States Navy wanting. The only ship capable of amphibious assault work was the *U.S.S. Manley* (APD 1), a four-stack destroyer that had been converted into a high speed transport. First commissioned in 1917, her torpedo tubes were removed and she was set up to carry four landing boats. In order to accomplish this task, two of her boilers had been removed and her cargo space redesigned to allow for the transportation of troops and landing boats to the battle zone.

Production of LSTs and LCTs began almost as soon as war was declared on Japan. At the urging of the British, the development of a ship that could carry and land troops on European beaches was undertaken. British specifications "called for the use of a ramp on either side for putting the men ashore" (Wheelock Memo). In accordance with these and other specifications, the shipyard of George Lawley & Sons in Neponset, Massachusetts developed the plans for the new LCI(L) (Landing Craft Infantry Large). With the approval of the Bureau of Ships, the first LCI(L) was commissioned on 9 October, 1942. The appearance of the LCI(L)s in the South Pacific occurred as early as April of 1943 (Dyer Vol. I, 501). The first 350 of these new vessels were armed with four 20mm guns. Hulls numbered 351 through 1098 had five 20mm guns.

Although the LCI(L)s were primarily designed to land troops on the beaches, it was obvious that additional firepower would be useful in softening up the beachhead. This became apparent with the invasion of Tarawa on 20 November, 1943. Japanese forces there had constructed their defenses in such a way that the flat trajectory of the gunfire from the destroyers, cruisers and battleships was unable to knock them out. Once the naval bombardment had finished, the Marines were unsupported as they made their landing. With so much of the enemy surviving the pre-landing bombardment, the Marines suffered great losses. One resolution to the problem of close support of the troops was to add firepower to the recently arrived LCI(L)s, since their shallow draft enabled them to get close to shore. The Navy began to experiment with conversions of some of these craft into gunboats. Captain Roy T. Cowdrey is credited with the experimentation that ultimately led to the development of LCI(R) (Rockets) ships. Serving as senior ship repair officer to Admiral Halsey, Cowdrey took two LCI(L)s, the *24* and the *68*, and added more armor, guns, and a large number of rocket launchers (Ladd 42). The two ships made their debut at the invasion of Cape Gloucester, New Britain on 26 December, 1943. Contributing their firepower to the assault, the new adaptations proved successful and ultimately over 100 LCI(R)s were produced. Additional hybrids were soon developed. One was designated the LCI(G) (Guns) and was produced in six different types, A through F, the letters designating different weapons combinations. A second support vessel, the LCI(M) (Mortars) was still

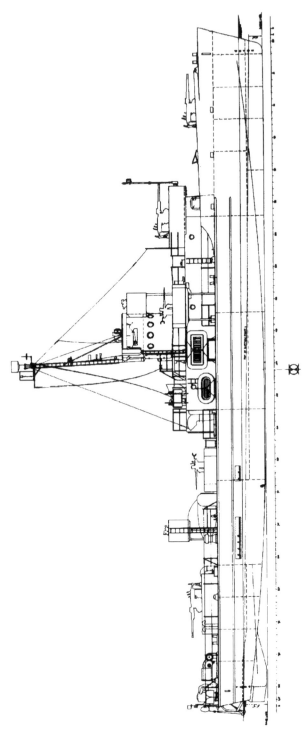

LCS(L)(3) Outboard Profile - Copy of Plan No. 1711-111-6 by George Lawley & Son Corp. Courtesy of National Archives.

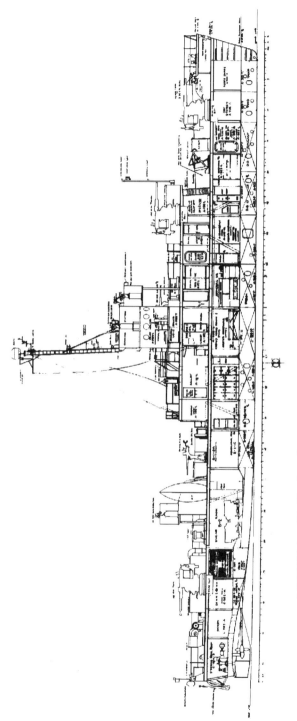

LCS(L)(3) Inboard Profile - Copy of Plan No. 1711-111-23 by George Lawley & Son Corp. Courtesy of National Archives.

another variation. Once modified, its armament consisted of one 40mm single, three 4.2 chemical mortars and four 20mm machine guns. Forty-two LCI(L)s were thus converted. LCI(D) (Demolition) ships were developed to carry Underwater Demolition Teams to the beaches and LC(FF) (Flotilla Flag Ships) were equipped with additional radar and communications gear so that they could fulfill their role as floating command posts.

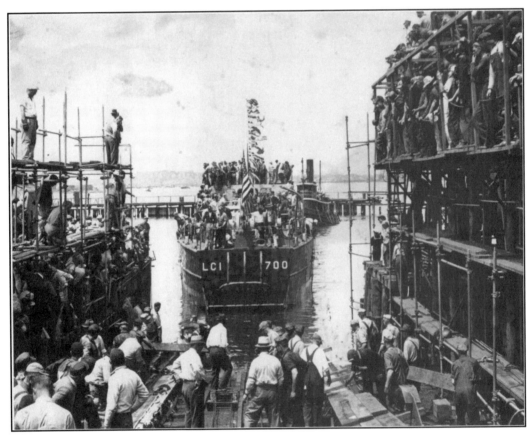

LCI(L) 700 **being launched at the shipyard of George Lawley & Sons, Neponset, Massachusetts. Photo courtesy of the Boston Public Library.**

The rocket and gun ships were considered to be temporary designs, since the original LCI(L) design was little changed with the exception of using the troop spaces for storage of ammunition and other supplies. A total alteration of the superstructure and arrangements was necessary so that the ship would be more capable of its assignment. To make this possible, the

LCI(L) plans were . . . modified to the LCS(L)(3) type . . . by George Lawley & Sons. The gun arrangements were revised; rocket throwers were installed; no landing ramp or bow doors were required; a revised and smaller deck house was installed; the flag ships of both classes were arranged to provide additional officer's quarters and radio and radar equipment (WWII History IV-6).

These vessels were constructed at three locations. In addition to the shipyard of George Lawley and Sons in Neponset (Boston) Massachusetts, which produced 47 of them, the remaining 83 were constructed in Portland, Oregon. There, the Albina Engine and Machine Works launched 31 and the Commercial Iron Works produced 52.

Portland during the war years was a busy place. Albina, at its peak, employed 5,200 workers and Commercial Iron Works 10,500. Both Albina and Commercial were on the Williamette River in Portland along with six other yards, all serving the needs of the war effort.

The two yards received their first Navy contracts of the war in 1941 and later on 10 December, 1943, Albina was awarded Contract NObs-1412 to build *LCI(L)s 1013* through *1033* and *LCS(L)s 61* through *78*. A later contract, NObs-1635, awarded on 5 April, 1944, was for the construction of *LCS(L)s 48* through *60*. Commercial Iron Works was granted Contract NObs-1258 on 24 September, 1943 for the construction of *LCI(L)s 725* through *780* and *LCS(L)s 79* through *108* (WW II Hist. C-1).

LCI(L) 402 **showing the later development of the landing apparatus. Earlier LCI(L)s had ramps on the sides for troop disembarkment. Also visible here is the small bow anchor and retrieval apparatus. On the LCS(L) ships, this gear had to be deleted in order to place a gun mount in the forward position. National Archives photo courtesy of Robert V. Weisser.**

LCI(G) 580 **on the Chesapeake, 6 May, 1944. This is an example of the Type D version, which mounted three 40mm, four 20mm guns and ten Mark 7 Rocket launchers. The rocket launchers were mounted on the infantry ramps on both sides. Photo courtesy of the National Archives.**

Ships exiting the yards displayed several varieties of paint scheme. They reflected the requirements of the Bureau of Ships Measures. In all, six camouflage designs were used for the LCS(L) ships Some sported a two-tone green camouflage pattern designed to break up the outline completely. Others were painted a solid Haze Gray or Navy Blue. Another paint scheme placed a darker gray on the bottom half of the ship which extended forward and then swept back. Still another pattern saw the ships painted Navy Blue from the deckline down and Haze Gray topsides.

Whatever their original paint scheme, it didn't usually last throughout the war. Haze Gray was a bit too visible at night and too easy for the enemy to see. It was not unusual for the ships to change their paint schemes periodically. The *LCS(L) 61* exited the Albina shipyard painted according to Measure 33 Design 14L, which was a combination of Pale Green and Ocean Green. She was later changed at Pearl Harbor to a Navy Blue bottom and a Haze Gray top (Measure 22) and toward the end of the war was painted a solid Navy Blue (Measure 21). The determining factor in these paint schemes was usually the geographic area in which the ship was operating. Ocean color varied from location to location and the proper camouflage paint helped protect the vessels.

LCI(R) 73 of the 7th Amphibious Forces, 28 May, 1944. Official U.S. Navy Photograph, courtesy of the National Archives.

LCI(R)s fire on Peleliu in support of landing by the 1st Marine Division, 15 September, 1944. Eighteen of these LCI(R)s, accompanied by four LCI(M)s participated in the landings. Official U.S. Navy Photograph courtesy of Robert V. Weisser.

LCI(L) 1013 - HULL No. 163
After Quarter Looking Forward
ALBINA ENGINE & MACHINE WORKS
PORTLAND, OREGON
JAN. 28, 1944

LCI(L) 1013 under construction at the Albina Engine and Machine Works in Portland, Oregon, 28 January, 1944. LCS(L)s and LCI(L)s had identical hulls, but the deck and interior arrangements differed. Albina was a major contributor to the production of LCI(L)s and LCS(L)s during the war. Photo courtesy of the National Archives.

Armament on the ships differed slightly, with the bow gun having three varieties. The first series of ships produced had a single 3"/50 gun which subsequently was changed to a single 40mm gun and eventually to a director controlled twin 40mm. Virtually all of the ships with 3"/50 guns were put to use in the Philippines and Borneo, and historian Ray Baumler has suggested that this armament was at the request of General MacArthur (Baumler Guns). The larger gun was useful in intercepting inter-island barge traffic and also in shelling shore installations. Ships engaged in the assault on Iwo Jima were all fitted with the interim single 40mm gun. Use of this gun was probably caused by a temporary shortage of director-controlled twin 40s (Baumler letter 4Nov97). Other ships, fitted with a twin 40mm gun in the bow were much better equipped to handle the *kamikazes* off Okinawa.

In all, half of the ships were equipped with either the single 3"/50 or the twin 40mm guns, and the other half with the single 40.

Gun Type	Ship Numbers	Date of Commission	Shipyard
3"/50	1-10	June to Sept., 1944	Lawley
	26-30	Aug. To Sept., 1944	Commercial
	41-47	Oct. , Nov., 1944	Commercial
	48-50	Aug., Sept., 1944	Albina
	58-60	Nov., 1944	Albina
	79-80	Nov., 1944	Commercial
Single 40mm	11-25	Sept. , Oct., 1944	Lawley
	31-40	Sept., Oct., 1944	Commercial
	51-57	Sept., Oct., 1944	Albina
	61-66	Nov., Dec., 1944, Jan., 1945	Albina
	81-89	Nov., Dec., 1944	Commercial
	109-124	Oct., Nov., Dec., 1944	Lawley
Twin 40mm	67-78	Jan., Feb., Mar., 1945	Albina
	92-108	Jan., Feb., Mar., 1945	Commercial
	125-130	Dec., 1944, Jan., 1945	Lawley

Whatever the reason for the armament, the new ships proved to be effective. With their new configuration and armament, the LCS(L)s were a decided improvement over their half-sister LCI(G)s. The 3"/50 guns proved useful against fortified shore targets and small Japanese ships. As an interim fit, the single 40mm gun without director control was not as powerful. The twin 40mm guns were the preferred armament for the radar picket boats during the Okinawa campaign. So impressive was the LCS(L)'s firepower that historian Walter Karig described them as "looking something like a Fourth of July fireworks when all weapons were blazing," (Karig 1949, 261) and Norman Friedman would claim that they "were the most heavily armed of the wartime gunboats (Friedman 222). Referred to frequently as "miniature destroyers" and "Mighty Midgets," the LCS(L) ships became well known after their initiation during the invasion of the Philippines which began in January of 1945. According to J. P. Murphy, the LCS(L)s had "the greatest amount of fire power per ton of any ship in the fleet" (Murphy 2). This was not surprising, since all this armament was mounted on the original inch-thick hull of the LCI(L). Vulnerable to attack as were all ships, their great firepower made them well able to defend themselves.

Some of those who would serve on the new LCS(L)(3) ships had already seen service on other landing craft in the European theater. Joe Columbus, who became the Chief Boatswain's Mate on board the *LCS(L)(3) 61*, recalls the first time he saw the new gunboat: "When I walked aboard the first LCS, I said 'wow.' It was all guns, no troops to worry about. We had a 65 man crew. It took more men to operate all the extra equipment. It had twin 40mm guns, 20mm guns and three .50 caliber machine guns as well as fire fighting equipment. No more worrying about carrying troops, it was going to be a lot different" (Columbus letter).

One of the unique features of the ships, shared with their sister LCI(L)s, was the ability to be beached. Since the LCI(L)s were designed to land troops, it was also possible to beach the new LCS(L) types if needed. In practice, the ship headed straight into the beach and dropped the stern anchor a couple of hundred yards out from shore. Mounted on the stern was a 1,000 pound Danforth type anchor which had the ability to hold in sand or mud. Under full power, the bow of the ship was run up onto the beach. With the anchor and cable trailing behind her, the ship was prevented from broaching. To get off the beach, the ship reversed its engines and hauled itself off with the stern winch. This type of maneuver was rarely performed by the LCS(L)s during the war. A beached ship was a stationary target and only under emergency conditions did LCS(L) captains beach theirs. A major benefit of their shallow draft was that it made it possible to run them in close to shore.

Naval amphibious strategy was still being developed at the outset of the Pacific war. Within a short period of time it became obvious that closer coordination of shipboard fire and landing operations was necessary. This became apparent at Tarawa when new strategies were devised. Older methods held that fire support ships should maneuver rapidly offshore while bombarding targets in order to avoid being hit themselves. At Tarawa, it was noted that ships could remain stationary and still deliver pre-invasion gunfire to the shore targets. According to Marine Colonel Donald M. Weller, the important lesson learned at Tarawa was that the landing of troops had to be closely coordinated with the lifting of naval gunfire support. He observed that the landings at Gallipoli would have succeeded rather than having been a disaster, if the operations had been properly coordinated (Weller 841). Too much of a time lag between the ending of naval gunfire and the landing of the troops allowed the enemy to recover and stiffen their defenses. After Tarawa, new methods were used that saw supporting craft, such as the newly modified LCI(L)s and eventually the LCS(L)s, lead the troop landing craft ashore and remain close in to render assistance with their rockets, 40mm and 20mm guns.

During the war, the new LCS(L) ships performed a variety of tasks. Since they were designated as support ships for landing craft, their usual duty involved going in close to shore just prior to the landing of troops. They ran to within a few hundred yards of the beach and fired a salvo of 120 rockets. They would then turn, run parallel to the beach and strafe the area with their twin 40mm guns and 20mm guns. After reforming off shore, they led the landing craft into the beach and fired off another salvo of rockets. At that point, they slowed down and allowed the landing craft to pass by them. For the remainder of the assault, they cruised inshore, firing at targets of opportunity in support of the infantry.

Although this was one of their standard tasks, it was not the first time they would see action during an invasion attempt. For several days prior to the landing of troops, the LCS(L)s frequently had other hazardous assignments. The approaches to many of the beaches were mined or contained underwater obstacles that had to be cleared away so that the troops could land. First on the scene were the minesweepers, which had the job of cutting loose the tethered mines that could destroy landing craft. Once their cables were cut and they floated to the surface, the LCS(L)s detonated or sank them with small arms fire or machine-gun fire. After having cleared the area of mines, the beach approaches were reconnoitered by swimmers from the Underwater Demolition Teams. Dropped off by small speedboats, these men swam into the beach towing explosive charges to clear away obstacles designed to prevent landing craft from depositing their troops on shore. Fire from the enemy could be great at times as they attempted to kill as many of the frogmen as possible. To cover them, the destroyers and other large ships off shore fired into the beaches to knock out as many guns as possible. However, their deep draft prevented them from getting close enough to identify small gun emplacements. This was the task assigned to the LCS(L)s. Cruising in close to shore, the *Mighty Midgets* were able to identify machine-gun nests and other small gun emplacements that were a hazard to the swimmers. With their 20mm and twin 40mm guns blazing, the LCS(L)s helped to insure the safety of the UDT men.

Once the initial assault had taken place, the beaches were usually clogged with wrecked vehicles and landing craft that had been hit by enemy fire. Using their stern anchor, the LCS(L)s dropped anchor in deeper water and ran in close to the beach. There they would attach lines to wrecked DUKVs and other assault landing craft. After pulling them out to deeper water, they sank them so that the beaches were cleared. Although they were frequently required to perform this task, LCS(L)s were not well-suited for it and had marginal success.

On rare occasions, the ships were beached in order to assist in shore based operations. At Iwo Jima, *LCS(L)s 53* and *54* were beached to fight a fire in an ammo dump close to the shore. The unique firefighting abilities of the ships were put to the test as hoses were run up on the beach and crews from the ships assisted in putting out the fire.

The greatest hazards for most of the LCS(L)s came at Okinawa, where they were assigned radar picket duty and had to provide anti-aircraft support for destroyers attempting to prevent attacks on the main landing area at Hagushi. In addition, they conducted regular patrols throughout the anchorage areas, destroying suicide boats and laying protective smoke screens for the anchored invasion fleet.

As the new LCS(L)(3) plans became available and the desirability of these ships was noted, existing orders for landing craft were changed and some ships that were originally destined to be LCI(L)s wound up as LCS(L)s. The Albina Engine Works in Portland, Oregon, had been awarded several contracts for LCI(L) ships. In June of 1944, the Navy directed a change from the construction of many hulls that were ordered as LCI(L)s to LCS(L)s (Roberts 257). In this way the Albina Engine Works produced the ships that became *LCS(L)s 61* through *78*. In all, Albina produced 31 of the LCS(L)(3) ships between 26 August, 1944 and 26 March, 1945. They were numbered *48* through *78*. Commercial Iron Works in Portland produced fifty-two vessels numbered *26* to *47* and *79* through *108*. The George Lawley and Sons Shipyard in Boston, Massachusetts produced a total of 47 of the ships. Lawley ships were numbered *1* through *25* and *109* through *130*. Although the average time to build a ship at each yard varied, it was usually about a month. Lawley set a record when it produced the *LCS(L)(3) 118* in only nine days. The demands of war required the rapid production of these vessels, however that sometimes caused problems. Some ship's Commanding Officers reported weak or improper welds in some sections of their ships and others reported shaft problems. In the *Monthly War Diary of LCS(L) (3) 61, 81, 82, and 83* dated 1 April, 1945, Lt. James W. Kelley, the Commanding Officer of the *61,* stated that:

> The *61* and *81* are having trouble with their shafts. There seems to be excessive vibration present along with the heating up of steady-rest bearings. Various types of grease have been tried, etc. We have checked everything we can but cannot find the trouble. We are trying to get dry docking here. If we cannot, the *61* and *81* will have to sail under protest.

LCS(L) 60 shortly after her launching on 7 October, 1944 at the Albina Engine and Machine Works, Portland Oregon. Photo courtesy of Ray Baumler.

LCS(L)s 92, 93 and *94* under completion at the docks of the Commercial Iron Works in Portland, Oregon in early January, 1945. Photo courtesy of Ray Baumler.

THE DEVELOPMENT OF THE AMPHIBIOUS SERVICES

As the needs of war became apparent and the ability to land large forces on foreign shores became a necessity, the Navy decided that a base to train crews for amphibious warfare was required. "Early in February 1942 the Commander in Chief of the Atlantic Fleet recommended that a training center for landing exercises be established in the Chesapeake Bay area" *(Building the Navy's Bases* 278). That summer, construction began on the first of these bases at Solomons, Maryland, with others to follow at Little Creek, Virginia, Fort Pierce and Panama City in Florida, Coronado and Morro Bay in California, Ocracoke, North Carolina and Galveston, Texas.

The base at Solomons was located at the mouth of the Patuxent River and situated on a small island to the south of the town. Organization there was haphazard and the rapid expansion of the base caused difficulties. Ultimately, the sinking of numerous wells by the Navy caused water shortages in the town and many of its wells were rendered unusable by saline infiltration.

The rush to complete the base at Solomons was necessitated by the imminent invasion of North Africa, a situation which led to problems. Hastily constructed, it had few of the amenities of the more established bases and morale there was typically very low. The base lacked any recreational facilities and water was in such short supply that in the beginning it was only turned on for a half-hour in the morning and in the evening (CINCAF ATC IX 10-2). There was adequate housing for the men in two story barracks, however the streets were unpaved. Liberty in the town of Solomons was less than desirable for permanent personnel stationed there, with the small fishing village unable to accommodate large numbers of servicemen. There was no liberty for crews in training.

Solomons Amphibious Training Base, Maryland. Aerial photo taken 14 September, 1944. Photo courtesy of the National Archives.

Articles appeared in the local papers making it apparent that residents, while supportive of the war effort, were quite concerned about the impact of so many Navy men on their small town. On 17 January, 1943, *The Baltimore Sun* ran an article noting how the "simple life" of Solomons had been changed (Footner 20), and on 10 June, 1943, a poem by Alberta Woodburn entitled "Is This Solomons' Anymore?" appeared in the local paper *The Calvert Independent* (Woodburn). The impact of the war on the small community was obvious.

However, if conditions for the town's people were difficult, life for servicemen on the base was also hard. Word began to circulate throughout the Navy that assignment to amphibious training was akin to being demoted. Referred to as the "Siberia of the Navy" and "Ensign Disposal School," assignment to amphibious training was considered undesirable duty. This was probably amplified by Captain Daniel E. Barbey's well known speech to Princeton graduates who were slated to become officers in the amphibious forces when he told them, "Those of you who go into the beach with the first wave will find yourselves in a fortunate position if you are able to man the second wave. After the second wave, there will be a few of you left to go in with the third. After that, no one knows who will man the craft" (CINC ATC IX-18). Barbey knew his subject well. Ultimately he would become MacArthur's leading expert on amphibious warfare and would retire as a Vice Admiral. Although his speech may have been poorly received at the time, his assessment of the hazards of amphibious warfare would prove to be all too accurate.

Word reached the Naval Academy as well. In the spring of 1944, Midshipmen seated in Bancroft Hall, about to have their dinner, were advised via an announcement over the public address system that 50 volunteers were needed for the amphibious service. Commander Edwin Thomas, future Commander of LCS(L) Flotilla 3, Group 8, had been sent to the Academy to recruit for the amphibious forces. At first the announcement was greeted with derision. However, word soon began to circulate that volunteers might actually get a position as a Commanding Officer or Executive Officer and a spot promotion to Lieutenant Senior Grade. Within a short time, 50 men from the Class of '45 had volunteered. Their classes had been accelerated and they were to graduate in June of 1944. Of the 50 men who volunteered, twelve served on LCS(L)s and became Commanding Officers, and the other 38 served on LSTs and LSMs. Only a couple of the men wound up as skippers on LSTs, and none filled that position on the LSMs.

As the base began its training program, crews for LCI(L)s, LCS(L)(3)s, and LCTs trained in the same classes with the same instructors. "The most famous of the training officers at ATB, Solomons was Commander Neill Phillips, USN" (CINC ATC IX-48). Phillips was a controversial officer whose emphasis on rules and regulations caused a general lowering of morale. However, he did get the job done

(CINC ATC IX-48). Phillips was given command of LCS(L)(3) Flotilla Four in December of 1944 and led his ships and men in the battles around Okinawa, where they distinguished themselves in action. Apparently, Phillips did not improve as a morale builder. On one occasion, as Commander of Flotilla Four, he boarded the *LCS(L)(3) 61* at 0200 in the morning for a surprise inspection of the officers' quarters. Not finding things to his satisfaction, he ordered the officers to clean their rooms in preparation for a follow-up inspection in the morning (Rielly interview).

Training at the base covered a number of subjects, as well as familiarization cruises on LCI(L)s and LCS(L)s. Although initially the crews trained primarily on LCI(L)s, in July of 1944 the training was expanded with the formation of the LCS(L) Training Group "under the command of Lieutenant Commander H. Heine, Jr." (*The Beachmaster Final Edition 36*). Six LCS(L)(3)s were eventually assigned to the base for use as training ships. *LCS(L)(3)s 1, 5* and *6* spent their entire service time in that capacity. *LCS(L)(3)s 2, 3* and *4* spent about six months as training ships and then at the end of February, 1945 departed for Okinawa, arriving there in the middle of June, 1945. The six training LCS(L)s each had a permanent crew of 23 men plus five officers to oversee the operation of the ships, many of whom had already seen action on LCI(L)s and LSTs. Additionally, Heine had a personal staff of four officers and eight enlisted men. The crew of the *LCS(L)(3) 61* had a typical experience when they trained on the *LCI(L)s 569* and *692* and *LCS(L)(3) 1* (Katz 2). Continued expansion of the program at Solomons from June to September of 1944, saw between 8,500 and 10,150 men on board the base (CINC AF ATC Vol. II).

LCS(L)(3) 1 shortly after her completion. She became the first of the LCS(L)s used for training at the Solomons ATB and remained there throughout the war. Photo courtesy of the National Archives.

LCS(L)(3) 6 **at New Orleans in the spring of 1946. She remained stateside for the duration of the war and served as one of the permanent training vessels for the Amphibious Training Command. Photo courtesy of James W. Kelley.**

TRAINING

Solomons was set up to train sailors for all types of amphibious craft. Crews that served on LCI(L)s and LSTs were trained there, as well as those who served on the LCS(L)(3)s. In addition to familiarity cruises on their future assignment ships, the sailors also studied the basics of seamanship and small boat handling.

Quartermasters gained practice in "shooting the stars" and plotting courses. Gunnery crews were given additional target practice. Damage control teams worked with the hoses and pumps that were an important part of the LCS(L)'s equipment. Although the future LCS(L) crews did a lot of their training on board the LCI(L)s, this did not matter. In fact, more could be gained by using the LCI(L)s for practice.

The wheel house and the engine room were about the same as an LCS. . . . they put 3 LCS crews in the troop compartments. Each crew took turns running the ship for several days. The LCI didn't have all the guns the LCS had so it was just a matter of letting the LCS crews get acquainted with the wheel house, engine room, mooring, docking, anchoring. For many of the crew this was their first ship (Columbus letter).

LCS(L) crews training their gunnery skills with the 20mm on board the *LCI(L) 1003* at Solomons ATB, 16 October, 1944. Photo courtesy of the National Archives.

LCS(L) crews practice fire fighting at Solomons ATB on 23 September, 1944. Photo courtesy of the National Archives.

During the approximately ten weeks that the crew spent at ATB Solomons, the men gained the skills that would be necessary for them to sail their LCS(L)(3) across the Pacific and into the war.

While many crewmen were training at the Solomons base, others were training at Fort Pierce in Florida. While the gun crews were trained, however, many other members of the LCS(L) crews were busy learning the skills that would enable them to defend the ship and carry out its offensive actions. After a six-week training period, they were assigned to assist on the guns during general quarters. The men destined to make up the gun crews were transferred to Solomons where they joined their future shipmates. Additional training was held for the entire crew after they received their new ship in Portland, Oregon or Neponset, Massachusetts. During that time they would become even more competent at running a United States Navy warship.

Crew's quarters on board an LCS(L). As with all combat vessels, the crew's quarters were cramped and little room was allowed for each man. Photo courtesy of the National Archives.

THE SHIP'S WORK

The crew of the LCS(L) ships normally consisted of six commissioned officers and 65 enlisted men who performed the various duties necessary to run the vessel in its prescribed manner. Supervising the operation of the ship were the officers. The Commanding Officer had overall responsibility for the ship, made decisions based on orders he received from the Flotilla Commander, and was the supreme authority in all matters relative to the operation of the ship and its crew. Subordinate to him was the Executive Officer who was second in command and typically served as the ship's navigator.

The Gunnery Officer was in charge of the ship's weapons systems and its ammunition. Keeping the engines in good running order and supervising the engine crew was the job of the Engineering Officer. Contact with other ships in the fleet was maintained through signals and radio and was under the supervision of the Communications Officer. An Additional Officer, frequently referred to as the First Lieutenant, rounded out the command structure. He was in charge of the deck crew, damage control and other duties associated with the running of the ship. Each of these officers had a senior enlisted man under him who handled the routine duties of supervising crewmen charged with specific tasks.

The day-to-day operation of the ship was handled by the Boatswain, Coxswain and the Seamen. They were the laborers of the ship and were responsible for numerous duties such as steering the ship, docking, anchoring, loading guns, ship maintenance and whatever various jobs needed completion. The Boatswain oversaw the conduct of drills and ensured that everyone was in the correct place and familiar with his assigned equipment. Since fire-fighting was an important part of training, he made sure that every man knew his fire detail assignment. He made daily inspections of the fire-fighting apparatus, life rafts, life preservers and other vital equipment. The Boatswain had a great deal of control over the crew and regularly inspected their quarters and all the interior compartments of the ship. On occasions, he ordered the compartments aired out and bedding taken topside for a few hours. When heavy weather threatened, he saw to it that lifelines were rigged on the ship in case the crew had to work on deck.

The chain of command for this section of the ship's company is shown below:

BOATSWAIN (1)

BOATSWAIN'S MATE (1)

COXSWAIN (1)   COXSWAIN (1)

SEAMEN (12)   SEAMEN (12)

Assisting the Engineering Officer was the Chief or senior Motor Machinist's Mate who oversaw the operation of the engine room. He was assisted by a Motor Machinist's Mate and a number of Firemen who ensured that the engines were supplied with fuel and maintained properly. Firemen were usually referred to as the "Black Gang" and performed the dirty tasks associated with the maintenance of engines. Theirs was a noisy, miserable job. Secured in their engine room compartment, the men were frequently made ill by the smell of diesel oil and stale air. According to Motor Machinist's Mate Edgar De Coursey of the *61*, "it was terrible duty, heavy odor of fuel oil, you had a hard time keeping your food down" (De Coursey interview). Normally, the engine room was staffed by two Motor Machinist's Mates, each of whom looked after the four engines on his side of the ship. Nearby was an Electrician's Mate, in case his services were needed. His post was in the next compartment which housed the two generators. It was particularly nerve wracking during general quarters as the men could hear guns being fired but could not tell if they were about to be hit. A provision had been made to assist them in escaping if the hull were flooded or the hatches jammed. Included in their equipment was a torch that they could use to cut themselves out if necessary. This was more of a morale builder than a practical tool. If a ship were hit by a suicide plane they probably wouldn't have enough time to use the torch. When the *LCS(L) 15* was sunk by a *kamikaze* at Okinawa, she went to the bottom within three minutes.

The Motor Machinist's Mates on duty sat or stood at a desk near the engine room telegraph, which was connected to the pilot house. The Captain or other officer on the conning tower gave orders to the Quartermaster in the pilot house. He transmitted the order to the Motor Machinist's Mates, who adjusted the engines, signaled back that they had received the order, and made an entry in the engine log book. Usually the ship ran on two to three engines per quad. When it was possible, one of the four engines was kept out for routine maintenance. Another responsibility for the Motor Machinist's Mate was the maintenance of a steam generator and a fresh water evaporator that could convert a thousand gallons of water a day.

The main engine room, starboard quad looking aft. Photo courtesy of the National Archives.

ENGINEERING SECTION ORGANIZATION

CHIEF MOTOR MACHINIST'S MATE (1)

MOTOR MACHINIST'S MATE (1)

FIREMEN (6)

The Gunnery Officer oversaw the work of the fire directors and the operation of the guns. On board the ship was one Fire Control man assisted by seven Gunner's Mates. During the actual working of the guns during combat or practice, they were loaded by Seamen. A variety of guns were fitted on the bows of the LCS(L)s. Many of the first LCS(L)(3)s delivered had 3"/50 guns in the bow. Still others had twin 40mm guns controlled by Mark 51 Gun Directors. Aiming the twin 40mm guns was the job of the Fire Control man who operated the Mark 51 gun directors which were located in tubs near the guns. These proved to be most useful against air raids by *kamikazes* at Okinawa. About half the ships had a single 40mm gun in the bow that was manually aimed. These were not as useful against aircraft and not as effective against shore targets as the larger 3"/50 guns. There were usually two men in the fire control tubs, one of whom was a formally trained Fire Control Man and one who was his assistant. When he was on target and wanted to shoot, the Fire Control Man would close a key on the director handles in front of him. Working below on the twin 40mm guns in the gun tubs were seven men: a gun captain, a trainer, a pointer, two second loaders and two first loaders. The pointer elevated the gun and the trainer moved the gun from side to side. Gun tubs were lined with 40mm ammunition clips, each of which held four rounds. When reloading became necessary, the damage control men passed ammunition cans from the ammunition locker. Each of these airtight cans held four clips or 16 rounds of ammunition

Aft fire control tub on the *LCS(L) 91*. Photo courtesy of Norman H. Wackenhut.

The guns had to be cleaned regularly, and in a war zone this required speed. While on patrol, the gunners tried to get by until they went back to anchorage. However, even then they were reluctant to break down more than one of the 40mm guns at a time, lest the ship be defenseless. On board the ship were a number of spare barrels, and the usual procedure was to switch barrels on the smaller guns and then clean the dirty one after it cooled down. This was not usually possible with the larger 3"/50 gun or the 40mm guns, since the barrels were quite long and heavy. Each gun had a special range of motion and cams in the gun mount automatically prevented it from hitting its own ship.

In order to determine when other ships or planes were nearby, radar was installed on the ship. Two men, a Radarman and a Radarman Striker, took turns standing watch on the screens to identify approaching ships or planes. One Radar Technician maintained the equipment.

The health and well being of the crew was looked after by the Pharmacist's Mate, who checked on the suitability of supplies and water, rendered first aid and diagnosed various health problems that the crew might encounter. His duties included the dispensing of medicines and, along with the Boatswain, he supervised the overall cleanliness of the crew.

LCS(L) 35 single 40mm bow gun. Official U.S. Navy Photograph courtesy of Charles R. Thomas.

LCS(L) 8 twin 40mm and single 3"/50 guns. Official U.S. Navy Photograph courtesy of the National Archives.

LCS(L) 35 port side 20mm gun. Official U.S. Navy Photograph courtesy of Charles R. Thomas.

Electrician's Mates were responsible for the electronic system of the ship, its operations and maintenance. Dependent upon them were the Communications Officer and the men he oversaw. They included Radiomen and Signalmen. Signalmen were skilled in the use of Morse code as well as signal lights and signal flags to send silent messages between ships. Ship's officers and Quartermasters also had some training in the use of signals in case their help was needed.

Quartermasters were responsible for assisting the Executive Officer in navigation, taking readings through the sextant and maintaining the charts. During general quarters they were on the ship's wheel and in the emergency steering room situated over the rudder area at the aft end of the ship. The Quartermaster Striker assisted in these jobs and, during general quarters, was assigned to the engine room telegraph.

Peter Panichi and Fred Berter peel potatoes on board *LCS(L) 61* while on mess duty at Yokosuka at the end of the war. Photo courtesy of Robert Blyth.

The galley of the ship held three members of the crew whose job was to feed the men on board. A Chief Cook was assisted by two additional cooks. It was an important job, since it involved the servicing of every member of the crew. As cook Joe Staigar of the *61* recalled, "If you were a good cook, most knew you. If a 'so-so' cook, everyone knew you" (Staigar letter). The Chief Cook was allotted $.87 per day per man. A standard was ground beef, which could be prepared in a number of ways, from hamburger or meatballs to meat loaf and other varieties.

Normally a cook's watch involved one day on and one day off with the cook on watch serving from 6 a.m. to 7 p.m. Hours were not always consistent, with men unable to eat at regular times because of seasickness and the uncertain routines caused by general quarters during combat conditions. When the first LCS(L)s were put into combat in the Philippines, it quickly became apparent that they were subject to extremely hazardous duty. From that point on they were given the same rations allotments as submarines, which also had dangerous assignments.

The cooks were assisted by Seamen assigned by the Boatswain. Mess duty usually lasted for one week at a time, with three Seamen assigned to assist with cleaning and preparing vegetables and general galley duties. Tending to the needs of the officers was a Steward's Mate, who maintained the officers' quarters and laundry and brought their food to them. He had to make the ship's fare look as palatable as possible.

The breakdown for the 65 man crew was as follows:

Boatswain - 1	Chief Motor Machinist's Mate - 1
Boatswain's Mate - 1	Motor Machinist's Mates - 4
Coxwains - 2	Firemen - 6
Seamen - 24	Electrician's Mates - 4
Fire Control Man - 1	Chief Cook - 1
Gunner's Mates - 7	Cook - 1
Radarmen - 2	Steward's Mate - 1
Radar Technician - 1	Pharmacist's Mate - 1
Signalmen - 2	Radiomen - 3
Quartermasters - 2	

Although Seamen had their assigned duties, which could be varied, some also were assigned permanently as strikers. A striker was non-rated and worked directly under a particular job assignment in order to learn a petty officer's skills through on-the-job training. Thus there was a striker working under each Quartermaster who was basically a Quartermaster in training. Strikers worked in other areas as well and might be found serving as cooks or on other duty.

Life at sea included a continual round of chipping paint and repainting the ship. Here crewmen John Sarsfield (on deck) and Stanley Wicks (on platform) work on maintaining the *LCS(L) 61* at Saipan Harbor, 12 December, 1945. Photo courtesy of Robert Blyth.

FROM SHAKEDOWN TO WAR

Crews leaving the Amphibious Training Base had a wide variety of experiences. After they left the confines of Solomons, some embarked on a trip across the country to Portland, Oregon to pick up their ships at either the Albina Engine and Machine Works or the Commercial Iron Works. Still others headed up the coast to Neponset, Massachusetts to board their new ship at the yard of George Lawley and Sons.

The bus ride from Solomons to Washington. D.C. was usually uneventful, however delays in Washington before the train left, sometimes gave crews time for liberty. Anticipating the worst, they were prepared for low-class accommodations, but some crews were pleasantly surprised to find that they would be traveling on Pullman cars featuring individual berths. Still others rode in troop carriers that were little better than cattle cars with bunks. Trains were frequently sidelined as freighters with higher priorities moved through and the crews spent the time "sleeping, playing poker with the porters, indulging, and writing letters" (Katz 2). As they traversed the country, they made stops at Chattanooga, Kansas City and Cheyenne as well as in some small towns. One notable stop was in the heartland of America at North Platte, Nebraska, where the town's people regularly showed their support of the armed forces by putting on a big feast featuring great food and treating the sailors as best they could.

The North Platte Canteen was founded on 25 December, 1941 to feed servicemen passing through the heartland of America. Local farm families turned the town's train depot into a large dining hall. Here, Navy personnel pass through the chow line, *circa* 1944. Photo courtesy of the Lincoln County Historical Museum.

The North Platte Canteen, as it came to be known, began feeding the troops in December of 1941 when residents of the town learned that a trainload of their local boys would be on their way west and would pass through the town on 17

December. They waited in vain since the train had been rerouted. Not wanting to waste the food, they fed the next trainload of servicemen who passed through. From that time on, it became a tradition. In time, over 100 surrounding towns contributed food. Walter Longhurst, of the *61,* recalls, "The train was there for an hour or two, the women had a spread of food out there — pies, sandwiches. They were all grandmas — all had sons in the service. They were all farmers" (Longhurst interview). Servicemen were invited to sign the Canteen registry which is today a proud part of the town's history.

After arriving in Portland the men had a short bus ride to the Portland Receiving Barracks, where they were assigned lockers and bunks. Portland was a hospitable town. Since there was no regular contingent of military personnel there, the citizens of Portland were glad to host their visitors. A favorite local attraction was George White's Service Center. Sailors able to pull liberty could find food, a lounge, dance floor, game room and dormitories in case they wanted to stay over. It was a welcome break for men who had been confined to Solomons ATB.

The activities at Portland were in preparation for receiving their ships, which they boarded for the first time. Launched only a short time before at the Albina Engine and Machine Works or the Commercial Iron Works, they were prepared for service within a few weeks. Launching ceremonies varied from yard to yard, however, they were fairly consistent.

One of the first considerations was the selection of a sponsor. A survey of the lists of sponsors indicates a wide variety of women chosen for the honor. At the Albina yard, *LCS(L) 73* was christened by Mrs. E. Snell, wife of the Governor of Oregon and *LCS(L) 76* by Miss F. Barbey, sister of Vice Admiral Barbey. With so many ships to launch, the yards soon ran out of distinguished guests, and almost everyone connected with the yards had a wife or sister involved in the ceremony. Mrs. A. Allen, wife of the Chief Timekeeper at Albina commissioned the *LCS(L) 48* and Miss B. E. Johnson, a yard employee, christened the *LCS(L) 59.* Popularity contests were run and one woman on each of the three work shifts also got to christen a ship. Most of the women were connected with the work of the yards in one way or the other, with wives, daughters and sisters of various foremen and company administrators heading the lists. Also selected for the honor were winners of War Bond contests and the wives of prominent local citizens.

Launching ceremonies were usually held around noon so that workers on their lunch hour could attend. Prior to the ceremony, the sponsor and company officials met in the Yard President's office. Flowers were presented to the sponsor and her attendants and the group then proceeded to the launching area.

After the playing of the National Anthem, appropriate remarks were made by the Master of Ceremonies or guest speakers, after which the sponsor, her attendants and distinguished guests were introduced, and a Chaplain or civilian Clergyman offered a prayer. After this, the sponsor took her position at the bow of the vessel, breaking a bottle of champagne across the bow just after the vessel started to move, at the same time pronouncing the words of christening. After the launching, the company usually gave a luncheon for the launching party, at which time a small gift was presented to the sponsor as a remembrance of the occasion (*WW II Hist*. VI-5).

LCS(L)(3)61- HULL No. 184
LAUNCHING
ALBINA ENGINE & MACHINE WORKS
PORTLAND, OREGON
OCT. 14, 1944

Mrs. E. D. Lusby, wife of the Pipe Shop Superintendent of the Albina Engine and Machine Works, christens the *LCS(L)(3) 61* on 29 November, 1944. Photo courtesy of the National Archives.

A few weeks later, after a ship had been outfitted, she was ready for commissioning. These ceremonies were usually brief, given the urgencies of the war situation. Typical was the commissioning of the *LCS(L)(3) 61* on 29 November, 1944. The entry in the *Log of the LCS(L)(3) 61* for that day reads as follows:

> 0915 to 1200 Captain L.D. Whitgrove representing the Commandant of the Thirteenth Naval District ordered Ensign James W. Kelley U.S.N., prospective Commanding Officer to read his orders. Ensign Kelley read his orders and assumed command. The Port Watch was set with Lt.(jg) Mark V. Sellis, USNR assigned the first Officer of the Deck Watch. The ship was placed in full commission (2).

Not noted for its sunny climate, Portland provided a dismal, rainy day. The ceremony itself was described as "brief, damp and unimpressive" (Pierpoint 1) and Longhurst added, "I don't remember what the guy said. He made a speech, we clapped our hands and that was it — raise the flag and we were official" (Longhurst interview).

Once the ceremony was over and hull number 184 had been transformed into *United States Navy Ship LCS(L)(3) 61*, the job of outfitting began in earnest. Crew members who had been living a leisurely life of short work days and plentiful liberty found themselves working around the clock to prepare the ship for war. Nightly liberty became a memory and the average crewman got off the ship only three nights a week. One of the first jobs for the crew was cleaning the cosmolene from the ship's guns. This was a messy job and the cosmolene went all over the deck, requiring that it be cleaned as well. The *61* remained at the Albina docks on the Willamette River from 29 November to 4 December, 1944, at which time she got underway for the Interstate Terminal farther down the river. There she received her supplies of ammunition and moved on to new docking at the Oceanic Terminal where the degaussing of the ship took place. Large electrical cables were passed under the hull in order to de-magnetize her so that she would not attract mines. Crew members took their watches and other metal items off the ship to ensure that they would not be affected by the process. Several days were spent in that area, taking short trips to familiarize the officers and crew with their vessel. On 10 December, 1944 the ship headed down the Columbia River and two days later began her cruise to San Diego for additional training and outfitting.

This was the first ocean cruise for many of the crew and a number of men became seasick leaving XO Powell Pierpoint to observe that "This first trip to sea was notable chiefly for the waste of provision, and effort by the ships cook" (Pierpoint 2). During this trip the crew experienced their first general quarters when they had a torpedo scare. Fortunately, it proved to be a false sighting and the cruise continued. The *61* arrived in San Diego on 15 December and remained there for training and outfitting until 12 January, 1945.

For those who went to pick up their ships at the Lawley Yard in Boston, it was a mixed experience. Boston was a great place to pull liberty, if it was granted. Crews that found their ships nearly ready usually had no time to enjoy the city, but for the fortunate crews who had a short wait, the city was a great place to be. Crews awaiting their ships were billeted in the Fargo Building, which had once been a warehouse for the Wells Fargo Company. A number of the men staying in the building had recently returned from duty in Europe. Sailors awaiting their ships were treated exceptionally well and rumors abounded that their chow was being prepared by local hotel chefs. Additional training was held in Boston and included fire-fighting and other subjects specific to the LCS(L)s.

Once they received their ship and it had been commissioned, they found themselves dodging the commercial traffic in heavily-traveled Cape Cod Bay. Exiting the area through the Cape Cod Canal, they then made their way to the Chesapeake and underwent further training. After shakedown cruises, the ships headed for the west coast to team up with other LCS(L)s in San Diego prior to heading for the war zone. Their journey frequently involved stops in Key West, New Orleans and the Panama Canal Zone.

Ships constructed at both Portland and Neponset gathered in San Diego for additional training prior to heading west to the war zone. Off San Diego and nearby San Clemente Island, the ships practiced various maneuvers and the crews honed their gunnery skills with their 40mm and 20mm guns and their rocket launchers. For example, the *61* set sail for San Clemente Island on the morning of 22 December, 1944 in the company of several other gunboats. Along the way they engaged in anti-aircraft firing practice, trying their 20mm and 40mm guns for the first time. Their .50 caliber machine guns would be installed later in Pearl Harbor. That evening they anchored in San Clemente Bay in ten fathoms of water. The following morning the crews practiced rocket attack runs on the beach, practicing with their ten Mark 7 rocket launchers. The units mounted on the LCS(L)s were capable of firing 120 rockets in four to eight seconds and were designed to saturate the beaches before the Marines went in. In combat conditions, LCS(L)s usually assembled and advanced towards the beach in a line to launch their rockets against the enemy. Training at San Clemente was designed to give the crews practice in judging the correct distance. Normal range for the rockets was about 1,500 yards. The launchers were not moveable but were arranged so that the rockets would cover a large section of the beach with a fan-like pattern of explosives. Additionally, the movement of the ship as it plowed through the waves would increase the dispersion of the rocket rounds. LCS(L)s usually began firing their rockets from about 1,000 yards out. Each rocket had a contact primer on the nose and was equipped with about ten pounds of anti-personnel explosives. On that day in San Clemente Bay, the *61* fired 48 rockets and also practiced with its 20mm and 40mm guns. Ships training off California during that time had been assigned to Flotillas One, Three and Four and included the *12, 18, 20, 21, 22, 23, 24, 25, 58, 59, 60, 61, 81, 82, 83, 84, 109* and *110.*

The *61* returned to San Diego on the 23 and remained in port until the 26 of December 1944, with the crew taking advantage of a 48 hour liberty. The next week was uneventful, with the exception of another 48 hour liberty over New Year's. On 2 January, 1945 the ship was dry docked to have her bottom painted. On the 10 and 11of January the LCS(L)s bound for the war zone loaded additional stores and ammunition. Crewmen were up until 2 a.m. finishing the work. On 12 January, 1945 they steamed out of San Diego headed for Pearl Harbor and ultimately to Okinawa. The *Log of the LCS(L)(3) 61* details the beginning of the voyage:

> 1200 Made all preparations for getting underway. 1214 Underway on all engines using various courses and various speeds in formation with USS LCS(L)(3) 20, 21, 22, 23, 24, 81, 82, and 83. 1450 Steaming on base course 240(T) 239(pgc) 224.5 (psc) standard speed 10.5 knots (22).

En route, the LCS(L)s engaged in practice firing and maneuvers, and life on board settled into a routine. Indications of how problems might be solved in the future soon became obvious to the officers and men of the small fleet. On Friday, 19 January, 1945, Fireman First Class Charles Wise of the *61* became ill and was diagnosed by Pharmacist's Mate Harold "Doc" Burgess as having appendicitis. His diagnosis was radioed to the command ship which had a doctor on board. Within a short period of time, the command ship came alongside and Doctor Witkerson jumped on board the *61* to confirm Burgess' diagnosis. Wise's condition continued to deteriorate and the following day permission was granted to the *61* to leave formation and proceed to Pearl at full speed in an attempt to arrive there before Wise's appendix burst. In the interim, Burgess administered morphine in order to ease Wise's pain. At 0915, on 20 January, 1945, the *61* detached from the convoy and headed to Pearl at full speed (fourteen knots). Although this was only a few knots faster than standard cruising speed, time was of the essence and the ship reached Pearl Harbor on the 21 of January. Fortunately, the hospital was only a few hundred yards from the beach and an LCVP came alongside to transfer Wise. He was lowered over in a stretcher basket and taken ashore (Longhurst interview). He later rejoined his shipmates on 15 February, just before his ship left for Okinawa.

The LCS(L) fleet tied up in Middle Loch, Hawaii, and the crews prepared for their first liberty after the journey. Hawaii was enjoyable, but the crews were required to be on board ship at night. Sailors in Hawaii had many opportunities open to them; many spent the days swimming at Waikiki Beach, souvenir hunting or horseback riding. Those who wanted to make a phone call home found lengthy waits and lines as long as two blocks for each telephone.

After a few days in Middle Loch, the ships were moved to other locations for re-supplying and to facilitate practice maneuvers. Shortly before they left Pearl Harbor, they were fitted with their radar and the last of their weapons, three .50 caliber machine guns. They were mounted port and starboard amidships on the main deck and one on the gun deck, aft of the conning tower on the port side. Some of the crews managed to get additional machine guns and mounted four or five of the weapons.

Six of the LCS(L)s had an unexpected first assignment. Designated as Task Unit 13.11.1, *LCS(L)s 23, 25, 61, 81, 82* and *83*, along with two destroyers, were to escort 36 LCTs and four YMSs to Guam. The LCTs were about 115 feet in length but their maximum speed was only eight knots. Although the LCS(L) was no speedboat, crew members found the standard 4.5 knot pace of these ships to be tedious as they slowly made their way across the Pacific. Quartermaster Bob Rielly, of the 61, checked the ship's course along the way and reported that because of their slow speed, the convoy "seemed to be going backwards" (Rielly interview). As the convoy settled into its daily routine, the men began to adjust to life at sea.

Normally the crewmen worked shifts which had them on watch for four hours and off duty for eight. During their time on watch, some had specific tasks and others had a variety of duties. In the eight hours that the men spent off watch, they were expected to do their regular jobs. Gunners spent their time breaking down guns and cleaning them to insure that they were in perfect working order. Quartermasters spent time updating the charts and cleaning and painting the inside of the pilot house. Most of the seamen had a number of chores, including basic ship maintenance. Preferred watch hours were from eight in the morning until noon and then again from eight in the evening until midnight. That allowed the most normal living conditions. After the eight to midnight watch was over, the crewman could turn in for a regular night's sleep. However, in the war zone, general quarters might sound at any time. If men were at their battle stations during their normal sleeping time, there was no compensation for lost sleep. They simply went back to work. On picket duty around Okinawa this proved to be difficult, with many of the men called to battle stations at night. In some cases they went without sleep for a couple of days in a row. Sometimes men could barely keep their eyes open on watch after prolonged sessions at general quarters.

Eating accommodations on board the ships were crowded. The mess area was small and only about 30 men could eat at a time. Normal hours for eating were from seven to eight in the morning for breakfast, noon to one for lunch, and from four to five in the afternoon for dinner. As men lined up for their turn in the mess hall, those who had the next duty were allowed to go first. Meals usually lasted about 15 to 20 minutes. One of the breakfast problems centered around the use of the toaster, since there was only one available. Many disputes erupted over who was next in line to use it. Coffee, the one indispensable item in the work place, was often bad-tasting. If the stainless steel tanks in which it was made weren't cleaned properly each day, a metallic taste permeated the brew. After they finished their meal, crewmen took their trays up to the next level for cleaning and waste disposal.

Once the last meal had been served, the crewmen assigned to their week of mess duty cleaned the area and it was then used for recreation. There the men could play chess, checkers or cards. Many of the ships had a resident expert in one of the games. On the *61*, Seaman Stanley Wicks fulfilled that role. Wicks had spent his boyhood on a Minnesota farm and had passed many a winter night playing checkers. Crewmen who played against him related how he would announce his ultimate victory after only a few moves had been made. Card games were popular, with some of the men bigger winners than others, causing occasional fights. Men also shot craps, however, this was definitely frowned upon since it was illegal. Normally officers avoided the area, leaving it to the Bosun to manage. The Bosun's additional duties involved acting as a peace keeper during occasional disputes.

Many of the men preferred to sit topside if the weather permitted. There they could relax and enjoy the trip across the Pacific, telling stories of their exploits before the war and their plans for civilian life afterwards. The small library on board the ship provided some reading material, which also helped to break the monotony of the voyage.

The berthing area was confined, with several rows of bunks lined up four high from floor to ceiling. Each man had a locker that measured twelve inches wide by eighteen inches deep by four feet high. Clothes had to be rolled carefully in order to fit into these spaces. Under the bottom bunk was a space of several inches where crewmen could stow their shoes. Some of the men with large feet made it through most of the war without proper foot gear. If shoes in their size could not be obtained, they wore an extra pair of socks with rubbers over them.

Men normally had a choice of which bunk they could have based on the principle of first come, first served. On the *61*, Quartermaster Bob Rielly chose a top bunk at the forward end of the crew compartment. Over his head was a round hatch leading to the deck. He reasoned that if there was an emergency, he would be able to get out much faster through the hatch, rather than fighting his way up the ladder with 40 other men. He greased the hatch regularly to make sure that his escape route was secure. Bosun Joe Columbus observed this one day and questioned what he was doing. After he heard the explanation, Columbus made sure that all the hatches were kept greased. Stored underneath the mattress bedding on each of the folding bunks was a hammock. When a crewman was transferred, he rolled his mattress and seabag in the hammock and carried it with him to his new ship.

Ventilation in the crew quarters was poor in spite of fans that moved the air around. Men were required to change their sheets regularly, however, some did not keep themselves or their gear clean. In crowded conditions this could be unpleasant. Bosuns had to keep after some members of the crews in order to prevent them from creating health problems.

The ship had a head area about ten by 15 feet. In this space were two showers, four wash basins, three urinals, three toilets and a washing machine. During some periods in the day it was quite crowded, however in the late evening a member of the crew might find that he had the space to himself. On some days showers were prohibited. Normally the ship carried enough water to permit washing, but sometimes the men ran too much water and went over the daily allotment. Situated in the engine room was a distilling mechanism that could produce 1,000 gallons of water a day, but captains usually did not like to deplete the supply by more than half, since the water was also used for drinking and cooking.

The first stop for Task Unit 13.11.1, which was headed for Guam, was at Johnson Island.

> Steaming as before on base course 260(T) 259(pgc) 240 (psc) at standard speed of 4.5 knots. . . . 1715 Sighted Johnson Island at 230 (T)distance twelve miles. . . . At 1813 sighted surf bearing 010(T), identified as novelty shoal. . . . From thence steamed on various courses and speed to anchorage of Johnson Island. At 2000 let go stern anchor in 54 feet of water and veered to 65 fathoms of cable (*Log LCS(L)(3) 61* 102).

Many landing craft and ships had dual anchor arrangements. Anchors in the bow could be used but, under most conditions, the stern anchor was a better choice. Mounted on the stern of the LCS(L) and LCI(L) ships was a huge Danforth type anchor, which had great holding power. LCI(L)s also had a smaller anchor and winch at the bow. However, this had not been installed on the LCS(L)s to make room for the Number 1 gun mount. Unless there was some special reason for doing otherwise, the gunboats almost always anchored by the stern. The bow anchor available to them was not very large and, if used, could be dropped over the bow by a couple of men. Normal anchoring practices required that a ship have a scope of about seven to one. Accordingly, a ship anchored in 50 feet of water would let out about 350 feet of anchor line. That enabled the flukes of the anchor to dig in and prevented the ship from dragging its anchor. Since the LCS(L)s were designed to be beached, their stern cables were longer and provided the necessary scope. They carried 900 feet of " wire cable on their stern anchor winch drum. LCI(L) and LCS(L) captains also felt that·they rode better when the stern anchor was used (Hill 677).

Johnson Island provided a brief break from the monotony of the convoy. At that time, its most imposing feature was its airstrip. The water was so clear in the anchorage that the bottom could be seen in 60 feet of water. One of the main concerns there was the refueling of the LCTs, which took up most of the time. During their two day stay, the crew passed the time catching fish and convincing natives to cut coconuts off the trees.

Having taken a brief respite from the voyage, on 22 February, 1945, the convoy pushed on to Majuro Atoll, where the crews were to enjoy their best liberty before arriving back in Pearl at the end of the war. On this leg of the voyage they crossed the International Dateline on 28 February and crew members were welcomed into the realm of the Golden Dragon. This tradition was a long standing one among Navy men of the world and signified that they were true sailors. On larger ships elaborate ceremonies were held. However, on a small ship such as the LCS(L)s, the passages were noted but not always celebrated.

The small fleet steamed into Majuro on 4 March, 1945. Majuro was a "fine little atoll" (Pierpoint 2). In addition to the opportunity to swim in tropical waters, the crew found a USO show awaiting them. Liberty on the island began the next day with crew members allowed access to the Naval Station there. An added bonus was a four beer allotment per man. The novelty of the coconuts had not worn off and many crewmen tried their hand at picking them and enjoying their consumption until the effects of coconut milk became apparent. That lesson having been learned, Navy chow once again became the standard fare. Task Unit 13.11.1 left Majuro on 7 March on the next part of their journey.

This leg of the voyage took the convoy to Eniwetok Atoll, "a forbidding, barren, sun baked wasteland" (Pierpoint 2). They arrived on 12 March. Liberty ashore was not allowed and the crews spent the next several days there swimming off the ship and catching up on mail from a newly arrived batch. Working parties were sent ashore to perform various tasks such as taking on provisions. However, the majority of the crews remained aboard ship.

The convoy left Eniwetok on 19 March, 1945 and arrived at Guam on 26 March. Guam was the terminal point for the escort duty of the LCTs. Pierpoint said of the smaller ships, "Their performance had been remarkable. During the entire trip they had only one breakdown, kept excellent station, and rated cheers from all hands for a difficult job well done" (Pierpoint 2). Shore liberty was not allowed but some of the men left the ships on working parties. With their ships re-supplied, the LCS(L)s left Guam headed for Ulithi Atoll.

At this point the LCS(L)s were able to resume their normal cruising speed of nine and one half to ten knots until the ships encountered some rough weather. According to the Commanding Officer of the *61*, Lt. James Kelley, "we hit the tail end of a typhoon. The ship took a list of 33 degrees but snapped out of it with ease. . . . even the most skeptical aboard have faith in the stability of an LCS now. The ship was very wet. In fact the stern was awash a great part of the time" (*CO LCS(L)(3)61 letter 1 April, 1945*). This bout with rough weather gave the crews increased confidence in the abilities of their ships, which would have other brushes with heavy weather in the future.

Once the storm had passed, the crews exercised at general quarters. This type of drill had been frequent during the voyage, along with various types of gunnery and emergency steering practices. Normally a general quarters drill lasted from a half-hour to an hour, at which time the ship was secured. Through this practice, the crew would be prepared for general quarters under combat conditions, a situation that would be the norm during their days on picket duty around Okinawa.

A mechanical problem arose and the *61* and *81* experienced excessive shaft vibration. Lt. Kelley noted that the ships would need to be dry docked and inspected in the near future. That problem having been identified, the ships entered the lagoon at Ulithi Atoll on 31 March, 1945, after a two-day cruise.

Ulithi was one of the Navy's most important bases in the closing stages of the war. It was occupied on 22 September, 1944 by the Navy after the Japanese had departed. An oval shaped assembledge of low coral islands, the atoll featured a deep lagoon ten miles wide (east to west) and 20 miles long (north to south) that was suitable as a staging area for future actions in the western Pacific. Within weeks of its occupation, seabees were at work transforming the islands of the atoll into a giant supply station that would prepare ships for the invasions of Iwo Jima and Okinawa. Up to 300 tons of material came in daily and the ships were able to take on fresh supplies. Situated only six degrees from the Equator, Ulithi was described as "another Eniwetok, only worse" (Pierpoint 3). At the northern end of the atoll were several small islands one of which, Mog Mog, was set aside for recreation. Mog Mog featured swimming, sports fields, and movies, and was noted by Radioman Larry Katz of the *61* as "having a hot swing band that plays every afternoon" (Katz 6). After several days in port, on 6 April, 1945, the 61 moored alongside the *U.S.S. Mindanao* (*ARG 3*). This association brought unexpected bonuses as crew members were able to obtain rare commodities in the tropics during wartime — cokes and ice cream.

**Enlisted men on liberty on Mog Mog at the corner of "Hollywood and Vine."
Official U.S. Navy Photograph courtesy of the National Archives.**

Easter Sunday provided a rare opportunity for Catholic crew members who were able to attend mass aboard a larger ship nearby. Motor Machinist's Mate Robert Blyth of the *61* described the visit:

> . . . the powers of command decided that crew members who were Catholic could attend mass aboard a large ship of unknown description. A small boat was sent around to collect our group to go to the larger ship, the sea was rough and boarding and getting back out of the small boat was scary, the thought crossed my mind that I might not have to worry about combat for I might not make it back aboard the LCS. I guess the Commander wanted to give us chance before Okinawa to give our souls to the Lord, we already knew who owned our butt." (Blyth letter).

While at Ulithi, the crews learned that they were to go to Okinawa. They were pleased to hear that they were finally going to a war zone, but somewhat dismayed that they had missed the actual invasion of Okinawa which had taken place on 1

April, 1945. Assumptions that the duty there would be somewhat routine circulated, with many thinking that intercepting inter-island barge traffic would be their main contribution. The late arrival on the scene was blamed on the special escort duty involving the LCTs and they "were cursed fluently and frequently by all hands" (Pierpoint 3).

Late in the afternoon of 9 April, with their ships re-supplied and their gunnery skills sharpened by frequent target practice, *LCS(L)s 23, 25, 61, 81, 82* and *83* set out for Okinawa in the company of two destroyers, an ARL (Repair Ship Landing Craft), and an ARD (Floating Dry Dock) with its accompanying tugs. They would finally get into the war.

The fleet assembles at Ulithi Atoll on 15 March, 1945 in preparation for the invasion of Okinawa. Official U.S. Navy Photograph by Ensign Steinheimer, courtesy of the National Archives.

The new amphibious warfare called for a special breed of ship. This need was filled by the development of the LCS(L)(3). Here the *LCS(L)(3) 72* is shown under way. Photo courtesy of the U.S. Naval Institute.

CHAPTER II

THE PHILIPPINES, IWO JIMA, AND BORNEO

After nearly three years of war, the Americans had made significant progress in the Pacific Theater. Sweeping westward in a two-pronged movement, the combined forces under General Douglas MacArthur and Admiral Chester Nimitz had come to a crossroads. In the southern areas, MacArthur had taken control of the islands around New Guinea while to the north, Nimitz had swept through an area from the Gilbert Islands to the Marianas. Ahead of them lay two prospective targets, Formosa and the Philippines. Formosa was considered to be the more valuable of the two targets since it was closer to Japan, and its capture would deprive the Japanese home islands of strategic materials from their southern holdings. In addition, the construction of air bases on the island would give the allies the ability to exact a heavy toll on Japanese areas in China proper and also to wreak havoc on the shipping lanes. It was thought to be the more heavily defended of the two and would be costly to take.

The Philippines were valuable, but for different reasons. MacArthur had vowed to return to the islands, therefore, their capture was considered to be of great psychological importance. America would be perceived as a nation that kept its word. Within the islands themselves, numerous guerrilla forces were in operation. Their assistance would make the retaking of the islands a much easier task. Once taken, the islands would be useful in the effort to deprive the Japanese of their southern sources of raw materials.

Both scenarios were presented to President Franklin D. Roosevelt in Hawaii in July of 1944. Nimitz asserted that Formosa was the logical target. However, MacArthur made the better argument and the invasion of the Philippines was ordered to begin on 15 November, 1944. The timetable was moved up when successful raids by Vice Admiral Marc Mitscher on Japanese air and naval bases in the Philippines destroyed a large number of planes and ships. Mitscher's raids were thought to have weakened the Japanese to the extent that further delay might allow them time to recover. Accordingly, MacArthur headed for the Philippines with a combined force of 600 ships and 250,000 men.

Operations in the Philippines presented unique problems. To begin with, the nation consists of approximately 7,100 islands which span 1,000 miles from north to south. Most of the islands are relatively small, with only 154 of them larger than five square miles. Movement between them was possible by sea, however not all were occupied by the Japanese. As a result of the geography of the nation, many amphibious assaults would be necessary, placing the LCS(L) ships in harm's way time and again.

Recapture of the Philippines began a few days prior to 20 October, 1944 with the taking of Suluan, Dinagar, and Homonhon by the Sixth Ranger Battalion. These small islands guarded the entrance to Leyte Gulf and were needed to insure that the assault on Leyte by four army divisions would go smoothly. Landings in the area were resisted by the Japanese as they sent a massive fleet to drive away the invasion forces. From 23 to 26 April, 1944, three crucial naval battles were fought in Leyte Gulf. When they ended, all hope that Japan had of restoring her sea power and avoiding eventual defeat was ended. The three-day struggle decimated her fleet, and she lost nearly 60 ships. With control of the seas firmly in the hands of their navy, the American forces proceeded with the invasion of the Philippines.

Expansion of the battle of the Philippines throughout the islands came just as the first units of LCS(L)s were ready to enter the war. Arriving on station at Hollandia, New Guinea, were the LCS(L)s that would become the backbone of Flotilla One. On 5 December, 1944, the *26, 27, 48* and *49* steamed into Humboldt Bay and began to prepare for their first patrols in a war zone. Joining them on 28 December were the *7, 8, 9, 10, 28, 29, 30* and *50.* Among the first of their type to be commissioned, they represented all three of the shipyards, Lawley, Albina and Commercial. All been placed in commission by September of 1944. One thing that the ships had in common were the 3"/50 forward deck guns that had been ordered specifically to intercept inter-island barge traffic and shell the landing beaches in the Philippines.

Once there, the Flotilla, headed by Flotilla Flagship *LC(FF) 778,* began to organize its activities. First on the list of chores for the newly arrived gunboats was a patrol of Humboldt Bay. Ever mindful of the threats from Japanese submarines, the Navy brass put a number of the LCS(L)s to work on anti-submarine warfare (ASW) patrol. Beginning on 13 January, 1945, *LC (FF) 778,* along with *LCS(L)s 9, 10, 28, 29, 30* and *50* steamed back and forth in the bay to protect the anchorage against the possibility of attack by Japanese submarines. Their effect, if any, was primarily psychological. With no depth charges, they had little ability to destroy their intended targets unless the submarine surfaced. Fortunately, none were in evidence and the ships simply practiced maneuvering in and out of the harbor. Around 10 January, 1945, the bulk of Flotilla One, including *LCS(L)s 7, 8, 26, 27, 48* and *49* left Hollandia and headed for Tacloban, Leyte to prepare for their first assault. Other elements of the Flotilla, including the *28, 29, 30* and *50* sailed on 24 January.

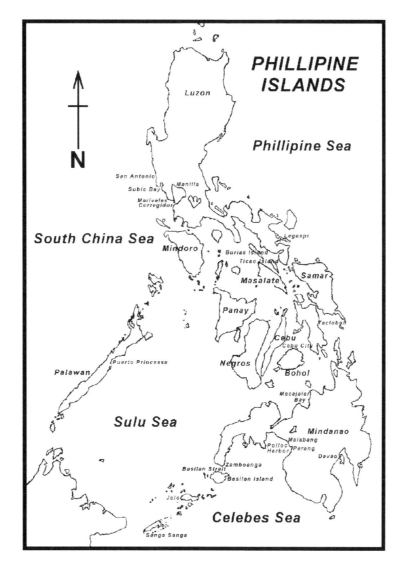

Locations in the Philippines were LCS(L) ships where engaged in action.

The first assault came at San Antonio in Zambales Province on the west coast of Luzon. A vital area, it contained an important naval facility on Subic Bay, as well as an airfield at San Marcelino. Capture of this area would cut off Japanese forces on the Bataan Peninsula to the south and make the capture of Manilla Bay, Corregidor, and the city of Manila an easier task. On 29 January, 1945, ships of Task Unit 78.3.8 entered the area to begin their work. This would involve the landing of 30,000 troops of the Eleventh Corps of the Eighth Army under Major General C.P. Hall in the area between San Felipe and San Miguel, Luzon.

Preliminary scouting in the preceding weeks had indicated that the area was not occupied by the Japanese and that the landing would be unopposed. However, nothing is certain in wartime. At approximately 0630, the assault force approached the landing area prepared for battle. Included among the fire support ships were *LCS(L)s 7, 8, 26, 27, 48* and *49*, along with *LCI(R)s 225, 226, 338, 340* and *341*. As they would do many times, they led the landing craft to the shore. Orders were received to hold fire unless fired upon and, fortunately for the landing craft and assembled support gunboats, no resistance was encountered. At 0832 the first waves of landing craft hit the beach and encountered only friendly natives waving an American flag. Once the troops were ashore, the gunboats assumed positions just offshore to protect the anchorage. They were to act as a screen against suicide boats which might attempt runs on the assembled ships. In order to safeguard the area, *LCS(L) 8* was ordered to nearby Silaguin Bay and Nazasa Bay for reconnaissance. Finding no enemy presence there, it returned to the screening area.

Grande Island guarded the entrance to Subic Bay, its capture would make access to the bay much easier. Task Unit 78.3.8 was also engaged in this operation. Forty-thousand troops of the XI Corps- 38th U. S. Infantry Division and the 134th Regimental Combat Team of the 24th Infantry Division, under the command of Major General Charles P. Hall and Brigadier General Chase, were scheduled to assault the beaches. However, the lack of enemy forces there made such a large scale assault unnecessary. Only one battalion of the 38th Infantry Division was sent ashore.

At 0815 on 30 January, the assault ships gathered at the rendezvous area. Once again, they preceded the landing craft to the beaches, but with no resistance encountered, they held their fire. Although the Japanese did have gun emplacements on the island, they had been neutralized by aerial bombardment. At 1150 the first wave of landing craft were ashore and the LCS(L)s and LCI(R)s lay to in order to provide covering fire if needed. By 1400 the area was secured and the gunboats left the fire support area to reconnoiter the rest of Subic Bay. These landings were the first of their type in which the LCS(L)s fulfilled their intended function, and they had done so without firing a shot or suffering a casualty. They would not be so fortunate in the weeks that followed.

LCS(L)(3) 28 **steams across Jaufeta Bay, Hollandia, New Guinea in January of 1945. She was one of the first group of LCS(L)s to enter the war zone. Photo courtesy of Ken Krayer.**

Corregidor stood as a symbol of American defeat in the islands. Its recapture was of great psychological as well as strategic importance. MacArthur had determined that the port of Manila would be useful in his campaign against Japanese General Tomoyuki Yamashita's 14ᵗʰ Area Army troops which were entrenched in the mountains of Luzon. In order to occupy Manila, it would be necessary to capture the islands guarding the entrance to Manila Bay, among them Corregidor. Heavily fortified, the "rock" was an important target. Just to the northwest of Corregidor, near the tip of Bataan Peninsula, was the small harbor at Mariveles. Its capture was necessary if Corregidor were to be taken. The town at Mariveles had an airstrip and nearby were the former headquarters of General MacArthur. Once again, Task Unit 78.3.8, including *LCS(L)s 7, 8, 26, 27, 48* and *49*, along with six LCI(R)s and two PCs (sub-chasers), was given the job of covering the landing. The invasion on 13 February commenced with shelling by destroyers and bombing by *B-24 Liberators*. Once their work had been completed, the LCS(L)s and LCI(R)s attacked the landing area with rockets and proceeded to strafe the beaches. A force was landed with minimal opposition at 1000 hours and the area seemed to be secure. Prior to this landing, *LCS(L)s 26* and *27* had performed routine mine clearing operations along with three minesweepers. This work involved firing on and detonating or sinking mines that had been cut loose by the YMSs, but fortunately none were encountered.

YMSs were motor minesweepers with wooden hulls, powered by twin 500 horsepower diesels and twin screws. The 136-foot vessels were produced in two versions, the first 134 had twin stacks, and vessels numbered 135 through 445 had single stacks. Since they were originally designed as fishing trawlers, they were perfectly suited for minesweeping operations. Trailing paravanes from each side, the doughty ships cut mines loose so that their escorts could either explode or sink them. Usually, they were assisted by the LCS(L)s or LCI(G)s. This hazardous duty took its toll on both minesweepers and LCS(L)s alike. In addition to firing on mines, the LCS(L)s part in the procedure was to provide covering fire if shore batteries opened up on the minesweepers. Normally, larger ships such as destroyers stood by offshore to add the support of their heavier guns, but their deep draft made it necessary to send in the LCS(L) fleet since they could get in closer to the shore line.

The assault at Mariveles began at 0753 on 13 February. *LCS(L) 48* approached Mariveles Bay near Gordo Point and fired at various on-shore structures with its twin 40mm guns. Assorted buildings and pillboxes on Caracol Point and Lilimbon Cove were blasted with a combination of rockets and 3"/50 shells. Steaming nearby, *LSM 169* struck a mine and the 48 went to her assistance. The other LCS(L)s and LCI(R)s made rocket and strafing runs on the beach and provided fire support for the troops as they landed. No resistance was encountered.

Once the landing had been accomplished, the six LCS(L)s involved anchored across the mouth of Mariveles Harbor to provide a screen for the landing craft on the beach. However, it proved to be a bad strategy.

At about 0305, 16 February, a terrific explosion occurred in the vicinity of the LCS(L)(3) 7 followed shortly by another explosion from the same locality. In rapid succession thereafter explosions occurred in the LCS(L)(3)s 49 and *26*, and after a short interval near the LCS(L)(3) 27. The LCS(L)(3) 48 got underway. A radio report was received from the LCS(L)(3) 27 that an attack by Japanese suicide boats was in progress, that she had sunk five of them and had been seriously damaged herself and was heading toward the western side to beach. The LCS(L)(3)s 7, 49 and *26* were seen to explode, capsize and sink. While this was occurring the air was full of shells and, in addition, it appeared that the harbor was under shell fire from Corregidor. Burning oil had the harbor under a pall of smoke. Commander LCS(L) Flotilla One had ordered all ships in the harbor to prepare to sortie, directed . . . LST 666 to send medical aid to the LCS(L)(3)

27, directed two . . . [PTs] present to pick up survivors . . . At this time the LCS(L)(3) 8 reported that she had sighted a midget submarine firing into the harbor during the period of action but that it had disappeared before she could take action (*War Hist. Flot. One* 3-4) .

The attack would prove to be the worst suffered by LCS(L) ships during the war. *LCS(L)s 7, 26* and *49* were hit by two suicide boats each and sunk.

LSM *169* burns off Mariveles Harbor as *LCS(L) 48* and a tug assist in putting out her fires. Photo courtesy of the National Archives.

Approximately 100 of the suicide craft had been hidden in the caves of Corregidor. Without the knowledge of the Americans, about 30 of them had set out for the harbor from their base on the island. Reports vary, but at least ten of the craft returned to their bases without engaging the Americans. Of the remaining 20, several were intercepted by American destroyers *U.S.S. Congyngham* (*DD 371*), *U.S.S. Young* (*DD 580*) and *U.S.S. Nicholas* (*DD 449*) and sunk, but a number of others got through. Under attack by four suicide boats, the *LCS(L) 27*, under the command of Lt. Risley Lawrence, sank three before the fourth exploded a few feet off the port side amidships, severely damaging her. "The only alternative to save the ship and the lives of the wounded was to run the ship on the beach. This was done with only the starboard engine in operation . . . On route to the beach a fifth suicide boat was destroyed by . . . [the] ship" (*LCS(L) 27 Action Report 7Mar45*). Beaching the 27 proved to be the right strategy, and she was saved. The ship sat out the next day's action, watching paratroopers jump onto Corregidor as the amphibious assault took place. Within a few days she had been patched up by Seabees and a tug pulled her off the beach. In due course, the tug struck a mine and a second tug was called in to tow the *27* to Subic Bay. By the time she was repaired, the war was over. However, she went on to perform patrol duties throughout the area.

The disastrous attack on the LCS(L)s demonstrated a weakness in their design. The guns mounted on the ships could not depress sufficiently, and it was difficult to fire on small targets such as the suicide boats as they made their runs. In his *Action Report of 17 February 1945*, the Commanding Officer of the *LCS(L) 48*, Lt. Denzil E. Widel, recommended that "small calibre machine guns be mounted on the bow and stern to cover blind spots in the 40mm and 20mm. It is felt that the machine guns placed in these positions will be adequate fire against Q-boat attacks. Four 50 calibre and four 30 calibre should be a sufficient number to do the work competently" (5). No official action was taken on this recommendation. However some LCS(L) captains took it upon themselves to mount extra guns when they were able to obtain them.

The battle for the capture of Corregidor continued, but only *LCS(L)s 8* and *48* were still combat ready and they joined in the assault. Included in the attacking force were *LCI(R)s 337, 338, 340* and *341*. During the assault, three of the LCI(R)s were hit by fire and the LCS(L)s had to fill in as best they could.

> . . . 0855(I) the paratroopers descended on Corregidor, while previous to this the cruisers, destroyers, and bombers had laid down a heavy barrage. We began our approach to the beach and several small calibre guns were firing on this vessel, however larger calibre guns were firing upon and striking the LCI(R)s. We maneuvered into position to fire several salvos of rockets into the west slope of the island, which spot we determined was the point of origin of mortar and machine gun fire. We then opened up with 20mm, 40mm and 3"/50 in this locality and succeeded in neutralizing several positions. For approximately two hours after the landing we made numerous runs on the west slope bombarding the area (*Action Report LCS(L) 48 17Feb45*).

The small size of the island made the drop by paratroopers of the 503rd Parachute Infantry Regiment a dangerous mission. A number of them were swept over the bay and had to be rescued by PT boats. Shortly after the first parachute battalion had made their drop, the amphibious assault forces landed. This unit was the 151st Regimental Combat Team under the command of Brigadier General Chase. Opposition to them was kept at a minimum by air attacks and continued shelling by the support ships. A second drop of paratroopers occurred shortly after noon, however, a third was canceled because of the difficulties encountered during the first two.

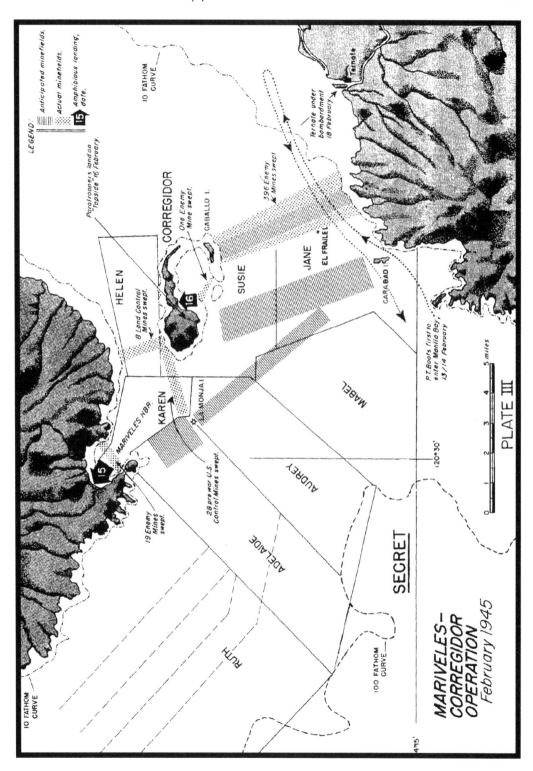

MARIVELES—
CORREGIDOR
OPERATION
February 1945

SECRET

PLATE III

LCS(L) 8 **stands by off Corregidor Island as paratroopers descend. Photo courtesy of the National Archives.**

Japanese defenders holed up in the maze of tunnels on Corregidor proved diffi-cult to dislodge. Continued firing into cave entrances by ships and artillery slowly took their toll until a huge explosion destroyed the magazines in Malinta Hill, thereby ending major resistance. Japanese losses were almost complete, with 4,500 dead and only 20 captured. Compared to 200 American dead and 400 wounded, the American losses seemed light. After twelve days, the island was secured and the task of clearing the Japanese from other islands like El Fraile, Caballo and Carabao, as well as from the city of Manilla, was undertaken. Most of the Japanese Army forces under General Yamashita had withdrawn from the area and its defense was under-taken by Japanese Navy personnel under the command of Vice Admiral Sanji Iwabachi. Although they fought fiercely, they were soon defeated.

During this campaign the *LCS(L)s 8* and *48* acted in consort with minesweepers to clear Manilla Bay of mines. On 25 February, 1945, as these operations were taking place, the *LCS(L) 48* was ordered to investigate a raft in the bay. As the gunboat approached the crew observed five Japanese soldiers on the raft who appeared to be dead. When they were only 50 yards away, one of their men accidently fired a submachine gun at the raft, setting off a grenade or booby trap. Several of the crew were injured by shrapnel and the ship let loose with 40mm and 20mm guns, putting an end to the threat. An observation plane dropped a smoke bomb near another raft in the bay and the *48* was ordered to eliminate it. This time she took no chances and blasted it out of the water, killing all four of the Japanese occupants *(LCS(L) 48 Action Report 26Feb45)*.

GUERRILLA OPERATIONS

The surrender of the Americans at Corregidor on 6 May, 1942 left the Filipino people in the hands of the conquering Japanese. Propaganda efforts on the part of the Japanese, stressing East-versus-West themes, fell on deaf ears as the Filipino people had formed close cultural ties with the West. Once the harshness of Japanese rule became evident, native resistance grew rapidly. Operating in the Philippines were a number of guerrilla movements, many led by officers who had served under Lt. General Jonathan M. Wainwright. As communications with the islands had been cut by the occupation, little was known about their existence. Gradually, word began to filter out that there was serious resistance throughout the islands and plans were devised to exploit the situation. By late 1942, contact had been established with a number of the guerrilla groups and plans for regular supply and assistance were drawn up. Since the power of the Japanese Navy was still significant, open attempts at supply were not possible and materials and agents had to be brought in by submarine. Eventually, as Japanese naval power declined and the campaign for the Philippines was underway, surface ships replaced submarines as the main supply vehicles. Delivering supplies, transporting guerrilla troops and various other duties fell to the LCS(L)s and LCI(L)s.

On 1 February, 1945, Lieutenants Donovan R. Ellis, Jr. and Albert C. Eldridge, Commanding Officers of the *LCS(L)s 9* and *10* respectively, learned that they had a new and unique mission. Designated as Task Group 70.4, along with the *LCI(L)s 361* and *363*, they were to replace the submarines of the Seventh Fleet as the contacts for Philippine guerrillas. The LCI(L)s were able to carry large stores of food and ammunition which were desperately needed by the guerrillas, and the LCS(L)s could provide the necessary firepower to protect them from the Japanese if need be. Up to that point, the two LCS(L)s had not seen much action. However, that was soon to change. On their first mission to Camiguin Island off the northern coast of Mindanao, the ships delivered much needed supplies to the guerrillas. Learning of an enemy installation on the opposite shore at Talisayan, the two commanding officers decided to pay it a visit.

> . . . Rocket bombardment of canal area began at 1503 and stopped at 1620 after 92 rockets had been fired from each of LCS 9 and 10. Effective straddling of the area where the Japanese are believed to have been building wooden barges was accomplished. No results could be fully observed because of the shallow water in the approach, but native and American Guerrilla officers commented that if there were targets there, they were hit. Strafing with 3" 50, both sets of 40mm and all 20mm resulted in the setting afire of 200 to 300 barrels of oil and gasoline. Between six and ten large buildings with metal roofs were burned down (*Log LCS(L)(3) 10* 78).

Later estimates indicated that 900 Japanese lost their lives in the attack (*Ship's Hist. LCS(L)(3) 10* 12-13).

Until 23 May, 1945, the small fleet carried supplies to Filipino guerrillas and attacked isolated Japanese garrisons and outposts. In some cases they simply showed up off the coast and shelled the encampment, but in others, the LCI(L)s landed guerrillas who proceeded to ambush escaping Japanese troops. One such raid occurred on 3 March:

> . . . 0945 Opened fire. 0958 LCSs opened fire. 1005 Open fire with rockets. 1009 Guerrillas ashore from LCIs. 1016 Began strafing beach. 1035 Opened fire with mortars. 1108 Cease firing. Stand by G.Q. . . . (*Log LCS(L)(3) 10* 130).

Continued harassment of the Japanese in the area by the LCS(L)s contributed to the efficiency of the Filipino guerrilla movement.

LCS(L) 10 and *LCI(L) 363* **load Philippine guerrillas. Photo courtesy of the National Archives.**

SOUTHERN OPERATIONS

While *LCS(L)s 9* and *10* were busy supplying guerrillas and harassing the Japanese as best they could on Mindanao, plans were being made for other amphibious assaults. Operation Victor III was designed to capture the island of Palawan. Troops of the 136th Regimental Combat Team of the 41st Infantry Division, led by Brigadier General Harold H. Haney, were scheduled to land at Puerto Princessa on Palawan Island on 28 February. A prisoner of war camp on the island had been the site at which the Japanese had burned alive 150 American prisoners on 14 December, 1944.

Control of the island would allow the construction of bases in range of the Japanese on Borneo and the Dutch East Indies. Garrisoned by 2,700 troops, the island promised to be a difficult target. Fortunately for the Americans, the Japanese followed a strategy that made the landing rather easy. In order to avoid bombardment by the larger ships, they abandoned the areas near the beaches and retreated into the hills. Basically unopposed, the assault provided another practice run for the LCS(L)s.

Arriving at the entrance to Puerto Princessa Harbor on 28 February was Task Group 78.2, under the command of Rear Admiral W. M. Fechteler. It consisted of *LCS(L)s 28, 29, 30* and *50*, four YMS motor minesweepers, twelve destroyers *U.S.S. Fletcher (DD 445), U.S.S. O'Bannon (DD 450), U.S.S. Jenkins (DD 447), U.S.S. Flusser (DD 368), U.S.S. Conyngham (DD 371), U.S.S. Smith (DD 378), U.S.S. Drayton (DD 366), U.S.S. Shaw (DD 373), U.S.S. Waller (DD 466), U.S.S. Sigourney (DD 643), U.S.S. McCalla (DD 488)* and *U.S.S. Abbot (DD 629)*, three light cruisers *U.S.S. Montpelier (CL 57), U.S.S. Cleveland (CL 55), U.S.S. Denver (CL 58)*, eleven gun and rocket boats, four APDs, one LSD, ten LCI(L)s, 20 LSMs and other miscellaneous small ships and boats. At 0630, the four YMSs and the *LCS(L)s 28* and *30* began the dangerous task of mine sweeping. Fortunately for the small ships, the area was relatively clear of any mines, thus eliminating one potential hazard. Assigned to Task Unit 78.2.6 were the four LCS(L)s, along with six LSTs, two LSMs, two LCI(R)s and three destroyers, including the *U.S.S. Flusser (DD 368)*. Patrolling along the shore, the LCS(L)s and the other ships fired on targets of opportunity near the town of Puerto Princessa. The first waves of infantry landed at 0845 without encountering any significant opposition.

Shortly thereafter, at 1010, both the *LCS(L) 28* and *30* were ordered to patrol up the Camuran River in search of enemy forces. The gunboats proceeded upstream until they hit shallow water and returned, the *30* was briefly grounded at the mouth of the river at about 1235. By evening the four LCS(L)s were anchored across the mouth of the bay. Mindful of the disaster at Mariveles Harbor only two weeks before, the sailors on board spent a nervous and watchful night. The campaign ended with a victory for the American forces, Puerto Princessa had suffered heavy damage and the enemy had withdrawn from the area.

Further to the east lay the islands of Ticao and Burias. Determined to secure the islands, Task Unit 78.9.10, consisting of *LCS(L)s 8, 48*, two LCMs and one LCI were assigned to the task of landing troops on both islands. On 3 March at 0615, the *LCS(L) 8* arrived off the beaches of San Fernando, Ticao Island in the company of an LSM and small landing craft. Native bonfires on shore guided the ships to their destination and the landing was unopposed. On 6 March, the *8* departed the area and picked up some wounded guerrillas at Allen, Samar Island. After transporting the guerrillas to San Fernando, the *LCS(L) 8* returned to Subic Bay.

As the *8* was accomplishing her mission, *LCS(L) 48*, along with *LSM 136* and *LCI(L) 448* were engaged in landing troops on Burias Island. The *48* and the *U.S.S. Douglas A. Munroe (DE 422)* then proceeded southwest and approached the town of Nabusagan about 0955. Apparently Japanese troops on shore mistook them for their own ships and began waving a Japanese flag to attract their attention. The LCS(L) began firing at a range of 1,200 yards with her 20mm, 40mm and 3"/50 guns. About the same time, the destroyer escort let loose. Gasoline and ammunition dumps went up in flames, and as they approached within 100 yards of the beach, they fired a barrage of rockets, completely obliterating the town. Troops from the 8th Army Americal Division occupied the town shortly thereafter and reported that the ships had accounted for 25 dead and 15 wounded Japanese. The *48* spent the next several days cruising between Ticao, Burais and Catbalogan islands, moving guerrillas and other troops to various locations.

Still another landing was planned for Zamboanga Peninsula on Mindanao on 8 March. This was considered to be the most important area of Mindanao for the U.S. forces to hold, since bases there would prove useful for the coming attack on Borneo. Zamboanga City, at the tip of the peninsula, was the focal point of the invasion. Reports from Philippine guerrillas indicated that there were about 8,900 Japanese troops on the peninsula, but that they had left the area around the city and would not oppose the landing. Not wishing to take chances, the Allies landed troops and sixteen *Corsairs* on an air strip 150 miles north of the city. From that location they flew air raids over the enemy areas in the company of *B-24 Liberator* bombers for two days prior to the landings.

Seven LCS(L)s from Flotilla One were assigned to the assault on Zamboanga as a part of Task Group 78.1. Along with eleven YMSs, two cruisers, *U.S.S. Phoenix (CL*

46), U.S.S. Boise (CL 47), thirteen destroyers, *U.S.S. Fletcher (DD 445), U.S.S. Nicholas (DD 449), U.S.S. Taylor (DD 468), U.S.S. Jenkins (DD 447), U.S.S Saufley (DD 465), U.S.S. Waller (DD 466), U.S.S. Philip (DD 498), U.S.S. Sigourney (DD 643), U.S.S. Robinson (DD 562), U.S.S. McCalla (DD 488), U.S.S. Bancroft (DD 598), U.S.S. Bailey (DD 492)* and two destroyer escorts *U.S.S. Rudderow (DE 224)* and *U.S.S. Chaffee (DE 230)* they prepared for the assault. Designated as Victor IV, the operation included *LCS(L)s 28, 29, 30, 41, 42, 43* and *50,* along with *LCI(R)s 225, 226, 337, 340, 341, LCI(M)s 362, 431, LCI(D)s 227* and *228* and other assault craft. They cleared the area in preparation for the attack, which was scheduled for 10 March.

Beginning on 8 March, *LCS(L)s 41, 42, 43* and *50* joined the minesweeping operations in Basilan Strait and areas near the landing beaches. On 9 March, beginning at 0730, the *LCS(L)s 41, 42, 43* and *50* assisted in minesweeping operations with the seven YMSs between Caldera Point and Zamboanga City. At 0920, the *43* was bracketed with mortar fire from the shore while cruising off San Mateo Point. In a series of four runs on the beach, the *43* let loose with everything she had, effectively putting an end to the attack. At 1125, lookouts on the other ships identified machine gun nests on Great Santa Cruz Island and the four LCS(L)s were sent to destroy them. *LCS(L) 42* swept eastward along the southern coast of Zamboanga Peninsula, taking her toll of enemy installations, including a 6" gun emplacement, pill boxes and machine gun nests. For the next several hours the gunboats cruised up and down the beaches, firing at targets of opportunity and providing covering fire for the hydrographic parties which were performing their tasks close inshore.

On 10 March the actual landings took place. Two beaches, designated Red and Yellow, had been selected although only one would be used in the actual invasion. This was an attempt to confuse the enemy and divide his forces. At 0850, after a severe pounding by the ships and planes of the allies, the amphibious assault began. Leading the landing boats in were the LCS(L)s and LCI(R)s, fulfilling the role for which they had been designed. Each of the guns on the LCS(L)s had a designated range and as that range was reached, the guns opened up. At the furthest range of 3,200 yards, the LCS(L)s fired their 3"/50 guns. Closing to 2,400 yards, the twin 40mm guns opened up, and at 1,100 yards, the 20mms. Rockets had a shorter range, and two salvos of 120 rockets each were fired off at ranges of 900 and 600 yards. Once this had been accomplished, the ships slowed and allowed the landing boats to pass them by on their way to the invasion beaches. Assaulting the beaches was the 162nd Infantry Regiment of the 41st Infantry Division under the command of Major General J. A. Doe. By 0915, the first waves had landed with only light opposition. Some mortar rounds fell in the general vicinity of the LCS(L)s, however, none were close enough to be considered a threat. In all, little resistance was encountered. The following day, the gunboats patrolled off the beach, strafing the areas ahead of the advancing troops as they attacked the town. *LCS(L) 42* strafed Pitogo as *LCI(R)s 340* and *341* delivered a deadly barrage to the town. With the landing site under control, the ships stood by for another two days and then left for the area around Semut Village.

LCS(L)s steam in for a rocket run on the beaches at Zamboanga Penninsula, 10 March, 1945. Photo courtesy of the National Archives.

At about 1030 on 16 March, *LCS(L)s 42* and *43* led an attack on Semut Village. Intelligence reports had indicated the presence of about 250 Japanese troops in the area. As the ships approached the area, they noticed a large number of people in the water. One swam out to the ships and reported to the Commanding Officer of the *43*, Lt. (jg) Earle Blakley, that he was the Mayor of the town and that the Japanese had left. Not wishing to cause unnecessary civilian casualties, Blakley radioed his report to command and asked for instructions. Not getting a reasonable response to his communication, he continued to radio the situation and ask for instructions. Finally the orders came back to attack the village, in spite of his message. Under orders, the two LCS(L)s fired into the village with their 20mm, 40mm and 3"/50 guns, causing a great deal of damage (Blakley interview). Unfortunately, the original intelligence was faulty, the Japanese had withdrawn from the area eight to ten days before. The toll on the natives was 19 dead and about 80 wounded. Crews and medical personnel from the ships went ashore and gave medical assistance. Their tasks in the area completed and the troops safely ashore, the LCS(L) fleet prepared for their next assault. Other areas around Zamboanga had also been attacked that day, among them Basilan Island, just to the south.

In addition to the above-mentioned landings, the ships of Flotilla One were active to the north and west of Mindanao as they participated in clearing the four main islands between the Visayan Sea and the Mindanao Sea. Arriving off Cebu City, Cebu Island on 26 March to participate in Victor II, was Task Group 78.2, which consisted of four APDs, 15 LCI(L)s, 11 LSMs, 17 LSTs, five LCI(R)s, *LCS(L)s 28, 29, 30* and *50*, along with two PCs, eight YMSs, one LCI(D), five destroyers, *U.S.S. Conyngham (DD 371)*, *U.S.S. Flusser (DD 368)*, *U.S.S. Shaw (DD 373)*, *U.S.S. Smith (DD 378)*, *U.S.S. Drayton (DD 366)* and four cruisers, *U.S.S. Phoenix (CL 46)*, *U.S.S. Boise (CL 47)*, *H.M.A.S. Hobart* and *H.M.A.S. Warramunga*. The fleet approached the target area near Talisay Town on the northeast coast of Cebu Island, and the cruisers and destroyers softened up the beaches with an hour and a half of naval bombardment. As usual, before an assault could begin, the area had to be cleared of mines. Beginning at 0200, *LCS(L)s 29* and *30* accompanied the eight minesweepers on their mission, effectively clearing the area. At 0815 on 26 March, *LCS(L)s 28, 29, 30* and *50*, along with other assault craft, led the landing boats towards the beach, firing their 3"/50s, 40mms and 20mms in turn. The first rockets were sent beachward at 700 yards out and the ships continued to strafe the beach. By 0830 the first waves of troops from the Americal Division (less the 164th Regimental Combat Team), under the command of Major General W.A. Arnold, had made it to shore and encountered some serious problems. Major General Takeo Manjome, in command of nearly 15,000 Japanese troops, had prepared the landing beaches well. Mine fields and tank traps greeted the invading Americans and slowed their progress considerably. Fortunately, the Japanese had retreated from the landing areas and consolidated their forces in the hills to the north of the city. During the landing operation, *LCS(L) 28* "took a 37mm hit in a cable reel just aft of the No. 5 20mm gun tub. The shell never went off, thus no one even noticed it" (Krayer 43).

Bohol Island, just to the east of Cebu was the target on 26 March. *LCS(L) 29*, along with two LCI(R)s, were assigned the task of supporting landings by elements of the Americal Division on Mactan Island, the Albuquerque area of Bohol and the Dumagusta area of Negros Island.

Prior to the landings it was essential to clear the area of mines, and the ships stood by as the YMSs did their job. Although they were prepared for anything, the ships encountered no resistance with the landings. With the area secured, the ships left for their next assault.

Targeted next was the town of Legaspi on the Albay Gulf. Assigned to the operation were the destroyers *U.S.S. Bailey* (*DD 492*) and *U.S.S. Bancroft* (*DD 598*), destroyer escorts *U.S.S. Day* (*DE 225*) and *U.S.S. Holt* (*DE 706*), two SCs, three APDs, ten LCIs, five LSTs, four LSMs, *LCS(L)s 8* and *48*, along with an LCI(R). The assault, scheuled for 1 April, 1945, was preceded by minesweeping operations in Legaspi Harbor. This was to be the last amphibious assault in the area.

LCS(L)s lead the landing craft ashore as the Americal Division assaults the beach at Cebu City, Philippines on 26 March, 1945. Photo courtesy of the National Archives.

The 158th Regimental Combat Team, under Brigadier General Hanford MacNider, landed to light opposition . Having captured the fortified area there, the Americans found themselves in position to control Bicol Peninsula. Beginning at 0630, the LCS(L)s provided cover for two LCVPs which were assigned the task of clearing the boat lanes. At 0845, the ships were fired upon by a gun emplacement which contained two 8" guns. Three rounds hit the water only 50 feet from *LCS(L) 8*. Both ships opened up with their 3"/50 guns and their twin 40mms, effectively destroying the Japanese gun emplacement. Leading the troop carriers in to shore, the LCS(L)s and the LCI(R) strafed the beach, and by 1000 hours the first waves of troops had reached land. No further resistance was generated and the LCS(L)s were ordered to perform minesweeping operations in the San Bernadino Straits for the next two days. After completing the task, they reported to Leyte for further assignment.

On 2 April, Task Unit 78.1.3, consisting of *LCS(L)s 41* and *42*, with *LCI(M)s 362* and *431*, were given the task of providing close fire support for the landing at Sanga Sanga Island. This island was located at the southernmost reach of the Sulu Archipelago and the 163rd Infantry of the 41st Division was scheduled to land there. As had happened with other operations in the Philippines, this one was unopposed and the ships were able to return to their anchorage in the Zamboanga area after a few days of minesweeping assistance.

To the south of Zamboanga Peninsula lay the islands of Basilan and Jolo. Joining other ships of Task Group 76.10, the *LCS(L)s 41* and *42*, the *U.S.S. Saufley (DD 465)* and the *U.S.S. Philip (DD 498)* set sail from the Basilan Straits anchorage at 1548 on 8 April. The following day, at 0650, the ships were at the line of departure for the landing on Patikul Point on Jolo Island. By 0853, the troops had landed without opposition and *LCS(L)s 41* and *42* awaited further orders. Since there was no danger to the invading troops or the landing site, the convoy returned to Zamboanga that evening and anchored in the Basilan Strait anchorage.

LCS(L)s 29 and *30* joined with seven LCI(L)s, one LCI(R), and six LSMs to form Task Unit 78.3.3. Their target was the city of Tagbilaran on Bohol Island. Sailing southward from their anchorage at Talisay on Cebu on 11 April, the small fleet arrived at the harbor at 0630. No resistance was encountered and the troops were landed without incident. The gunboats remained in the area and departed the next morning.

A few days later, on 20 April, the same task unit was ordered to support the landing of the Americal Infantry Division at the Danao area of Cebu Island. The four hour run from their anchorage began at 0200, and by 0600 they had arrived at their staging area off Danao Point. At 0630, they commenced their run on the beach, firing their 3"/50 and 40mm guns as they led the landing boats ashore. Coming within rocket range, they each fired off a salvo of 120 4.5-inch high explosive barrage rockets and then slowed their progress to allow the landing craft in to the beaches. At 0702, the first LVT hit the beach, quickly followed by the other troop carriers. The ships lay to, awaiting further orders and prepared to intercept enemy craft. However, no resistance was generated towards the Navy ships.

Still another assault took place at Polloc Harbor, Mindanao on 17 April, 1945. Referred to as the Malabang-Parang Operation, it also was completed without resistance. Assigned to the mission was Task Group 78.2, which consisted of the light cruisers *U.S.S. Montpelier (CL 57)*, *U.S.S. Denver (CL 58)*, *U.S.S. Cleveland*

(*CL 55*), 16 destroyers, *U.S.S. Conway* (*DD 507*), *U.S.S. Eaton* (*DD 510*), *U.S.S. Stevens* (*DD 479*), *U.S.S. Young* (*DD 580*), *U.S.S. Cony* (*DD 508*), *U.S.S. Sigourney* (*DD 643*), *U.S.S. Flusser* (*DD 368*), *U.S.S. Aulick* (*DD 569*), *U.S.S. Conyngham* (*DD 371*), *U.S.S. Charles Ausburne* (*DD 570*), *U.S.S. Braine* (*DD 630*), *U.S.S. Robinson* (*DD 562*), *U.S.S. Claxton* (*DD 571*), *U.S.S. Dyson* (*DD 572*), and *U.S.S. McCalla* (*DD 448*) as well as numerous LSTs, LCI(L)s and *LCS(L)s 23, 28, 48* and *50*, along with a number of other assault ships and craft. Guerrilla activity on the island had forced the 43,000 Japanese troops, under Lieutenant General G. Morozumi, into a defensive posture. With the countryside in the hands of some 25,000 Filipino guerrillas under the command of Colonel Wendel W. Fertig, the Japanese resistance was of limited quality. Lt. General Robert C. Eichelberger determined that a landing at Illana Bay near the towns of Malabang and Parang would be the best course of action since Japanese strength was concentrated to the east on Davao Gulf. There, Army troops of the X Corps (24th & 31st Infantry Divisions), under the command of Lieutenant General F. C. Siebert, stormed ashore on 17 April. Participating in the assault were *LCS(L)s 28, 43* and *50*. Again, the ships had expended much effort and ordinance against an enemy who was simply not there.

Lt. Colonel Robert Amory was assigned the task of exploring the Mindanao River, which was supposedly navigable to a distance of 35 miles inland. Sent on the mission, which began at 0830 on 18 April, were five LCM(G)s, one LCM(R), three LCS(L)s, 24 LCMs and 14 LCVPs. Captain Rae E. Arison, in charge of the close support unit, attempted an in-depth reconnaissance by taking some of the LCIs, LCMs and PGMs up the river. This was believed to be the best way to get troops inland since the highways were little more than dirt roads. Unfortunately some of the ships were grounded and not freed for several days. However, by the end of the journey they had managed to place their troops in an advantageous position.

On 26 April, Task Unit 78.3.34, which included *LCS(L) 29* and an LCI(R), participated in the landings at Sibulan on Negros Oriental Island. Steaming from their anchorage at Cebu City, the ships screened the convoy of landing craft as they made their way westward through the Tanon Strait toward their target. These landings were accomplished by the Americal Division under Major General W.A. Arnold, acting in consort with the ships of the Seventh Amphibious Force. Dumaguete Airfield, on Negros Island, had been used by the Japanese Fourth Air Army. Fortunately for the Americans, their earlier strikes in the area had eliminated the Japanese aircraft. The Japanese followed the strategy that they had used on other islands and withdrew to the center of the island, leaving the Americans in control of the northern part.

The last major island in the area to be attacked by the Americans was Bohol. Task Unit 78.3.3, including *LCS(L)s 30*, along with seven LCI(L)s, one LCI(R) and six LSMs were given the job. Resistance was light and units of the Americal Division quickly secured control of the island on 11 March, 1945. By 0730, the LCI(L)s and the LSMs had unloaded in the dock area at the town of Tagbilaran. The troop carriers left the area and the LCS(L)s were ordered to moor alongside the dock, in case their services were needed. They left the following day.

General Morozumi's troops had managed to slow the progress of Major General Martin's 31st Division forces as they advanced up the Sayre Highway in the northern part of Mindanao. In order to assist Martin, MacArthur decided to land troops on Macajalar Bay to further distract the Japanese. An amphibious landing by the 108th Regimental Combat Team of the U.S. Fortieth Infantry Division was scheduled for 10 May, 1945. Task Unit 78.3.48 arrived at 0600, before the rest of the invasion fleet to engage in minesweeping operations. The destroyer *U.S.S. Meade* (*DD 602*) covered the unit with heavy fire from its guns as the inshore unit cleared the area of mines. *LCS(L) 30* performed routine fire support for the minesweepers as it cruised behind them. This chore was completed by 0730, just as Army *B-25 Mitchels* were bombing and strafing the town of Tagoloan.

At 0800, the assault began. Providing fire support were the *LCS(L)s 30, 42, 79* and *80*. The fire support ships saw to it that the "landing area and flanks were covered with 3"/50, 20mm, 40mm and 4.5" rocket fire to a depth of approximately 400 yards" (*LCS(L) 80 Action Rept. 14 May45* 1). After slowing to allow the LVTs to pass through on their way to the beach, the LCS(L)s hove to and patrolled the beach searching out targets of opportunity. Fortunately for the landed troops, there was no resistance and the area was quickly secured.

After completing 14 major and 24 minor amphibious landings in 44 days, Eichelberger's troops managed to consolidate the American control of the Philippines. Although resistance in the area was light and casualties kept to a minimum, the value of the assaults in the southern Philippines has been questioned by historians (Spector 526-527). Many feel that the strategic value of the islands was not as important as the psychological need to liberate all of the islands and thus fulfill MacArthur's promise to the Philippine people.

IWO JIMA

Standing mid-way between the Marianas Islands and Japan, the island of Iwo Jima served as an advance warning post for the Japanese. Flights of *B-29s* originating in the Marianas could be picked up on Japanese radar and the Japanese mainland alerted. To give their attacking bombers a better chance, Air Force planners gave a wide berth to the island, making the modification of their cargo necessary. Fewer pounds of bombs and greater supplies of gas had to be carried in order to make the longer trip possible. Additionally, bombers on the return flight faced a long arduous journey through the area, particularly if they were damaged or low on fuel. If Iwo Jima were in friendly hands, it could serve as an emergency landing strip and save many bomber crews from a watery grave. Accordingly, in the fall of 1944, the Joint Chiefs of Staff determined that Iwo Jima would be useful as an air base with the potential of striking Japan and other targets in the western Pacific.

Knowing its importance to the Americans, the Japanese built intricate defenses on the island, evacuated its civilians and bolstered the garrison to around 21,000. Elaborate underground tunnels and fortified gun emplacements were constructed and the two-and-a-half by four-and-a-half mile island became a fortress. Measurements were taken from each gun position, and the entire island was laid out on a giant grid, enabling gunners to zero in on any section of the island from their positions. Any invading force would be easily targeted.

Major General Harry Schmidt, the leader of the Marine units assigned to the assault, recognized the extent of the defensive capabilities on Iwo Jima. He requested a ten day period of naval bombardment before landing his troops. Other campaigns were underway about that time and such a lengthy undertaking was not possible. The bombardment was cut to a three day period prior to the invasion.

Assigned to the attack on Iwo Jima was Task Expeditionary Force 51 under the command of Vice Admiral Richmond Kelly Turner. It included nine battleships, eight heavy cruisers, five light cruisers, seven escort carriers and thirty-one destroyers. A division of that force, the Amphibious Support Force, was under the command of Rear Admiral W. H. P. Blandy. Operating in that division were the LCS(L) ships of Flotilla Three, under the command of Captain T. C. Aylward. Included in this division were four Task Units, designated as 52.5.1, 52.5.2, 52.5.3, and 52.5.4. The first two Task Units consisted of LCI(G)s and Units 3 and 4 were LCS(L)s. Task Unit 52.5.3 contained *LCS(L)s 32, 33, 34, 35, 36* and *51* and *LC(FF) 988*. Task Unit 52.5.4 was comprised of *LCS(L)s 31, 52, 53, 54, 55, 56* and *LC(FF) 484*.

These units had practiced the assault at Kahoolawe, Hawaii between 12-18 January, 1945 and rehearsed again in the Tinian-Saipan area between 11-13 February. They left Saipan late in the afternoon of 15 February and arrived off Iwo Jima at approximately 0400 on 19 February. Their assignment in the invasion of the island was to make two rocket runs on the beaches as a prelude to landing troops, to provide call fire and harassing fire as the troops ashore required it and to assist in the salvage of small craft and equipment. It was anticipated that many of the smaller landing craft would be hit by fire and would soon clutter the beaches. Removal of these obstacles was necessary if additional troops and supplies were to be landed.

An additional problem had to be solved in preparation for the landing of troops. Intelligence reports indicated that the Japanese defenders had buried a number of gasoline drums along the beach front and would ignite them as the troops landed. Just prior to the troop landings, the LCS(L)s would have to fire their rockets in an attempt to eliminate the threat.

> This initial salvo was intended to ignite any electrically wired gasoline drums which were believed to be arranged on the beaches' edge so as to set up a "wall of flame" ahead of our first assault wave just as it reached the beach. The tremendous rocket barrage almost perfectly placed over the questionable area produced no visible effect indicating that the "wall of flame" idea had been discarded and the gasoline drums removed sometime previously" (*LCS(L) 31 Action Report* 10Mar45 1).

At sunrise on 16 February, 1945, the Japanese saw the extent of their attacker's power. For three days, the guns of battleships like the *U.S.S. New York* (*BB 34*), *U.S.S. West Virginia* (*BB 48*), *U.S.S. Arkansas* (*BB 33*), *U.S.S. Idaho* (*BB 42*), and *U.S.S. Nevada* (*BB 36*) along with those of cruisers like the *U.S.S. Tuscaloosa* (*CA 37*), the *U.S.S. Vicksburg* (*CL 86*) and those of the smaller ships pounded the island with the hope of destroying its defensive capabilities.

On 17 February 1945, one day prior to the landing, the Japanese made an error that would ultimately cost them dearly, but would also cost the LCI(G) fleet as well. Initial plans called for LCS(L)s accompanied by LCI(G)s to lead the assault forces into the beach, laying down fire support as the Marines landed. Before the troops could land it would be necessary to clear away any underwater obstacles. One of the jobs assigned to the LCI(G)s was the delivery of Underwater Demolition Teams to the shallows. Working in as closely as possible, the LCI(G)s deposited their frogmen in the water and proceeded to fire their rockets and guns at the shore emplacements. As the LCI(G)s worked over the beach emplacements with their rockets on the second day of the bombardment, the Japanese mistakenly perceived them as the beginning of the assault on the island. Opening up with their larger guns, they damaged all twelve of the LCI(G)s. In so doing, the Japanese revealed their gun positions prematurely and the larger ships off-shore were able to knock out a number of them.

The LCS(L)s were off Iwo Jima early on the 19 of February. Sunrise came at 0707 and revealed the effects of the bombardment by the heavier ships. Conditions were perfect for the gunboats. A calm sea, light winds and slight swells accompanied a sunny day. Although there was a great deal of smoke and haze over the island from the shelling, the sky was clear, giving the ships unrestricted visibility of their target areas. At 0730 the gunboats took position off the beach, preparatory to their first rocket run. Original plans called for the twelve LCS(L)s along with the twelve LCI(G)s to lead the landing craft to shore. Unfortunately, only one of the LCI(G)s was operational and so the bulk of the work fell on the *Mighty Midgets*. Two miles offshore, troop ships began unloading their cargo of Marines into the landing boats as the LCS(L)s stood by. At 0730, 90 minutes prior to H-hour, they made their first run. Among the gunboats in the assault was *LCS(L) 53*. Her log for that day records the events:

0600   Sounded general quarters in preparation for initial assault on Iwo Jima.

0700   Making various courses and speeds to get in position for assault on Green Beach.

0730   Proceeding to Green Beach, speed 12 knots; LCS(L) 31, 52, 53, 54 in Green Beach area. Gun boat support units one, two, three, and four moved in simultaneously. At 2500 yards from beach opened fire with 40mm batteries. At 1600 yards from beach opened fire with 20mm and 50 caliber machine guns. At 1200 yards from beach secured 40mm No. 1 to fire rockets. At 1150 yards fired ranging shots. At 1000 yards fired first salvo of 120 rockets. All gun boats turned left and retracted beach at 900 yards. Fire continued with all guns while within range of beach and hot rocks. Little enemy opposition was observed. Few 50 calibers and mortar shells landed near but no hits. . . . (38).

As the LCS(L)s were making their rocket run, the beaches were bombed by a flight of 15 *B-24 Liberators* and then by a flight of *Corsairs*. At 0827 the ships were at the line of departure for the troop assault. Once again they headed towards the beach, firing with their 40mm, 20mm guns and finally launching rockets. Six-hundred yards behind them, the first assault wave followed. The gunboats turned and strafed the beaches as the landing craft passed through their line, bringing the Marines in to the beaches. Later reports would credit the attack from the LCS(L)s as instrumental in keeping Japanese activity to a minimum, thus saving the lives of many of the troops involved in the landing.

0830   Started in on second run at speed 4 knots. At distance of 1200 yards made turn of 30 degrees to launch salvo of rockets. Launched second salvo when within 900-850 yards and immediately reloaded. Second salvo included 120 rockets. At 700 yards launched 40 rockets in third salvo. All guns continued to fire at beach and strafed side of mountain. Many pill boxes were observed on return from beach. Two fires were started by our gun fire.

0900   First wave hit beach and continuous waves followed. Some increase in enemy resistance was noticed, but no hits were observed.

1040   Received orders to cease firing and stand by for call fires.

L.D. Howard
Ens. USNR (*Log 53* 38).

Japanese gunners began to fire back at the ships and within a short time *LCS(L) 51* been hit by a Japanese anti-tank gun. Under the command of Lt. H. D. Chickering, the 51 kept at her task of covering the Marine assault as her damage control team extinguished the blaze. LCS(L)s continued to patrol up and down the beach, at times coming within 150 yards of the shore.

LCS(L) 33 found herself bracketed by mortar fire. One round landed 50 feet ahead of the ship and two others just to port and starboard. Two men were wounded by shrapnel from these mortar rounds. The *33* also took two hits from gun emplacements on Mt. Suribachi, which caused minor deck damage to pumps and rocket launchers. *LCS(L) 32* also was hit by shrapnel from these attacks, but not damaged. Fortunately, the LCS(L)s would suffer no significant damage at Iwo Jima.

Enemy fire was heavy from a number of caves on Mount Suribachi and the surrounding areas. The *Mighty Midgets* spent the rest of the invasion day patrolling up and down the beaches, firing into caves, pillboxes and other enemy installations. Frequently, they were so close to the beaches that they were able to observe troop concentrations, tanks and other targets. Many of these were successfully attacked with rockets or 40mm or 20mm fire. Their ability to get in close to the shore and spot enemy targets made them invaluable in subduing enemy resistance and in thwarting enemy counter attacks. This was a pattern of attack that would be standard operating procedure for the LCS(L) ships in an amphibious assault. On their first run they would hit the beach area with rockets, turn and run broadside to the beach and then strafe it. They would then regroup for a second run, leading in the landing craft. After firing their next salvo of rockets, they would slow down so that the troop carriers could pass by and go in for the landing. As the troop carriers passed, they would turn again and strafe the beach. Patrolling inshore during the landings, they would continue to fire over the heads of the troops and cover them as best they could, at the same time identifying enemy gun emplacements for the larger ships.

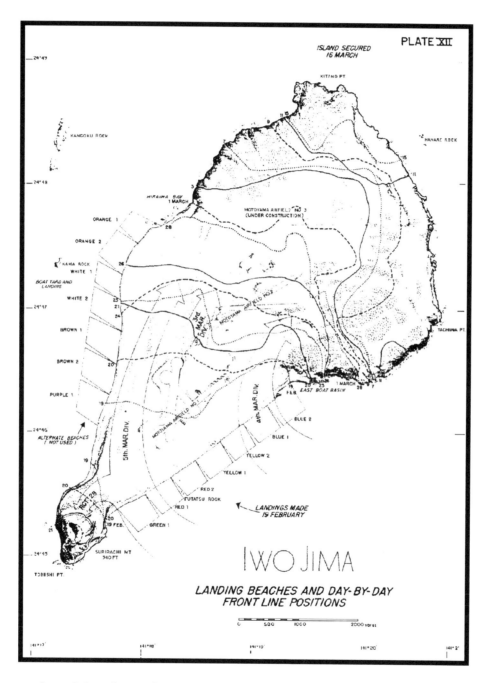

Assault beaches and progress ashore at Iwo Jima (OPOA February, 1945).

A line of LCS(L)s cruise off Mount Suribachi during the invasion of Iwo Jima. Photo taken by a plane from the *U.S.S. Saginaw Bay (CVE 82)* on 19 February, 1945. Official U.S. Navy Photograph courtesy of the National Archives.

Targets of opportunity presented themselves in the form of enemy troops and vehicles, as well as gun emplacements ranging in size from machine guns and mortars to artillery pieces. The twelve LCS(L)s in the action were equipped with single 40mm bow guns which, along with their twin 40mm and 20mm guns, proved effective in obliterating many of the enemy installations. Marine observers on board the LCS(L)s were assigned the task of directing fire from the Navy ships to targets on shore.

Marine teams in action ashore identified targets that were in their path and radioed their grid coordinates to their counterparts on the LCS(L)s. If the target was within the capability of an LCS(L), she added her supporting fire and wiped out the obstacle, usually a small gun emplacement or pillbox. If the enemy target was too large, the information was passed farther offshore to the battleships, cruisers and destroyers which then demolished the larger target. In order to give them the best vantage point, the LCS(L)s, with all guns blazing, brought the Marine observers close to the beach in order that their observations would be more accurate. This tactic was extremely effective. In his action report, Lt. Ken F. Mahacek, Commanding Officer of the *LCS(L) 31* wrote:

> Twenty-five to 100 of the enemy were definitely destroyed by this vessel's gunfire during these first two days. Rockets were able to reach into the ravines at the base of the mount to neutralize mortar emplacements and the close range enabled the 40 and 20 millimeter batteries to keep the many caves and pill boxes silent during the early advances. Harassing fires both night and day kept the enemy guns down and hampered any attempts to counter-attack under cover of darkness. Fire control was only difficult during days of rough weather when the pitch and roll of the vessel hampered accurate, sustained fire on definite targets (*LCS(L) 31 Action Report 10Mar45* 5).

LCS(L) 33 **cruises in the South Pacific, prior to the invasion of Iwo Jima. She was later sunk at Okinawa on 12 April, 1945. Photo courtesy of the National Archives.**

LCS(L)s 34 and *36* **head into the beach at Iwo Jima, 19 February, 1945. Official United States Navy Photograph, courtesy of the James C. Fahey Collection, U.S. Naval Institute.**

Specific targets could be identified during the daylight hours and a number of ammo and supply dumps were destroyed by fire from the LCS(L)s. So much ordnance was fired by the little ships that many had to replace their ammunition on a daily basis.

Lieutenant General Tadamichi Kurabayashi had prepared the island well. Many of the gun emplacements were well-protected in hardened bunkers. Once the landing was under way, the amphibious assault forces found themselves under the Japanese guns on Mount Suribachi. This fire was extremely effective, since the Japanese had measured each area of the island and were able to hit targets with great accuracy. Many of the guns were difficult to spot until they opened fire. In order to identify the enemy gun positions, a new tactic was employed that teamed the LCS(L)s with destroyers or cruisers. As an LCS(L) cruised near shore, she would be fired upon by one or more of the shore gun emplacements. At such a close range, LCS(L) gun crews could easily spot their attackers. Firing tracer rounds into the gun emplacement identified its location for the waiting destroyers offshore, which then proceeded to destroy it with heavier ordnance from their larger guns. *LCS(L) 51* reported, "Spotting fire for cruiser Vicksburg on pillboxes located on the face of the quarry. Silenced two positions and cruiser demolished four more, following our tracers" (*LCS(L) 51 Action Report 10Mar45 2*). Acting as bait for Japanese gunners was hazardous duty to say the least, however, only *LCS(L) 33* was hit by shore fire, wounding six of her crew. Fortunately, the damage to the *33* was not serious and she was able to continue on her mission.

After the initial landing of the Marine troops, the LCS(L) ships played a variety of roles. The small size of the island made it possible for them to constantly patrol inshore delivering harassing fire to the enemy positions all night long. Continual runs were made against enemy targets that could be identified.

One of the more difficult tasks for the *Mighty Midgets* was the removal of damaged landing craft and vehicles from the beach area. Dropping its stern anchors in deeper water, an LCS(L) would head for a wrecked LCVP or DUKW that was stuck on the beach or in the shallow surf. Attaching heavy lines from its bow to the damaged craft was the most difficult part, both physically and psychologically. In order to accomplish this, sailors from the ships frequently had to get into the surf area or on the beach among the bodies of American Marines who had been killed in action. Anchored in close to the beach, the LCS(L)s were sitting targets for Japanese artillery and mortars. Many of the tasks were performed under fire, lending urgency to the situation. After this unpleasant task had been accomplished, the LCS(L) would back off the beach using a combination of its anchor winch and engines. The damaged craft was then pulled into deeper water and sunk. LCS(L)s proved to be unsuitable for the task. In many cases they damaged their skegs, rudders, props and hull. Towing cables frequently parted and winches burned their clutches, rendering them unusable. In many of the action reports filed by the LCS(L)s at Iwo Jima, this was a common complaint. The Commanding Officer of *LCS(L) 32*, Lt. Jewel M. Evans, wrote:

> It is submitted that the construction of the LCS type of vessel makes it totally unadaptable to salvage duty. The main engines are not powerful in relation to the length and weight of the ship and it's shallow draft makes it extremely unmaneuverable. No gear has been furnished such as a powerful windlass, booms, and towing tackle, which are essential to successful salvage operations. This ship operated as a salvage vessel for 6 days, accomplished practically nothing in the performance of it's salvage duties, but suffered minor damages to itself and destroyed a considerable amount of deck gear. It is recommended that LCS type vessels be used exclusively for fire support missions and not be used as salvage vessels" (*LCS(L) 32 Action Report 10Mar45 6*).

To which Lt. J.C. Boone, Commanding Officer of *LCS(L) 33*, added "much embarrassment is felt on our part when called upon to do a job for which we are not fitted" (*LCS(L) 33 Action Report 10Mar45 11*).

A survey of the damage suffered by the gunboats at Iwo Jima is revealing. Most of their problems came from either salvage duty or the transfer of materials from larger ships. Lt. A. B. Cooper, Commanding Officer of *LCS(L) 55* noted:

> The allowed necessity of exchanging supplies and ammunition between ships of LCS(L)(3) types, and larger vessels such as B.B.s during this operation proved most damaging to both hull, gun tubs, stanchions supporting gun tubs, and handrails. It is suggested that the LCI or LSM type ships to be used for transporting supplies and ammunition for LCS(L)(3) type ships as the difference in superstructure of each type vessel offers no protection from pounding and crashing together in an open sea where it is most often necessary for such exchange of supplies to be made (*LCS(L)(3) 55 Action Report 10Mar45* 5).

In addition to the hazards caused by their larger sisters, the LCS(L)s also had to dodge friendly fire. *LCS(L) 32*, anchored off the island on 24 February, 1945, found herself in the middle of a shower of 20mm shells, which had been fired by nearby ships. A couple of days later, the *35* also reported herself in danger from shells overshooting their targets and landing nearby. Still another LCS(L) was hit by a shell from an American plane, putting a hole in her conn.

At Solomons ATB, the crews of the ships had engaged in fire-fighting practice. They had assumed that it would involve fighting fires on board ships at sea. However, at Iwo Jima this was not the case. Many fires were started on shore and needed to be put out. LCS(L) ships were called to this duty as well. On 21 February, *LCS(L) 36* was assigned the task of suppressing fires in tanks and construction equipment that had been hit by enemy fire. At 1335, the ship was beached next to a wrecked LSM and a party was sent ashore to fight a fire. Leading two two-and-a-half inch lines and two one-and-a-half inch lines ashore, all available men turned to for the task. Within an hour,

> Fires in five tanks were put out. One burning crane was salvaged. The ammunition fire was extinguished. Mission completely successful. Intensive action by own aircraft protected ship from enemy fire at time of beaching. All men aboard. Ship backed off beach, having received several holes in bosun's locker by bumping against derelict tank while beached. The Damage Control party plugged the holes and pumped water out of the bosun's locker. A wave of amphibious craft was able to proceed immediately to beach Blue One as a result of this fire-fighting action (*LCS(L) 36 Action Report 10Mar45* 3).

The following day, the firefighting capabilities of the *53* were also put to the test. An ammo dump near the beach had been shelled by the Japanese and was on fire. Contained in the dump were hand grenades, 5.0 rockets and small arms ammunition. Exploding munitions made the job even more hazardous. "From the midst of the fire the party rescued a dazed and shocked Marine. He was treated on board and transferred to Medical Guard later in the morning" (*LCS(L)(3) 54 Action Report 14Mar45* 2). *LCS(L)s 53* and *54* were ordered to assist in putting it out. This was a difficult task, as the heavy surf made the landing difficult. Dropping her anchor off shore, the *53* inched towards the beach and grounded herself among the damaged tanks and landing craft. Hoses were run from her firefighting stations forward up into the beach area and a shore party was sent in to use them against the fire. Nine men from the *53*, led by Ensigns John Sterling Jr. and Stuart Manegold, along with another crew from the *54*, fought the blaze for an hour and a half, amidst exploding ordnance and extreme heat.

Hot shells cast out of the fire landed among them. They threw this live ammunition down the embankment into the water. Several exploded after being tossed aside. The deep loose volcanic sand impeded their progress and made the handling of the fire hoses a laborious job. However, the sand proved to be a boon, for just as the last glow of the fire was being put out a Jap *Betty* glided in at mast height and dropped a stick of four bombs scarcely 75 yards from the scene. The bombs burrowed deeply and exploded harmlessly, showering areas with sand (*Hist. LCS(L) 53* 2).

Mitsubishi G4M2 bomber. Code named *Betty* by the Allies, the plane had a top speed of 266 m.p.h. at 13,780 feet. It was used by the Japanese from 1940 until the end of the war and went through three versions. Photo courtesy of the National Archives.

Japanese troops saw the venture as an opportunity to fire mortars and small arms ordnance at the ship and its firefighting crew. When the blaze was extinguished, the men and equipment were hauled on board and the ship backed off the beach. Bronze Stars were awarded to the men of the firefighting party who risked their lives in this endeavor.

The final assault on Mount Suribachi on 28 February, 1945 was preceded by an intense 30 minute barrage from all available American guns, both ashore and shipboard. In that capacity, the LCS(L) fleet expended a major amount of ammunition. Three days later they were privileged to see the capture of the summit which culminated in the raising of the American flag. It would not be the end of the fighting on Iwo Jima, however, the psychological significance of the event was great.

Throughout the campaign, the new LCS(L)s had demonstrated their value. They had assisted in leading the assault waves into the beach and provided covering and support fire for them. In addition, their shallow draft had given them the ability to get in close to shore and spot enemy positions, and their guns and rockets had caused much damage to the enemy installations and forces on the island. In several cases, they had even put their fire fighting capabilities to the test, running their ships up on the beach and fighting fires on the shore. When not performing the above-mentioned tasks, they engaged in laying smoke screens for the transports anchored off shore. There were larger, more heavily-armed ships in the battle, but perhaps none were so versatile as the *Mighty Midgets*.

Their task completed, the LCS(L)s departed the island by the middle of March, 1945. Some were sent to Saipan and others to the Philippines for their next assignments.

BORNEO

Early in their planning for expansion throughout Asia, the Japanese had recognized their one major weakness, a lack of raw materials. The Japanese home islands did not possess many of the strategic materials necessary to develop their industrial capacity. Looking to the south, they found rich sources of rubber and petroleum, which seemed theirs for the taking. In the aftermath of the attack on Pearl Harbor they expanded southward through the Philippines, the East Indies and South East Asia. One particularly rich prize was the island of Borneo with its great reserves of oil. Balikpapan, on the Dutch held southern part of the island, and Brunei, on the northwest coast, were centers of oil production and had been quickly seized by the Japanese.

Although there were serious disruptions to the delivery of oil supplies to the Japanese mainland by 1944, the decision to take the oil producing areas was put off until nearly the end of the war. Re-conquest of the Philippines was considered a higher priority. Once the islands had been retaken however, the decision to capture the Japanese held areas on the island of Borneo was made. In addition to depriving the Japanese of their resources, the area could provide air bases for future attacks into Southeast Asia and access to the rich oil fields at Balikpapan, Brunei, and Tarakan Island.

The assault on various areas of the island of Borneo took place from 27 April to 20 July, 1945. Previous assaults in the southern Phillippines had been notable for the lack of beach obstacles. Mines had frequently been a hazard, however, the landings on Borneo would prove problematical as well. In addition to more extensive mining operations, many of the landing sites were protected by underwater obstacles that could only be cleared by UDT teams. Amphibious assaults on the island generally followed a familiar pattern. Several days prior to the invasion, minesweepers (YMS) ranged throughout the prospective invasion areas clearing minefields so that amphibious assault craft and ships would be free to operate in the area.

Following the clearing of mines, frogmen from the Underwater Demolition Teams swam in to map the beach approaches and clear underwater obstacles. Theirs was an extremely hazardous duty and in the southern areas it was even more so. Added to the hazards of enemy fire were poisonous sea snakes and sea-going alligators. These teams had to be deposited only a few hundred yards off shore, and the LCS(L) ships had to be nearly as close in order to cover their activities.

The pattern of action in the Borneo Campaign followed the standard plan of attack. Participating in the campaign were ships of Flotilla 1 and included *LCS(L)s 2, 8, 28, 29, 30, 41, 42, 43, 44, 45, 46, 47, 48, 50* and *60*. First in the line of targets for the invasion fleet was the island of Tarakan. Between 27 April and the actual invasion on 1 May, *LCS(L)s 8* and *28* worked in conjunction with YMSs in clearing and destroying mines in Tarakan Bay prior to the landing of troops. Operations there proved to be quite hazardous, with the *YMS 329* striking a mine and taking heavy damage and 19 casualties. Occasional shore fire harassed the minesweeping operations as well.

Four LCVPs sweeping in shallow water reported being fired on with the fire coming from the town of Linkas. The order was given for them to vacate the area and we [LCS(L) 48] took aboard an officer from one of the LCVPs who had observed the fire in order that he might spot the targets for us. The five LCS(L)s closed the beach and strafed the beach and approaches. We continued fire for an hour and a half and during this time we noted several pill boxes, gun emplacements, anti-aircraft guns and various installations, the beach proper seemed to be heavily defended (*LCS(L) 48 Action Report 1May45* 2).

The 48 was fired on from shore, but fortunately was not hit. Her biggest hazard in that location was friendly fire. An Army *P-38 Lightning* passed over with a bomb stuck in her racks. As she passed near the ship the bomb dropped in the water only about 150 yards from the *48*. No damage was done, but it was too close for comfort. On 30 April, a minor landing on nearby Sadau Island was accomplished with little resistance or activity on the part of the LCS(L)s. Assigned to this task were *LCS(L)s 8, 48* and *50.*

The actual invasion of the island of Tarakan was scheduled for 1 May at 0700. At 0530, the larger ships, under the command of Admiral Berkey, assembled off shore at about 0700 and began an hour of pre-landing bombardment. Lending their power to the invasion were the cruisers *U.S.S. Phoenix (CL 46), U.S.S. Boise (CL 47), H.M.A.S. Hobart* and the destroyers *U.S.S. Taylor (DD 468), U.S.S. Nicholas (DD 449), U.S.S. O'Bannon (DD 450), U.S.S. Fletcher (DD 445), U.S.S. Jenkins (DD 447),* and *H.M.A.S. Warramunga.* The landing ships assembled, loaded with troops of the 26th Australia Infantry Brigade under the command of Brigadier Whitehead A.I.F. At 0800 the assault force, led by the LCS(L)s headed for the beach. As the *Mighty Midgets* neared shore, they fired their salvos of rockets and raked the shoreline with all available guns. After 15 minutes of firing, they slowed their speed to allow the landing craft carrying the Australian troops to pass by them and deposit the men on shore. Small arms fire emanated from the shore and the two LCS(L)s responded. However, the landing forces encountered no significant opposition and the LCS(L)s were ordered to standby off shore on picket duty. In all, 18,100 Australian troops had been landed with minimal casualties. The Japanese had followed their previous tactics and withdrawn from the immediate beach area to escape the guns of the assembled fleet.

The following day, *LCS(L)s 8* and *28* were ordered north to another section of Tarakan Island to support minesweeping operations by YMSs. At about 1530, the minesweepers came under attack from shore batteries. *YMS 481* was sunk and *YMSs 334* and *364* were damaged. In addition, *YMS 363* struck a mine and had to retire from the action. *LCS(L)s 8* and *28* responded by returning fire to cover the minesweepers. Unfortunately, the two gunboats were outranged by the shore batteries and could not prevent damage to the YMSs. Minesweeping operations were halted and the ships withdrew out of range of the shore guns. Having assisted in securing the target area, the LCS(L)s spent several days on picket duty and covered the clearing of damaged LCTs and LCVPs from the beach area.

LCS(L) 28 explodes a mine off Tarakan Island, 1 May, 1945. Photo courtesy of the National Archives.

Next on the list of invasion targets were several areas in Brunei Bay. As the *LCS(L) 43* headed into the area, she noticed 15 to 20 radar blips on the screen. Further investigation indicated that they were Japanese landing craft, each carrying from 50 to 100 troops. Radioing back to command for instructions, the *43* was ordered to sink them. Within a short period of time all the Japanese troop carriers had gone to the bottom (Blakley interview). The ships also assisted in the landing of the 9th Australian Division in three locations, Brunei Bluff, Muara Island and Labuan Island near Victoria Town. "The ultimate objective of the operation was to secure Brunei Bay as an advanced fleet base, to take from the enemy vital rubber and oil reserves, to establish air bases, and to reinstate the British Civil Government" (*LCS(L) 60 Action Report 12Jun45* 1). Stiff resistance was anticipated here. The invasion fleet of 184 ships, included *LCS(L)s 43, 45, 46, 47, 58, 59* and *60*, along with cruisers, destroyers, destroyer escorts, minesweepers and other assorted amphibious attack vessels. The actual assault by Australian troops under Major General G.F. Wooten A. I. F., was scheduled for 10 June, so the fleet practiced its usual activity for several days prior to the landing. Minesweepers, covered by LCS(L)s, patrolled back and forth in Brunei Bay locating and cutting loose anti-ship mines. Crewmen on board the LCS(L)s and LCI(L)s fired rifles or automatic weapons at the mines in order to detonate them. Preparatory firing on the beach by the heavier ships was undertaken to eliminate any possible resistance. In addition to the ship attacks, a dozen *B-24 Liberators* dropped bombs on the invasion site.

The following day, 10 June, 1945, allied amphibious forces executed a standard attack. *LCS(L)s 58, 59, 60, LCI(G)s 69, 70*, and *LCI(R)s 31* and *34* preceded the troop carriers, closing to within 1,000 yards of the beach and then letting go their salvo of rockets. After their rocket run was completed, the LCS(L)s turned and ran parallel to the beach, strafing everything in sight. After regrouping and making another rocket run on the beach, they held position as the troop carriers landed. As their action was underway, the cruisers and destroyers fired their heavy guns farther inland, adding to the effect. All this destruction was either highly effective or not necessary, since the Australian troops were able to land without much resistance. Once again, the Japanese had withdrawn to the interior. Within a short period of time, the LSMs and LSTs were able to complete their landings and began to unload. In all, four landings occurred in the area at Victoria Town, Labuan Island and two sites near Brockton City. Little resistance was met and the area was secured within a few days. The assembled fleet remained there until the first of July. During that time they engaged in picket duty, minesweeping and general patrolling. Still another invasion was attempted at Borneo on 20 June in the Miri-Lutong area. This was an important oil production center and its capture would be damaging to the Japanese. Active in this operation were the *LCS(L)s 42, 45,*

46, 58 and *60.* As with other operations the assault was preceded by minesweeping operations. In this area, the waters were heavily mined. Operating with YMSs on 13 June, the *LCS(L) 45* destroyed 29 mines with small arms fire and the following day accounted for another 26. In the midst of this operation, crewmen on the 45 saw a lone Japanese *Betty* go after a destroyer and drop several bombs. Fortunately they missed and the plane flew away. Between the 15 and the 17 of June, the 46 accounted for an additional 29 mines.

LCS(L) 50 **makes a rocket run at Tarakan. Photo courtesy of Ken Krayer.**

By 20 June, 1945, the way was clear for the assault. At 0900 the attacking force got underway. Once again, the LCS(L)s and their companion LCI(G)s and LCI(M)s laid down a heavy barrage on the beach areas accompanied by offshore fire from larger ships, and once again, the landing was unopposed. "It consisted of three waves of LVTs and one of DUKWs, preceded by ships of the Support Unit in a line abreast from left to right as follows: *LCI 72, LCS 46, LCI(R) 71, LCS 60, LCI(R) 74, LCS 58,* with *LCI(M) 359* and *431* on the left and right flanks respectively" (*LCS(L) 60 Action Report 21Jun45*). Eighteen-hundred Australian troops were landed without casualties.

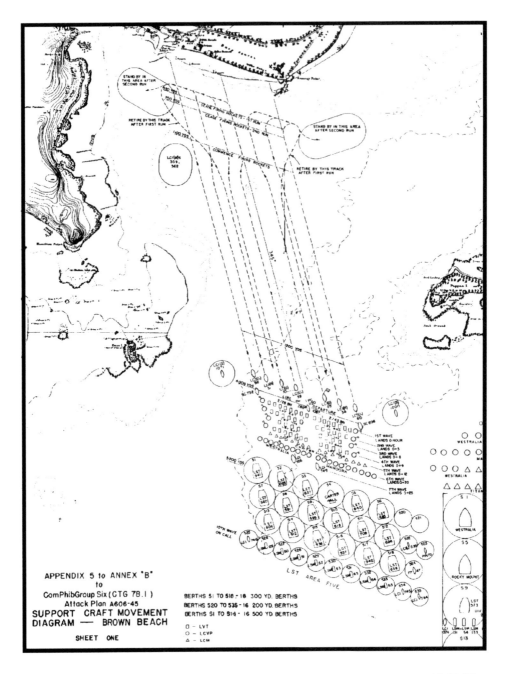

Attack Plan for the invasion at Brown Beach, Brunei Bay on 10 June, 1945. The attack was led by *LCS(L)s 58, 59, 60, LCI (G)s 69, 70* and *LCI(R)s 31* and *34*. (*ComPhibGroup Six Attack Plan*).

The final assault on the island of Borneo took place on the southeastern coast at the port city of Balikpapan. Serious concern was voiced among the allied leaders "because of the belief that the Japanese intended to use it as a tryout of new defense techniques which would be employed to resist the Allied invasion of the home islands" (Barbey 316). Participating in that assault were the ships of Task Unit 78.2.8, which included *LCS(L)s 8, 24, 28, 29, 30, 41, 43, 44, 48* and *50*. Scheduled for 1 July, the invasion was preceded by eleven days of work by minesweepers, underwater demolition teams and gunfire designed to soften the area's defenses.

A Japanese gun emplacement was located on a cliff overlooking the horseshoe shaped bay that was to be the sight of the landing. Since this particular weapon was mounted on rails in a tunnel in the cliff face, the Japanese were able to withdraw it after each shot, making it hard for the ships off shore to hit it. *LCS(L) 43* received the job. The rationale was that the LCS(L) could get in close to shore and that the gun would be unable to depress sufficiently in order to hit her. A negative aspect of the mission was that the area had not been cleared of mines and the ship would be under fire until she came close enough to be in the safe zone. Lt. (jg) Earl A. Blakley, CO of the *43*, gave orders to Quartermaster Evans to plot a careful course into the area. The *43* went in under the cliff face, dodging shells from the gun which bracketed her. Gunner's Mate Coombs took careful aim and fired a few rounds. Unfortunately, the gun was withdrawn and it was not possible to hit it. The ship's Gunnery Officer timed the movement of the gun and the next round caught it just as it came forward to fire, knocking it off its tracks and killing the crew.

Its mission accomplished, the *43* still had to withdraw safely. The Quartermaster had carefully plotted the course in and it had to be followed precisely in order to get out. As the *43* was almost to the edge of the mined area, the Quartermaster informed the CO that they were being pushed slightly off course by the current. The ship continued on course after making a few adjustments. A few minutes later a loud bump was heard on the hull, followed shortly thereafter by an explosion ten yards off the stern. They had set off a mine. Fortunately, the mine exploded after they had passed over it and the ship and its crew escaped harm. As CO Blakley looked back at the area, he noticed that his men had taken off life jackets and helmets as though they were no longer at General Quarters. He ordered the Bosun's Mate to place on report all who had violated orders (Blakley interview).

The LCS(L)s had occasion to use their anti-aircraft capabilities as Japanese planes attacked them in the midst of their activities. Continual firing by American ships into the shore areas for an extended period eliminated much of the opposition. Along with the naval gunfire, *B-24 Liberators* bombed enemy emplacements in the area. Two weeks of such activity took place with the shore defenses being decimated. However, not all resistance was quelled. LCS(L)s were supporting UDT operations on 28 June near the beach when they came under fire from shore batteries about 0945. Several shells came uncomfortably close to the LCS(L) line before *LCS(L) 8* took a hit through the base of the conn on the port side. One officer and two enlisted men were wounded by shrapnel. The ships returned fire, maneuvered, and eventually managed to quiet the shore batteries. A short while later, at 1045, they were fired upon again. Once more the *8* was hit, this time below the water line. A live shell was found lodged in the base of an electric generator, which was put out of commission. EM3c John C. Black was wounded in the attack, but in spite of his wounds, he managed to plug the hole and save the ship from further damage.

On the 29 of June, *LCS(L)s 8* and *28* were engaged, along with other LCS(L)s, in the support of underwater demolition teams when they were fired on by shore batteries. At about 1020, the *8* came under fire and took three hits, wounding seven crewmen. As she withdrew from the area, the *LCS(L) 8* surveyed her damage. Her engines were not functioning and she had to be towed to Morotai for repairs. Other vessels suffered as well.

> On D-Day minus 4, minus 3, and minus 1, close support fire was given by LCS(L)s for reconnaissance and underwater demolition operations at the Klandasan beaches in the Balikpapan area. Enemy return fire was encountered on each of these three days, but no direct hits were suffered by this vessel [LCS(L) 29]. In all cases the enemy fire lasted for short periods and was discontinued when fire of close support vessels was intensified. At about 2025 on the night of D-Day minus 5, six Japanese planes attacked ships anchored in the assault area, and this ship participated in the anti-aircraft fire. Three of the planes were destroyed as a result of the fire from the ships. Heavy fire by destroyers and cruisers, and bombing and strafing by planes also were an integral part of the support of underwater demolition operations (*LCS(L) 29 Action Report 2Jul45* 1).

The invasion took place on 1 July, 1945 and was the last amphibious invasion of the Pacific War. Thirty-three thousand Australian troops of the 7th Australian Division (plus Corps Artillery), under the command of Major General Milford A.I.F., landed to light opposition and the area was secured. For the ships of the Seventh Amphibious Force, it was their 56th landing in two years and their last.

Additional landings and pursuit of Japanese troops that had moved inland seemed superfluous. News from the Joint Chiefs of Staff indicated that the final assault on the home islands had been authorized. For that venture, every available ship and man would be needed. Additional efforts in the islands were no longer necessary.

CHAPTER III

THE KAMIKAZES

One of the greatest dangers of the war was the *kamikaze* or "Divine Wind." Originally used to describe the typhoon that had blown away the Mongol invasion of 1281, the term became synonymous with the Japanese suicide attacks on allied forces. This concept was incomprehensible to the American forces at the time and the mind set of the Japanese was at best described as "different." How their ethos came into existence is worth examining if we are to understand the *kamikaze* in the context of World War II.

The Japanese military class, or samurai, had its origins during the Nara period of Japanese history (AD 710-784). The land distribution system of the times made it possible for large land holders to use their workers for defense when necessary. Gradually, over the course of the next several centuries, political changes occurred that caused the formation of large estates (shoen) guarded by full time warriors. These full time warriors formed a new class in Japan and were to have a great impact on its culture from that time forward. Prior to 1185, the Emperor and his court held a nominal rule over the Japanese countryside. The large estates were so powerful that, in actuality, the Emperor had little ability to control them. Eventually two clans, the Minamoto and the Taira, fought for control of the country. Emerging victorious at the final battle in the Straits of Shimonoseki, the Minamoto, under the leadership of Yoritomo Minamoto, assumed control of the government in AD 1185. This placed the samurai class in control of the country. Samurai rule lasted until 1867, when the four major clans of Tosa, Hizen, Satsuma and Choshu overthrew the ruling Tokugawa Shogunate and began Japan on its road to modernization. During the previous seven centuries, the values of the samurai class gradually filtered down to the common people and became the ethos under which the Japanese lived. This ethos was known to the outside world as the code of *Bushido*. The *Bushido* code was relatively consistent throughout the seven centuries of samurai rule and included frugality, stoicism, honor, benevolence, obedience, a sense of duty, a war-like spirit, loyalty, courage, a sense of morality, self-discipline, decorum, sobriety, honesty, practical ethics, and the study of war and administration.

Western intervention by Admiral Perry in the 1850s, caused great consternation among the Japanese and was a major factor in the overthrow of the old system ruled by the Tokugawa clan. The Japanese perceived the need to modernize in the face of Western intervention, and restructured their traditional values in order to assist them in their survival. As they modernized, they attempted to maintain their culture in the face of growing changes in their society brought about by Western technology and their own modernization. The reemphasis on their martial ideology came as they went to war with Russia in 1904. In his work, *Bushido The Soul of Japan* written in 1905, Inazo Nitobe attempted to remind the Japanese of their traditions. In order to compete with the West, they had modernized their nation and expanded in Asia to make themselves militarily and economically stronger. This had caused changes in the nation which, when coupled with industrialization, made the new Japan a very different place than the Japan of old. Perhaps it is through the revival of the martial ideology that the Japanese were able to preserve the unique "Japanness" of their being in the face of many pressures from the outside. Certainly the martial ideology might have been used to hold the culture together in the face of the destructive Western elements.

In Japan's pre-war period, classic tales of samurai adventures became quite popular, and novels such as Eiji Yoshikawa's *Musashi* were widely read. Martial ideology in the 1930s caused some changes in school textbooks with the emphasis placed on reverence for the Imperial line and a religious bent imparted by the myths of the divine origins of the Japanese nation. With the increasing involvement in overseas Asian campaigns in the 1930s, that enthusiasm was channeled into a sense of mission in East Asia that demanded loyalty in the form of military service.

In addition to stories in their texts that indicated the desirability of the samurai-like virtue of loyalty, schools also held military drills and the practice of martial arts was increased. The government also passed a number of decrees that were basic admonitions designed to foster the martial spirit and value system. Such decrees as the Educational Reform of 1941 (Imperial Ordinance No. 1483) and the *Ministry of Education: Policy on Instruction* were designed to increase national spirit in the face of the wartime threat. In effect, the traditional values of the *Bushido* code had been brought forward in time from the period of samurai rule to the World War II era. One of the major concepts of the code that helps to understand the *kamikaze* in the war was the idea that a warrior's life did not belong to him. As with the samurai of old, the modern warrior's life was focused on self-sacrifice in the name of his country. What better way to demonstrate this concept than to crash one's plane or ship into the enemy, thereby fulfilling this centuries' old ideal? The modern samurai who had volunteered for the mission even wore an item of clothing dating to earlier times. Samurai warriors of old wrapped white cloths around their heads before donning their helmets. These *hachimaki* cloths often carried inscriptions. Originally they kept perspiration out of the warrior's eyes and helped control their long hair. During World War II, they were used by the *kamikaze* pilots as a reminder of the warrior tradition.

Although Westerners have labeled the actions of the *kamikaze* pilots as suicide, the pilots themselves did not regard their actions that way. Former member of the *Kamikaze Corps*, Saburo Sakai wrote:

> To the enemy our men seemed to be committing suicide, they were throwing their lives away uselessly. Perhaps it will never be fully understood by Americans, or anyone in the Western world, that our men did not consider that they were throwing away their lives. . . . This was not suicide! These men, young and old, were not dying in vain. Every plane which thundered into an enemy warship was a blow struck for our land. Every bomb carried by a Kamikaze into the fuel tanks of a giant carrier meant that many more of the enemy killed, that many more planes which would never bomb or strafe our soil (Sakai 346-347).

This mind set was difficult for their American opponents to understand, but it was deeply rooted in a cultural ideal that had been held in high regard for many centuries. With that understanding, let us examine the *kamikaze* actions during World War II.

Kamikaze attacks began in October of 1944, when Admiral Takijiro Onishi arrived in the Philippines to take charge of the Air Fleet. Onishi "was horrified to find that there were fewer than 100 operational planes in the entire Philippines . . . He therefore concluded he had no choice but to implement the plan for sending Special Attack Groups to make suicide strikes" (Costello 501). The most important targets for the *kamikazes* at that time were the allied carriers. However, later in the war they would be used against any target of opportunity.

As the war progressed and the Japanese lost the Philippines, the invasion of Okinawa seemed imminent. The loss of so many of its ships and planes during the Marianas Turkey Shoot, had left Japan with a severe shortage of experienced pilots. Combating the American airmen would be difficult with green pilots. Short cuts were taken during the training of replacement pilots, and their actual flight time upon graduation was only about 200 hours as compared to 800 before the war (Hoyt 1993, 20). This situation drove the Japanese high command to consider an expansion of the suicide corps, and in late spring of 1945, it organized additional units to attack the American invasion forces in and around Okinawa.

Suicide weapons were of various types and not limited to aircraft. Much of the LCS(L)'s duty during the Okinawa Gunto Campaign included "fly catching" or "skunk patrol." Flies or Skunks was the term given to the suicide boats used by the Japanese against ships anchored in Hagushi Bay and other locations. Referred to by the Japanese Army as *Maru-ni* (Liaison Boats) or by the Japanese Navy as *Shinyo* (Ocean Shakers), the small craft were used by both services. The United States Navy classified them as *Q-Boats,* and the U.S. Technical Mission to Japan at the end of the war did not differentiate *Shinyo* from *Maru-ni* craft.

The Japanese developed seven varieties of these boats in 1944 and designated them as *Types 1, 2, 3, 5, 6, 7*, and *8*. Two of the types were in use by the end of that year, the *Type 1* and *Type 5*. *Type 1* boats had two variations, the first was about 23-and-one-half feet long with a five-and-one-half-foot beam. These V-bottomed hulls were produced in either wood or steel. They were not placed in use as suicide boats. The second, designated as *Type 1 Model 1*, was about 16-and-one-half-feet long with a five-and-one-half-foot beam and made of wood.

> Only Type 1, Mod. 1, and Type 5 Shinyo boats were actually used as suicide special attack boats. Types 2, 3, 6, 7 and 8 were in design and experimental stages in an endeavor to attain better performance. Type 4 was never designated because of the superstition attached to "Shi," its Japanese pronunciation, which can also mean "death" (*U.S. Naval Tech. Mission* 1).

The design of these boats was derived from the 18-meter torpedo boat in use by the Japanese, which was designed by S. Makino for the Navy Ministry (*U.S. Naval Technical Mission* 5). Powered by 67 or 70 horsepower Toyoda or Nissan automobile engines, they could attain speeds of 23 knots. Although they had a 250 mile range, most of their targets were not that far away. Navy boats carried an explosive charge of 270 kg in the bow and two crude rocket launchers, one of which was mounted on either side of the cockpit. The explosive charge was armed just before attempting to ram a ship. This charge had little protection from defensive fire, and the Commanding Officer of *LCS(L) 85* wrote that he fired three shots from a .3- caliber rifle, and that the third shot apparently hit the explosive charge. Although the suicide boat was 300 yards away, the "concussion was so great that it rocked the ship a slight bit and a slight jar was felt" (*LCS(L) 85 Action Report*

18Apr45 1). Since these craft were constructed of plywood, with no protective armor in front of the explosive charge, they were easily blown up by a single shot from a rifle. Still others were shot full of holes by LCS(L) gunners and sank before they could reach their targets.

The Type 1, Mod. 1 Shinyo was equipped with a net cutter extending from the bow to a raised stanchion on the stern. It also had two 12cm rockets mounted on two primitive wood launching troughs on either quarter, to be fired against enemy attacking boats, attacking airplanes, or the intended victim, and to serve as a morale booster (*U.S. Technical Mission* 12).

A second type of *Shinyo*, designated the *Type 5*, was also put into service. They were 21 feet long and also constructed of wood. *Type 5s* had twin six-cylinder Toyoda engines and were capable of 25 knots. They carried the same explosive charge and rockets as the *Type 1* but had a slightly longer range. In addition to the rockets, the *Type 5s* had improved net cutters and some mounted a "13mm machine gun . . . just forward of the cockpit for increased protection, fire power, and morale" (*U.S. Technical Mission* 12). Also equipped with a radio and a two man crew, they were designed as division leaders (*U.S. Technical Mission* 1).

Boats used by the Army had racks behind the driver which carried two depth charges as the explosive agent. After approaching a target at a high rate of speed, the craft would swerve and roll the depth charges off the stern. If the driver was lucky, he would have time to get away before they detonated. On 9 April, 1945, the destroyer *U.S.S. Charles J. Badger* (*DD 657*), suffered just such an attack while on a fire support mission off Okinawa. Her engines knocked out by the blast and shipping water, she was towed to Kerama Retto for temporary repairs and then sent to the states. She had been effectively put out of the war by a suicide boat. *LCS(L) 37* also reported the use of depth charges as an attacking method. On 28 April, 1945, the *37* saw a suicide boat approaching at a speed of about twenty knots. When it was only a few feet off the side of the ship, it swerved away and a depth charge rolled off the rear racks. Set to go off at a shallow depth, the charge exploded under the hull of the *37*, causing considerable damage.

Production of these boats by numerous shipyards led to slight variations in hull design, construction and fittings. Official U.S. Navy photographs in this writer's collection show four different profiles and deck arrangements. At least three types of engines were known to be used: (1) a small chevy-type valve-in-head engine, (2) a twin eight cylinder valve-in-block Ford type engine and (3) a six cylinder valve-in-head engine (*Baumler letter 12 Aug., 1996*). It is probable that these variations of hull shape, power plant and other features were caused by the availability of materials as well as production in a variety of shipyards. According to Millot, 6,000 of them were produced by the end of the war (155). Official reports indicate that, "they were manned by middle school boys about 15 to 16 years old. It is reported that an ample supply of volunteer pilots was obtained because of the special privileges, early responsibility, fast promotion, and the promise of a posthumous monetary reward to the volunteer's parents" (*U.S. Technical Mission to Japan* 7). Operators of these craft usually tried to attack at night, and a favorite method was to get in between two ships so that any fire directed at them might also hit the defending ships. Other tactics were described in the *Log of the LCS(L)(3) 84*: "It is noted that small boats lay in water with little or no movement until they are closed for investigation. They attack then at high speed at bow or slightly off bow"(54).

First used against the LCS(L)s in the Philippines in January and February of 1945, the boats were usually destroyed before they reached their targets. However, in the attack on 16 February, 1945 in Mariveles Harbor, about 30 of the *Shinyo* attacked the LCS(L)s guarding the harbor. *LCS(L)s 7, 26* and *49* were sunk and the *27* was severely damaged.

***Maru-ni -Type 5* under power with driver showing empty racks. This boat was used by the Japanese Army and carried two depth charges on the racks behind the driver. As the boat approached within a few feet of the target, it swerved and dropped the depth charges next to the ship. This example is being tested by U.S. Army personnel shortly after its capture at Kerama Retto. Photo courtesy of the National Archives.**

A captured *Type 1 Model 1 Shinyo* on the beach at Okinawa. This type of suicide
boat was used by the Japanese Navy and carried a charge in the bow which
detonated upon impact with the target vessel. Photo courtesy of the National
Archives.

As the invasion of Okinawa commenced, the American forces enjoyed some
good fortune. When they captured the Kerama Retto Islands on 25 March, 1945,
their attack came so swiftly that they captured more than 350 suicide boats before
they could be put into action. Most of these boats had been hidden in caves along
the coast, well back from the entrances so that they would be hard to find (*Kerama
Isles* 4). Unfortunately, in exploring the caves and inspecting some of the captured
boats on Aka Island, a group of high ranking Army officers happened upon one
that was booby trapped. The ensuing explosion killed five of them and seriously
wounded three others.

In spite of the fake invasion attempt on the southeast coast of Okinawa, the
Japanese correctly predicted the invasion in Hagushi Bay. To prepare for it they
stationed *Shinyo* boats in a small river (Bisha Gawa), and prepared to meet the
invasion fleet. During the night of 31 March, 50 *Shinyo* were sent to attack the
approaching American ships. Fleet gunners took aim and successfully blew them
out of the water. Of the 50, only one hit a target. *LSM 12* was the victim, and
within a few days she had gone to the bottom. Still another, larger base had been

established on Motobu Peninsula, and this base also caused problems for the fleet as they supported the invasion of the island.

Less numerous and not as effective was the class of midget submarines known as *Ko-Hyoteki* (*A-targets*). Although photographers and writers seemed fascinated by them, the total number of all types of these craft actually delivered was estimated at only 438 (Fukaya 863). The *Ko-Hoteki* had been under development since the 1934 and were not originally designed as suicide craft. Later developments along this line would see them used in that manner. By war's end, only two successful missions had been completed by these miniature subs, both against British ships at Diego Suarez between Madagascar and India.

The largest of this type, the *Koryu* (*Scaly Dragon*) carried a crew of five. It was 86 feet long with a beam of nearly seven feet, displaced 58 tons and was armed with two 18" torpedoes in tubes. Capable of eight knots on the surface and 16 knots when submerged, the vessel had an extreme range of 1,000 nautical miles at its lower speed of eight knots. Its sturdy hull allowed it to dive to a depth of 330 feet. The decision to use a five man crew indicates that the purpose of this vessel was similar to that of a full sized submarine. Its development came too late in the war to be of use to the Japanese, with the first of its type completed in January of 1945. Subsequent war-induced production problems limited actual completion to 115 (Kemp 113). However, its late entry and the limited production of torpedoes probably would have required that it eventually be fitted with an explosive warhead, the crew limited in size, and its use reserved for suicide attacks. As it occurred, none of the *Koryu* were ever used in action.

A smaller sub, the *Kairyu* (*Sea Dragon*), carried a crew of two and at 57 feet was shorter than the *Koryu*. *Kairyus* displaced 20 tons and had the ability to dive to 650 feet, but their speed and range were not as great as that of the *Koryu*. Originally they were armed with two 18" torpedoes mounted externally. Carrying a two man crew, they had a speed of seven-and-one-half knots on the surface and ten knots submerged. At their lower speed, they had an extreme range of 450 nautical miles. As with the *Koryu*, their production came too late in the war to be placed into service. In all, only 212 were delivered to the Japanese Naval establishment. Since torpedo production lagged towards the end of the war, they were also designed with a 1,300 -pound external warhead for ramming enemy ships. Although not originally designed for the suicide corps, they became a part of the program toward the end of the war since they could not carry out their original functions.

Still smaller was the *Shinkai* (*Sea Shaking*) submarine which was only about 30 feet long. It was designed to attach magnetic explosives to the underside of ship hulls.

U.S. Navy Personnel inspect *Kairyu* suicide submarines at Yokosuka Naval Shipyard, 11 September, 1945. Photo courtesy of the National Archives.

The initiation of suicide attacks by the Japanese air corps had a profound effect on the naval forces and made navy men want to emulate them, leading to the development of the *Kaiten* (*Changing Heaven*) manned torpedo. This was designed for the Navy Ministry by K. Mimizuka (*U.S. Naval Technical Mission* 5). Based on the *Mark 93, Model 3 Long Lance* torpedo, *Mark I Kaitens* were 48 feet long and packed a 3,200 pound warhead. They were shorter than some of the midget subs and had a range of 23 miles, a top speed of 30 knots, and could extend their range to 78 miles at twelve knots. *Mark II* and *IV Kaitens* were 54 feet long. They had a range of 83 at 20 knots or 25 at 40 knots and carried a warhead in excess of 3,200 pounds. *Mark I Kaitens* carried a crew of one and *Mark IIs* and *IVs* had a crew of two. A *Mark III* was experimental and never went into production. It was commonly believed that frogmen straddled these torpedoes and rode them into their intended targets, however this is not quite accurate. Fitted with a miniature conning tower and an escape hatch, they were designed to be guided to within 50 yards of their target and then abandoned to make the final run. "Standard Kaiten attack approach procedure was to run about one meter below the surface of the water, take an occasional look with a retractable periscope, and dive to about five meters prior to striking" (*U.S. Technical Mission* 22). The subsequent explosion would have killed anyone in the water at such a close range, so in all probability, the pilot would have ridden it to his death. An end to a naval career in this manner needed an incentive. Accordingly, the *Kaitens*

> were manned by 18-to 20-year-old youths who, after about three months training, became Ensigns. As in the case of the Shinyo boats, volunteers were reported to be plentiful because of fast promotion, special privileges, and the promise that their family would receive about ¥10,000 as a posthumous award. No doubt, many of the pilots were in no position not to volunteer (*U.S. Naval Technical Mission* 22).

Japanese *Kaiten Mark 2* or *4* manned torpedo. This example was built in 1945 and is shown on display at the Washington Navy Yard in 1974. It measures 54 ½ feet long and is 4 ½ feet in diameter. Photo courtesy of the U.S. Naval Historical Center.

Frequently they were transported to within attacking range on the backs of specially-fitted submarines which could carry from four to six of them. The strategy was to locate a ship underway or in an anchorage and then release the *Kaiten* in its path. At a range of about 500 yards the *Kaiten* would surface and set its course for the target ship. With its 40 knot speed, the miniature sub would surely hit its target. In the two instances where these weapons were used successfully, each pilot followed the tradition of his airborne comrades in arms and stayed aboard till the end. One successful mission took place at Ulithi, where the tanker *Mississinewa* was struck and sunk, and a second off Okinawa, where the destroyer escort *U.S.S. Underhill* (*DE 682*) was attacked and sunk. About 50 of the *Kaiten* actually saw service. Their lack of success during the war has been attributed to difficult steering characteristics and the lack of experience of their pilots. Near the end of the war, as a last resort for the protection of the home islands of Kyushu and Honshu, the Japanese were constructing bomb-proof caves near the suspected invasion sites. These caves usually faced into the harbor or bay so that they would not be vulnerable to fire from attacking ships. Each cave held one or two *Kaiten* mounted on launching dollies which rode rails to the water in order to launch the manned torpedoes.

Kaiten on launching tracks. Photo courtesy of U.S. Naval Historical Center.

A Japanese midget submarine. Both the Japanese and the Germans developed these toward the end of the war. They could be used as manned torpedoes or to tow mines into place. Their limited range would have made it likely that they would have been used in defense of the home islands. Photo courtesy of the National Archives.

Lowest on the scale of technology were the *fukuryus* (*crawling dragons*). They were frogmen who wore light diving gear and either swam underwater or crawled along the bottom in an attempt to attach explosives to the bottoms of American ships. Their breathing apparatus was crude but allowed them to remain underwater for several hours.

Units of *fukuryus* were developed towards the end of 1944, but they were not observed in action in any of the campaigns. It is thought that they were a last ditch defense effort in case the home islands were invaded. According to Richard O'Neill, underwater pillboxes were under construction in the shallows of each projected invasion site. As allied landing craft neared the shore, *fukuryus* would exit their underwater bunkers and, using long poles, strike the undersides of landing craft with impact charges (O'Neill 270-271).

In addition to the weapons noted above, the Japanese had developed a new, airborne weapon, the *Oka* (*Cherry Blossom*), which was literally a flying bomb. After considering types of unmanned rockets, such as the *V-2* used by the Germans, the Japanese high command determined that they could not be used accurately against the ships of the American invasion fleet. It was decided that a piloted bomb would be more effective. *Okas* were made of plywood with aluminum bodies about 20 twenty feet in length. Their 16 foot wingspan and high speed did not give them a great deal of maneuverability. Powered by three rocket engines, which could be fired consecutively, they reached speeds of 403 miles per hour in level flight and up to 576 miles per hour in their dive to destruction. They had a range of only about 23 miles and carried a 2,646 pound warhead. Nestled beneath a twin engine bomber, usually a *Betty*, they were released near the target to complete their mission. The only flaw in the *Oka* plan was that in carrying it, the bomber was slowed considerably. On one early mission, eighteen bombers equipped with *Okas* were sent out and all were shot down. Quickly dubbed the *Baka* (*Fool*) by American forces, the rocket bomb was not as successful as the more conventional *kamikaze* aircraft. Within a short time it became obvious to the American forces that this weapon, although potentially dangerous, would have little effect on the outcome of the war. The record for the *Okas* were quite poor but they still did manage to take their toll. On 12 April, 1945, the destroyer *U.S.S. Mannert L. Abele* (*DD 733*) became the first ship sunk by an O*ka* when she was hit while patrolling on Radar Picket Station 14, about 70 miles northwest of Okinawa. A bomb, carried into her interior by a *kamikaze Zeke* had exploded and broken her keel just aft of the Number 2 stack. Within a minute or two she received her death blow from a second hit by the *Oka*, which struck her on the starboard waterline. The blast broke her completely in two. As men went into the water, the two halves of the destroyer went to the bottom.

A Japanese *Oka* or *Baka* piloted bomb captured at Okinawa. Photo courtesy of the National Archives.

On the same day, both the *U.S.S. Stanly* (*DD 478*) and the *U.S.S. Jeffers* (*DMS 27*) were damaged by *Okas*. The *Stanly* was heading for Radar Picket Station 1, north of Okinawa. The *U.S.S. Cassin Young* (*DD 793*) had been hit by a *kamikaze* and the *Stanly* was sent to aid her. While fighting off a swarm of *kamikazes*, the *Stanly* was attacked by two *Okas*. The first hit her above the waterline near the bow and the second narrowly missed her. Fortunately, the warhead of the *Oka* passed completely through the ship before exploding in the water on her port side. The *Jeffers* was also on radar picket duty that day. The *Oka* that damaged her crashed in the water nearby, and fortunately did not make a direct hit.

Japanese crew members relax prior to taking off in their *Betty* bomber. Underneath the bomber is an *Oka* piloted bomb. Photo courtesy of the U.S. Naval Institute.

The *U.S.S. Shea* (*DM 30*) arrived on radar picket duty early on the morning of 4 May. At about 0854, enemy *Betty* bombers were spotted in the area. One was shot down by the Combat Air Patrol, but within minutes an *Oka* was sighted heading straight for the *Shea*. She took the hit on the starboard side of her bridge, causing serious damage to her steering and some gun mounts. Fortunately, the warhead passed completely through the ship before it exploded. There was little solace, however, as the attack caused the death of 27 men and wounded 91 others. The following day, 5 May, still another ship was attacked by an *Oka*. Crewmen on the *U.S.S. Gayety* (*AM 239*) observed an *Oka* closing with their ship at a high rate of speed. Her gunners were able to destroy the piloted bomb only 15 yards off her port bow. The ensuing explosion wounded three men and knocked out the port 40mm gun. On 10 May, while on patrol at Radar Picket Station 15, the *U.S.S. Hugh W. Hadley* (*DD 774*) was struck by a bomb, two *kamikazes* and an *Oka*. Badly holed by the attack and suffering casualties, she still managed to survive.

Although they could claim to have sunk one ship and damaged five others, the *Okas* were not as effective as the Japanese had hoped. Their high speed and lack of maneuverability made it possible for ships to avoid being hit by them, and as one Associated Press correspondent reported, "They attain high speeds, . . . but the boys who fly them don't get a chance to practice, and so there are lots of misses" (*Japanese Rocket Bombs*). In fact, their extreme speed and design would have been difficult for a veteran flyer to handle, let alone a green pilot. Accordingly, the Okas were not a great threat to the American fleet.

A second version of the piloted bomb was the *Oka 43*. Based on the German *V-1 buzz bomb*, it was launched from a ramp. Although they were not used at Okinawa, their ramjet engines gave them a range of 130 miles, making them a potential threat to an invasion fleet heading for the main islands of Japan. British experience had indicated that this type of flying bomb was not as dangerous as the *Oka*. Since they were not as fast, British *Spitfires* regularly caught up with them and shot them down. Accordingly, their effectiveness in battle would have been limited.

The American strategy for the invasion of Okinawa required that Americans land in the center of the island and divide the Japanese forces. Their assault came on the western side of Okinawa in Hagushi Bay and they deployed as quickly as possible. So rapid was their advance that they overran many of the airfields that contained *Okas*, denying the Japanese full use of them. As Hagushi Bay filled with landing craft, supply ships and other vessels, it became a prime target for the Japanese suicide corps. LCS(L)s, which had been designed for close-in support of landing craft, such as the LCI(L)s and LSTs, found themselves with additional duties guarding against suicide boats and swimmers, as well as suicide planes. LCS(L) action reports and deck logs for the period covering the Okinawa Gunto Operation indicates a number of missions referred to as "anti-small boat patrols," during which time the ships traversed Hagushi anchorage and the surrounding islands in search of suicide boats and swimmers. Dispatches and communiques referring to "fly catching" are common as well. Throughout the deployment at

Hagushi, *kamikazes* were a constant threat. Many hit their targets and many were destroyed. However, this was only the beginning.

In desperate straits, the Japanese high command decided to launch an all out suicide attack on the Allied forces off Okinawa. The offensive was termed the *Ten Go* (*Heavenly Operation*) and was designed to send large numbers of suicide planes against the American forces. Individual planes, known as *kikusui* (*floating chrysanthemums*), were aimed at the Hagushi anchorage and were to prevent supplies and reinforcements from landing. Organized in small groups of from four to six planes, with fighter escorts to protect them, the *kamikazes* flew in from Formosa and Kyushu. Additional targets included carriers, however, other ships were considered targets of opportunity. Some Japanese sources estimated that "7,852 aircraft (2,393 of them *kamikazes*) were sent against Western forces between 6 April and 22 June [1945] in both *kikusui* and small-scale attacks. Of this number, 2,258 never returned home" (Frank 171). Still other Japanese sources extend the beginnings of the suicide attacks back to 3 March and list different numbers (Nagatsuka 175). Samuel Eliot Morison's totals for *kikusui* come in at 1465 as shown below.

		(Number of Planes)		
Attack No.	**Date**	**Navy**	**Army**	**Total**
1 (*Ten-Go*)	6-7 April	230	125	355
2	12-13 April	125	60	185
3	15-16 April	120	45	165
4	27-28 April	65	50	115
5	3-4 May	75	50	125
6	10-11 May	70	80	150
7	23-25 May	65	100	165
8	27-29 May	60	50	110
9	3-7 June	20	30	50
10	21-22 June	30	15	45

(Morison 233).

Morison's figures refer only to the massed suicide attacks of the *Ten-Go* campaign. Japanese sources show slightly different figures. In addition, there were numerous other individual or small group suicide attacks, as well as conventional ones by torpedo bombers, fighters and other planes. In response, the American forces set up a line of radar pickets around Okinawa in an attempt to thwart the Japanese flyers. Manned primarily by destroyers, LCS(L)s, PGMs and LSM(R)s, the radar pickets were charged with early detection of the raids and guiding the

Combat Air Patrols (C.A.P.) to intercept the incoming planes. Within a very short time, the picket ships themselves became primary targets.

> Naval casualties in this operation, because of the persistence and weight of enemy aircraft suicide tactics, were the highest in the history of our Navy for any single operation. For the first time in the history of amphibious warfare naval casualties for the first two or three weeks of the campaign exceeded those of the assault troops on the beach (*Action Report, Capture of Okinawa Gunto* 15).

Japanese *Val* dive bombers prepare for a mission against the American forces. Photo courtesy of the National Archives.

CHAPTER IV

OKINAWA AND
THE BEGINNING OF TEN-GO

The capture of Okinawa was considered to be the final step toward the eventual invasion of Japan. Situated only 350 miles southwest of Japan, the island offered bases from which American planes could attack the home islands, as well as Japanese installations in Formosa and China. Harbors on the island would provide staging areas for the fleet and the vast amounts of material needed to supply the invasion forces. Another obvious benefit was that it would deny its use to the Japanese, who could interfere with the campaign against their homeland. The scheduled date for its invasion was 1 April, 1945.

For the month preceding the invasion of Okinawa, LCS(L)s and other ships of the attack force practiced their role in the assault. In the southern areas, rehearsals were held in the Cape Esperance area of Guadalcanal. Further to the north, in the Philippines, other ships were busy practicing assault tactics in San Pedro Bay, Leyte. Rocket runs were staged and crews on the ships trained with their rockets and guns.

From staging areas at the Ulithi Atoll, Saipan, and San Pedro Bay, the combined fleet of 1,213 ships and 182,112 assault troops set sail on the morning of 25 March, 1945 for the invasion of Okinawa. First to be taken were the islands of the Kerama Retto group to the west of Okinawa. These islands would serve as a supply and repair area and would prove useful as the invasion went on. Captured or destroyed in the invasion of Kerama Retto were 359 suicide boats, which would have posed a great threat to the invasion fleet. Troops landed on the islands on 26 March, 1945 and on Keise Shima on 31 March. Keise Shima, only 12 to 15 miles from the targeted invasion beaches at Hagushi in Nago Wan, on the western side of Okinawa, was close enough to cause great problems for the invasion fleet as it passed by. Accordingly, its capture was deemed necessary. Once taken, two batteries of 155mm guns were placed there to aid in the assault on the main island of Okinawa.

American plans called for the initial landing of two Army and two Marine divisions in the Hagushi area on the western coast. It was hoped that Japanese attention would be diverted to the opposite side of the island where the Second Marine Division, supported by naval gunfire, would fake an invasion attempt and then join the main force at Hagushi. Two additional Army divisions would be held in reserve and land later in the fray. These four Army and three Marine divisions formed the Tenth Army, which had been created specifically for the campaign. Lieutenant General Simon Bolivar Buckner was assigned command of the land forces and the naval command was handled by Admirals Raymond A. Spruance and Richmond Kelly Turner. Facing them was the Japanese 32nd Army under the command of Lieutenant General Mitsuru Ushijima.

The invasion of Okinawa proper began on 1 April, 1945. For six days prior to that date, American battleships and cruisers unleashed a devastating naval barrage designed to cause as much destruction to the Japanese defenders as possible. Participating in the bombardment were "Ten battleships, nine cruisers, 23 destroyers and 175 LCI gunboats of various types . . ." (Dyer Vol II 1103).

Arriving off the coast of Okinawa the evening before, the invasion fleet maneuvered for position during the night. On the morning of D-Day at Okinawa, reveille went at 0330 on the assembled LCS(L)s of Flotillas Three and Four. On the eastern side of the island, at its southernmost tip, LCS(L)s from Flotilla Three and Four, including the *31, 52, 53, 54, 55, 56, 62, 64, 84, 87, 109, 110, 111, 114, 115, 116, 118* and *119* along with other landing craft and assault ships, prepared for the diversionary landing that would last for two days. At about 0555, as the ships were about 15 miles off the southern coast of Okinawa, they were attacked by two suicide planes. One was shot down, but one struck *LST 884* on the port quarter. The explosion started a large fire and her captain gave the order to abandon ship. Over 300 Marines went into the lifeboats, along with the ship's crew and officers. *LCS(L)s 115, 116, 118* and *119* were ordered to assist in putting out the fires. *ATR-80* and the *U.S.S. Van Valkenburgh* (*DD 656*) attempted to put them out, but their fire equipment was not suitable for the task. The destroyer moved off and ordered the *LCS(L) 118* to take over. As the *118* moved into position, she and her sister ships trained their hoses on the raging fires. By 0657 it was obvious that the ship would have to be boarded in order to fight the fires effectively. Crews from all four LCS(L)s boarded the LST, and amid exploding bazooka, mortar, 40mm, 20mm shells, hand grenades, flame throwers, gasoline, and other explosives, managed to put out the fires. The task had taken over four hours and so much water had been pumped into the ship in order to drown the fires that she had taken a ten degree list. With ground swells bouncing the ships around, the LCS(L)s received a battering.

As the fires were being fought, the other ships of the diversionary assault force were preparing for their first run on the beach. At 0830 on 1 April, they began their attack. Fifteen-hundred yards from the beach they made smoke and began firing their 40mm and 20mm guns. No targets of opportunity presented themselves and there was no return fire. Behind them were a number of landing craft resembling an assault force. A few hundred yards off Saskibaru Saki, the ships abruptly turned and headed back out to sea. The entire exercise took less than an hour. When it was over, the ships retired to a point about three miles off the beach and spent the day in screening duties and anti-skunk boat patrol. On the following day, 2 April, 1945, the diversionary force once again went through the motions of an assault with no return fire. By mid-afternoon, the ships were on their way to the actual invasion site at Hagushi, to Radar Picket Duty and to Kerama Retto.

On the western shore of Okinawa, the situation was different. There the full scale invasion was underway. LCS(L) ships were assigned as part of the Inshore Fire Support Group. It was to be a classic assault on the beaches, with the recently designed LCS(L)s assuming the role for which they had been created.

The action was initiated early on the morning of 1 April, 1945. As *LCS(L) 19* and her companions were headed for the landing site, a Japanese torpedo bomber made a run on the assembled ships. The Japanese plane launched a torpedo at the *U.S.S. Gendreau* (*DE 639*) that passed only 50 yards in front of *LCS(L) 19*. Fortunately the torpedo missed, and the ships escaped unharmed.

Tension associated with the coming battle put everyone on edge. Unfortunate incidents occurred, some with deadly effect. At about 0530 one of the cruisers in the invasion fleet launched its observation plane, an *OS2U Kingfisher*. Heavy anti-aircraft fire was present in the area and the plane headed away from it on its observation run. Unfortunately for the pilot, he came in at a low altitude and headed for some assembled LCS(L)s, LSMs and LSTs. At first, most ship's gunners thought his plane was Japanese and prepared to fire. The Gunnery Officer on the *LCS(L) 18* identified it as American and the *18* held her fire as did the *17*, but the gunners on both the *21* and *22* were too jumpy. A 40mm gun on the *LCS(L) 22* and a 20mm on the *LCS(L) 21* opened fire and got off a number of rounds before the officers could stop them. Whether or not they contributed to the mishap is not clear, as fire from the LSTs and LCMs had already caused the plane to burst into flame. It "crashed west of the LST's and lay burning on the water for several minutes" (*LCS(L) 18 Action Report 14April45* 9). This would not be the only American plane brought down by friendly fire, and it pointed out one of the many hazards of war. Other planes had close calls later that day. In some cases LCS(L)s had to delay launching their rockets at the beaches because of low-flying planes heading in to the beach on bombing or strafing runs. Great concern was voiced over the possibility of attacks by suicide boats. This raised another friendly fire hazard. Many ships reported being hit by small arms fire and machine gun fire that had been aimed at suspected targets and had ricocheted off the water. It was recommended that extreme caution be urged in the fleet areas.

At 0630 the larger ships of the invasion fleet began a heavy naval bombardment of the landing area. By 0800 the actual invasion was underway. LCS(L)s, LCI(R)s and other gunboats made rocket and strafing runs on the beaches, leading the first wave of landing craft. A harbinger of things to come appeared at about 0820. *LCS(L) 12* noticed a small boat coming out of the mouth of the Bisha Gawa (Bisha River) and fired on it. Smoke from the guns obscured the target and when it lifted a few moments later, the boat was gone. Apparently it had been destroyed.

Shells from the larger ships off-shore, battleships, cruisers and destroyers flew overhead as the troops assembled to assault the beaches. In the lead were the LCS(L)s and other fire support ships. They led the charge into the beach followed by the Marines and Army men on board the LCVPs, LCMs and other assault craft. Stationed about 100 yards apart, the LCS(L)s attacked the beaches. The landing areas had been divided into a number of designated beaches, Green, Red, Blue, Yellow, Purple, Orange, White and Brown. Each beach was divided in to several sectors. Those not assaulted by LCS(L)s were taken under fire by LCI(R)s or LCI(G)s. *LCS(L)s 32, 33, 34, 35, 36* and *51* were assigned to attack Purple Beach 1. Brown Beach 4 was attacked by *LCS(L)s 24, 37, 38, 39, 40* and *57*. *LCS(L)s 11, 12, 13, 14, 15* and *16* were assigned to attack Yellow Beach 1. Attacking Red Beach 1 were *17, 18, 19, 20, 21* and *22*.

At a range of 1,400 yards, they let loose with their barrage of 4.5 rockets, laying a fan-shaped pattern of explosives on the landing beaches. Firing of the rockets was continuous until the ships were only 400 yards from shore. This insured that the area from the shoreline to about 1,000 yards inland was covered by rocket fire. At a range of 400 yards, the LCS(L)s slowed and the troop carriers passed by them. Some of the vessels lay bow-in to support troops if needed, while others turned broadside to the beach and raked it with fire from their twin 40mms. *LCS(L) 20*, moving in with the troop carriers, came under mortar and machine-gun fire from the beach, however, only one man was slightly injured. Most of the heavier Japanese guns had been moved away from the beaches. As the ships began their rocket and strafing runs, little return fire was encountered. The Japanese kept down. However, as the gunboats turned to head back out to sea, they found themselves under attack by mortars. None of the LCS(L) ships were hit by mortar fire, although some did have close calls. Machine-gun fire splashed in the water about them and at 0844, the *LCS(L) 34* was bracketed by mortars and raked by machine-gun fire. About the same time, the *LCS(L) 17* had the same experience, with several large explosions as near as 30 yards off her stern.

LCS(L)s 12, 13, 14, 15 and *16* line up for the assault on Yellow Beach 1 during the invasion of Okinawa. Photo courtesy of the National Archives.

Virtually all of the ships in the attacking force experienced the same problem. Smoke and dust from shells, rockets and their own guns made visibility poor. In many of the action reports LCS(L) skippers noted that they frequently could not see the target areas on the beach because of this.

Fortunately for the invasion fleet, the Japanese had adopted a strategy that would lead to light resistance on the beachfront. In spite of that strategy, they still managed to cause trouble. *The History of the USS LCS(L) 62* indicates that the damage control party from the ship was kept busy fighting fires and assisting with the salvage of many of the small landing craft that participated in the invasion (1). Ships at the extreme southern end of the invasion beaches seemed to have an easier time of it. Those from Group 9, commanded by Lieutenant Commander B. Thirkield, experienced no return fire at all. Some ships of Group 8, such as the *LCS(L) 16*, also were not fired upon. Recognizing that his forces were outnumbered by the American invaders, and cognizant of the great firepower possessed by the American fleet,

General Ushijima had decided not to oppose the landing but to move his troops inland, out of the range of the naval guns. Ushijima had established a number of concentric defensive perimeters around Shuri. As a result the Japanese defenders escaped the effects of naval shore bombardment. Still, resistance was offered in some locations. *LCS(L) 38* cruised the area off Brown Beach, identifying and "firing shells at Japanese pockets of resistance" (*LCS(L) 38 Ship Hist*. 1). Other hazards existed as well. Both the *38* and the *57* hit coral reefs, damaging their screws.

Such a large assemblage of ships made an obvious target for the aircraft of the Japanese Army and Navy. At 1907 the *LCS(L) 36* sighted three *Vals* closing in from 400 yards. The ships opened up and one of the planes went down. The *36* was credited with an assist. A few minutes later, at 1912, about six Japanese planes attacked the area. One "did a left wing-over and made a suicide dive into the battleship, *U.S.S. West Virginia*," (*LCS(L) 33 Action Report 4Apr45* 2) 500 yards to port of the *LCS(L) 33*. Both the *32, 33* and the *51* fired at the plane. The *33* took another under fire with its starboard 20mm guns and it splashed 400 yards off the starboard quarter. One of the planes hit the attack transport *U.S.S. Alpine* (*APA 92*) and she was soon ablaze. Within a short time, the *LCS(L) 32* was next to her, using her fire fighting apparatus to help put out the fires. She had been hit in an open hatch in the forward area, starting fires in her hold. *LCS(L) 32* was able to pump water on the blaze through a large hole in the transport's hull. It was estimated that the *32* pumped 260,000 gallons of water into the hull before the fire was brought under control. *LCS(L) 51* stood by and the next day helped to pump her out.

Within a few days, it became obvious that the main danger to the LCS(L)s and their companion invaders would not be shore-based fire. Rather, it would come from suicide boats and planes manned by men determined to give their lives to destroy their enemy. One of the primary concerns during the invasion of Okinawa was the need for protection of the American fleet from these dangers. The anchorage at Hagushi was a prime target for attacks by suicide boats and planes.

Suicide boats were a major problem for the invasion fleet and a number of destroyers and support craft had to be assigned to the inshore screen in order to cope with the threat. Usually "a destroyer type patrolled a mile to the seaward of each group of four to five in support and as a source of illumination . . . In addition to the above, a number of LCSs patrolled on a line approximately perpendicular to the shore line on the flanks of the transport areas" (*Action Report, Capture of Okinawa Gunto 26 March to 21 June 1945* 11). Assigned to the inshore patrol screen from 1 April to 2 April were six LCS(L)s. None were used for this task between 3 April and 17 April, with the task assigned to LCI gunboat types. From 18 April until 12 June, the LCS(L)s were again assigned to the patrol screen and an average of seven could be found on duty each day.

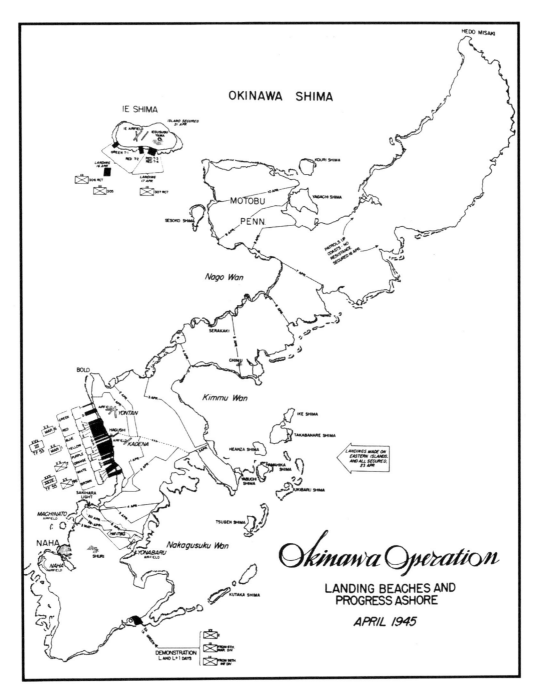

Landing beaches during the invasion of Okinawa (*Opns. In Pacific April, 1945*).

The Hagushi landing beaches on invasion day. Photo courtesy of the National Archives.

In order to intercept planes flying from Southern Japan, China and Formosa, the Navy set up radar picket stations around the island. The close radar pickets were only 20 to 25 miles from the Hagushi anchorage and the distant stations 40 to 70 miles out. Their job was to track incoming enemy aircraft, warn the anchorage area and guide American aircraft to them so that they could be intercepted. The original planning called for 15 picket stations. This was soon changed to 16 and ultimately minor changes were made that resulted in designations such as 15A and 16A. Although these stations were listed in the invasion plans, they were never occupied completely. From 1 April to 15 May, stations 1, 2, 3, 4, 7, 10, 12, and 14 were used. By 15 May, radar installations at Hedo Saki and Ie Shima had been completed and some of the picket areas were covered by the land based radar. Accordingly, from 16 May to 15 June, stations 5, 7, 9, 15 and 16 were manned. From 16 June to 21 June only RP stations 5, 7, 15A, and 16A were patrolled by the picket ships. RP stations 6, 8, 11, and 13 were never used.

In the beginning days of the battle for Okinawa, few ships could be spared to man these stations. From 1 April to 9 April, only one destroyer and two LCS(L)s were on each picket duty assignment. With such a limited number of ships, mutual fire support was difficult. In order to cover the area assigned to it, the destroyer usually remained right on station and the two LCS(L)s were spaced one-third of the way to the next station. By 10 April, it was possible to use additional ships on RP duty and one to two destroyers and two to four support craft were used. The use of many LCS(L)s on the inshore screen, led to a variety of ships used on the RP stations. LSM(R) ships were added to picket duty and some of the stations had a combination of destroyers, LSM(R)s and LCS(L)s. In addition to these ships, PGMs were also used on picket duty from 18 April to 26 April and again between 9 May and 20 May. With the arrival of additional LCS(L) ships from the states it became possible to exclude the other support craft on the RP stations. From 22 May on, each station was usually manned by three destroyers and four LCS(L)s. The total number of LCS(L) ships on RP duty each day varied during the invasion, with the low numbers of eleven to twelve in the first week of April to a high of 30 to 31 in the first week of May. As the battle began to wane and the Japanese *kamikazes* became fewer in number, an average of 20 LCS(L)s could be found on the RP stations by the end of May and the beginning of June.

LCS(L)s 109 and *110* were assigned to Radar Picket Station 3, along with the *U.S.S. Colhoun (DD 801)*. Arriving on station near daybreak on 2 April, the ships soon had an enemy plane to fire on. They missed and the plane went on its way. A few minutes later, at 0630, the destroyer assigned the *109* to check out nearby Yoron Shima to see if they could spot suspected radar installations. The LCS(L) found some camouflaged antennae and reported back to the destroyer which quickly obliterated the installation. Around noon, the *Colhoun* was relieved by the *U.S.S. Cassin Young (DD 793)*. The remainder of the day there was uneventful, with no enemy planes coming within range.

Only two days after the actual invasion of Okinawa the first *kamikazes* were downed by LCS(L)s. Patrolling on Radar Picket Station 1, north of Okinawa, *LCS(L)s 62* and *64* along with the *U.S.S. Pritchett (DD 561)*, came under attack at 0130 on 3 April. The *Pritchett* shot down the first plane about that time. At 0315, a *Dinah* flew over the *62* and she fired on the plane. Although it was hit, it did not go down. At 0325, the *62* observed another *Dinah* off her starboard beam. This time her fire was deadly and the plane went down. Opening fire on another plane at 0405, the *64* recorded her first splash. The ships searched the area, recovering the body of one of the Japanese pilots, along with navigation material and charts.

The following day, the *Pritchett*, which had been damaged by a near bomb miss in the attack, was replaced by the *U.S.S. Bush (DD 529)*. At 1800, the station came under attack by four Japanese planes. The *Bush* got one of the planes and the C.A.P. Corsairs took out the other three.

LCS(L) Commanding Officers quickly learned the best methods of coping with the hazards of radar picket duty. They found that if the ships were close together they could lend assistance to each other and increase fire support. Accordingly, they frequently steamed in diamond, single file or triangular formations and tried to stay within 1,000 yards of each other. At a speed of six knots or less, they left little wake and were harder to spot from the air. Once under attack, they were advised to use flank speed in order to avoid planes. Opening fire at a range of 6,000 yards gave other ships a warning and would tend to throw off the pilot of the attacking plane. Continuous night firing was discouraged, since the tracer paths would help the enemy spot the ship. It was recommended that ships fire upon only if discovered and then only in short bursts. If a ship was hit, usually the safest place to be was on board. In many cases, casualties were amplified when men went overboard and went through the screws of the ship. In some cases, this accounted for half of the casualties suffered (*LCS(L) 114 Action Report 12Aug45* 3).

Control of each station was under the authority of the fire-director destroyer. This ship contained the command post for the entire picket group and was responsible for coordinating the actions of the destroyers, the LCS(L)s and the Combat Air Patrol. In the LCS(L) group, one ship was designated as the command ship for that group and guided the actions of the others.

Since the destroyers soon became prime targets, it was necessary to have the Combat Air Patrol overhead in order to assist the pickets when they came under attack. Plans called for from four to six planes, but in actual practice, frequently only two could be spared. Once the sun had set, it was not possible for the Combat Air Patrol to cover the ships unless they were one of the few planes equipped with radar. This coverage only became reliable after 14 April, 1945. On some occasions C.A.P. planes were hit by friendly fire.

When cruising on picket duty, the destroyers and the support craft formed separate groups. Normally steaming in a quarter echelon or triangular formation, the destroyers easily outdistanced their LCS(L) escorts since their speed was much greater. They would then circle back to join with them again. At first the difference in speed was not obvious to some of the destroyer captains. Lt.(jg) Powell Pierpoint, Executive Officer of the *61*, recalled one such incident:

On one of our early tours on picket duty the senior destroyer . . . was on the short wave radio trying to organize the team. This was before the destroyers realized that, at any speed over 10 knots they left a rooster tail that a kamikaze could see from ten miles away in the pitch dark. A part of the message to the other destroyers and the four LCSs was: "Speed one will be 10 knots, speed two will be 20 knots, speed three will be 25 knots and speed four will be 30 knots." The senior LCS skipper . . . quickly radioed back: "Will require 15 minutes notice prior to reaching speed four" (Pierpoint letter).

The superior speed of the destroyers also led to a certain amount of disdain on the part of their captains, however, within a short period of time that attitude changed.

Until the attack on 12 April, the writer felt that the LCSs assigned to him were wonderful moral support, especially handy to pick up the pieces after that one suicider got through. But as far as additional AA support was concerned, it was felt that they were almost more trouble than they were worth. They got lost at night, wouldn't always stay where they were put and were too slow to keep within mutually supporting distance of the destroyers. After the way they took care of a group of Vals on the 12th , the writer would particularly desire to have them in any kind of engagement (*Secret Information Bulletin No. 24* 81-37).

At Radar Picket Station 4, on 3 April, *LCS(L)s 111* and *114* patrolled along with *U.S.S. Mannert L. Abele (DD 733)*. At 1725, the ships were attacked by several Japanese planes. One went down in flames, a probable assist by the *LCS(L) 111* and a half-hour later, the destroyer accounted for another. Still another plane attempted a bomb run on the destroyer, but intense gunfire from the ship and her support craft drove it off course and the bomb missed

That same day, *LCS(L) 67* was on Radar Picket Station 2 between Iheya Jima and Yoron Jima. Six small enemy boats, probably suicide craft, appeared on the radar screens between the islands of Iheya Jima and Okinoyerabu Jima. With their speed estimated at about 35 knots, they easily outran the LCS(L).

On 3 April Radar Picket Station 1, to the north of Okinawa, came under deadly attack. Patrolling there were the *U.S.S. Bush (DD 529)*, the *U.S.S. Colhoun (DD 801)*, and *LCS(L)s 64* and *87*.

At 1700 the Bush was hit by a suicide Val and almost immediately hit by another. The Colhoun commenced taking survivors from the now sinking ship. At 1724 the Colhoun was hit by one Val, at 1732 by 2 more and at 1741 by a 4th Val. We, the U.S.S. Cassin Young and the U.S.S. LCS(L)(3) 87 proceeded to her assistance immediately . . . *Ships History LCS(L) 84* 3).

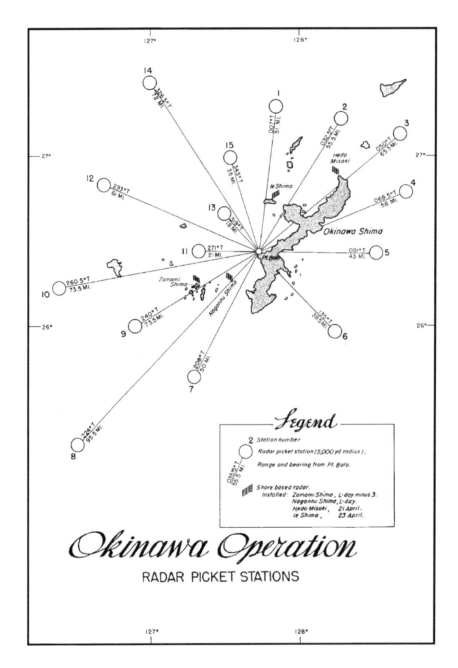

Within a few days after the invasion of Okinawa, the Navy set up radar picket stations around the island to monitor incoming Japanese aircraft. The destroyers and LCS(L)s on picket duty soon became targets. (*Secret Information Bulletin 24* 81-3*)*

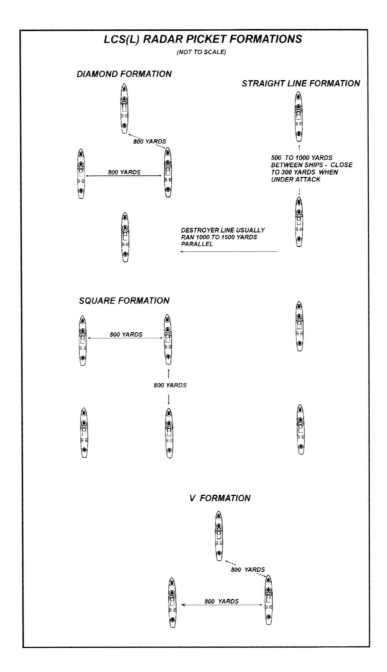

Destroyers, LSM(R)s and LCS(L)s on radar picket duty used a variety of formations designed to provide covering fire for one another. Problems arose in keeping the formations once the ships came under attack because of the great differences in speed between the destroyers and the landing craft.

The *LCS(L) 64* picked up an additional 95 survivors from the destroyer. After the initial hit on the *Bush*, which disabled her, the *64* had attempted to tie up to her, but with the Japanese attack continuing, she had to stand clear as the *Bush* took the additional hits which would lead to her sinking. The little gunboat maneuvered continually about the destroyer, firing on the attacking Japanese planes. She hit one plane and it went down, her second splash during her tour at RP 1. Still another *kamikaze* targeted the *64* and she continued to take evasive action. The plane hit the water close to the ship, covering her fantail with water and splitting open her side. Pumps were manned and the *LCS(L) 64* continued on her patrol.

The *Colhoun* made it to nightfall and was still afloat. Attempts by the *U.S.S. Cassin Young* (*DD 793*) to take survivors off the damaged destroyer were prevented by heavy seas. Attempts by *LCS(L) 84* were more fruitful. At 2015 she managed to stay alongside the destroyer long enough to take off 228 men, including 17 wounded. Continually pounded by the roll of the destroyer, she finally pulled clear. There was no hope left for the *Colhoun* and at 2358, *U.S.S. Bennet* (*DD 473*) sank her with gunfire. Prior to that, the *LCS(L)s 64* and *87* managed to remove the remaining 36 members of the crew (*Phillips, War Hist Flot. Four* 5). *LCS(L) 64* continued searching the area and rescued 95 survivors of the *Bush* including Commander Westholm, its Captain (*Log LCS(L) 64* 6Apr45). These rescues were attempted under the most trying of conditions. In most cases, where enemy planes were in the area, it was too hazardous to stop. Crewmen lashed themselves to the ship and threw lines to those in the water as they passed. Ropes were looped so that they would be easier for the men to grasp. Many men from the destroyers and other picket ships were rescued in this manner. This was one of the worst nights for the destroyers off Okinawa, but demonstrated the effectiveness of the LCS(L)s in rescue work.

On 5 April, while patrolling on Radar Picket Station 10 with the *U.S.S. Hudson* (*DD 475*) and *LCS(L) 116*, the *LCS(L) 115* made contact with an enemy sub at 0150. The gunboat headed for the sub, which was about 8,000 yards off with the intention of ramming her, however, when she closed to 1,400 yards, the submarine disappeared from sight. The *Hudson* reported on the scene, picked up the sub on sonar and dropped depth charges. Shortly thereafter, the *U.S.S. Gendreau* (*DE 639*) and the *U.S.S. Bowers* (*DE 637*) joined in the search. Debris was found floating on the surface, and the next day an oil slick three miles long covered the area, giving evidence that the sub had been destroyed.

About the same time, from 4-5 April, the *LCS(L) 110* shot down a *Judy* off Okinoyerabu Island where she had been patrolling. Following that, she steamed in the vicinity of the island and sighted what appeared to be an observation post on top of a ridge near the shoreline. Enemy personnel, telescopes and communications lines leading from the post were visible. Requests for an air attack were made, but the aircraft picked the wrong target, and the destroyer *U.S.S. Cassin Young* (*DD 793*) was called in to put an end to the installation. Located on the eastern shore of the island were the villages of Oyama and Wadonari, which appeared to house a communications center and other military targets. *LCS(L) 110* approached to within 200 yards of the shoreline and strafed the villages with 40mm and 20mm guns, starting fires with incendiary shells. About the same time, the villages got a working over by several planes, and secondary explosions gave evidence that enemy munitions stores had been hit.

LSM(R)s were often seen on radar picket duty along with the destroyers and LCS(L)s. *LSM(R) 194*, shown here, was sunk by a *kamikaze* at Radar Picket Station 1 on 4 May, 1945. Photo courtesy of Ron MacKay.

The next several days brought increased air attacks against the invasion fleet and the radar pickets. LCS(L)s were not primary targets at first, but that was soon to change.

During this same period enemy aircraft were to a large extent ignoring the presence of the LCS(L)s on the radar picket stations. On a few occasions they were observed to break off their attacks as if surprised by the heavy fire which they received from these small ships. Later, after 6 April, 1945, their tactics were to change radically in respect to LCS(L)s. The enemy's planes attacked LCS(L)s as often and as savagely as other types. Suicide attempts against the support craft were made with ever increasing frequency (*Phillips, War History Flot. Four* 4).

TEN-GO 1

April 6-7, 1945, was the beginning of the first of the *Ten-Go* operations which saw a total of 355 *kamikaze* planes sent toward the American forces at Okinawa. Two-hundred and thirty were navy craft and 125 were army planes. At the inception of this massive raid, the American fleet suffered its greatest losses in a single day. Six Navy ships were sunk and an additional 20 hit by suicide planes. Among the ships sent to the bottom were three members of the amphibious force, the *Hobbs Victory*, the *Logan Victory* and the *LST-447*. At Radar Picket Station 10, the *LCS(L) 115* shot down a Japanese *Betty* bomber.

On 9 April, at RP Station 4, the ships there came under attack by four Japanese planes. Present were the *U.S.S. Sterett* (*DD 407*) and the *LCS(L)s 12, 24, 36, 39, 40* and *119*. Both the *Sterett* and the *24* were hit by *Val* suicide planes, with the destroyer taking the hit amidships and the *LCS(L) 24* on top of her mast (*Log 24* 204). Both made it safely back to Kerama Retto for repairs, escorted by the *U.S.S. Jeffers* (*DMS 27*) and the *LCS(L) 36*. Three Japanese planes were downed in the fray.

No safety was to be found in the anchorage at Hagushi. Early in the morning of 9 April, *LCS(L) 118* was moored starboard side to *LCS(L) 116*, which was moored in turn to the port side of the attack cargo ship *U.S.S. Starr* (*AKA-67*). At 0425 an explosion sent all hands to general quarters. A suicide boat had attacked the *Starr* on her starboard side but had run into a cluster of her landing craft that were tied up there. It exploded without hitting the ship. The Japanese survivors were being taken under fire. Two Japanese soldiers hiding in the debris were killed and the ships secured for an hour before general quarters was sounded again. This time, enemy aircraft were in the area and the LCS(L)s covered the anchorage with smoke (*Log 118* 276).

Gradually, as the landing site at Hagushi became more secure and the fighting moved inland, more destroyers were freed from shore bombardment duty and could be assigned to the radar picket stations. By 10 April, 1945, most of the radar picket stations had at least two destroyers and four support ships such as LCS(L)s or LSM(R)s.

LCS(L)s 15, 16 and *24* were assigned to RP 7 along with *U.S.S. Brown* (*DD 546*). On 11 April, they were attacked by three *Zekes*. One was shot down by the destroyer and the LCS(L)s fired on others, but no other hits were recorded. For the next few days, occasional attacks by individual planes took place but the action was inconclusive.

TEN-GO 2

Ten-Go 2 began on 12 April, 1945 and continued into the next day. One hundred and eighty-five planes, consisting of 125 from the navy and 60 from the air force, descended on the American ships at Okinawa. Radar Picket Station 1, which by this time had been nicknamed "coffin corner," continued to be a hot spot. On 9 April the *LCS(L)s 33, 57, 114* and *115*, along with destroyers *U.S.S. Cassin Young (DD 793)* and *U.S.S. Purdy (DD 734)* were assigned there. On 10 April, the *57* rescued a Marine pilot who had gone down in the area. While patrolling the station on 12 April, the picket ships came under attack at 1330 by approximately 30 *kamikazes* consisting of *Vals* and *Nates* (*War History Flot. Four* 5). The *Cassin Young* was hit by one plane and shot down a number of others. The *Purdy* shot down six and suffered damage from an armor piercing projectile. Both destroyers were able to make their way back to Kerama Retto for repairs.

At 1347 *LCS(L) 57* was attacked by eight planes. The first plane made a run on the *57* and dropped a bomb about 200 yards from the ship and missed. Struck repeatedly by the forward 40mm and 20mm guns, the plane crashed into the sea 50 yards off the port quarter. Two waves of four planes each then attacked from the east. One made a run on the ship from forward. Rounds from the *57's* guns apparently killed the pilot and his plane glanced off the number 2 gun tub, crashing 25 yards to port. At 1352 the aft twin 40 accounted for two *Nates*. Still another *Nate* headed for the port side of the ship.

> This plane was taken under fire by 2 port 20mm and after twin 40mm using director control switching to tracer control as the plane approached. Plane was hit and exploded about 10 feet from the ship. Although this hit probably saved the ship, the force of the explosion blew a hole 8 feet in diameter in the port quarter extending 3 feet below the water line, blew four men from the gun crew into the water, rendered the after twin mount 40mm inoperative, damaged steering, [and] destroyed internal communications . . . (*LCS(L) 57 Action Report 15Apr45* 3).

The impact caused serious internal damage to the ship, starting fires and flooding the ship. She soon was listing ten degrees to starboard, but her crew brought the fires and flooding under control. Two men had been killed and six wounded. Using emergency steering, the ship maneuvered through the area rescuing the men who had been blown overboard. *LCS(L) 33* steamed to her aid and assisted with the search. The *Cassin Young (DD 793)* spotted the men and informed the LCS(L) as to their location. It then steamed off. After notifying the destroyers of her condition, the *57* was ordered back to port for repairs and was finally able to anchor at 0020 of the next morning (*LCS(L) 57 Action Report 15Apr45* 5). Her Commanding Officer, Lt. H.L. Smith, was awarded the Navy Cross for his outstanding leadership that day.

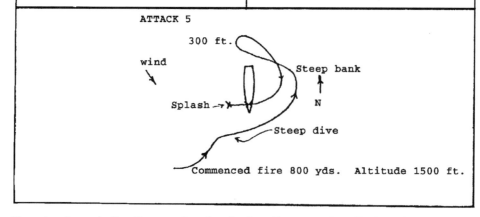

Drawing from Action Report showing the *kamikaze* **attack at Radar Picket Station 1 on 12 April, 1945** (*LCS(L) 57 Action Report, 13 April, 1945*).

LCS(L) 33 fared no better. Under attack by three *kamikazes*, she downed the first one and had a close miss by the second, which took off her radio antenna before crashing into the sea. Unfortunately, this was not to be her day. A *Val* struck the starboard side of the *33*, setting her on fire. The call to abandon ship was made and the crew went into the water. Number *33* continued to circle slowly to port before she blew up and sank in front of her crew. She was the fourth LCS(L) to go down in the war, but she would not be the last. After shooting down two *Vals* with two probables, *LCS(L) 115* circled the area picking up 69 survivors, one dead member of the *LCS(L) 33* and a Japanese pilot. She had accounted for one *Oscar* herself and had two assists. *LCS(L) 114*, which had shot down two planes and made two assists, took the more seriously injured to port. *LCS(L) 57* went to Kerama Retto on 13 April for repairs, where she remained until 28 May. She was effectively put out of action for the remainder of the war by the attacks. In recognition of her valiant struggle, the ship was awarded the Presidential Unit Citation.

In assessing the battle afterwards, the Commanding Officer of the *LCS(L) 115* noted several lessons that were learned from the encounter:

A. Suicide pilots do not seem to be experienced flyers, and have probably never had the experience of operating an aircraft at the rate of speed attained in a suicide dive, from a position angle of 30 degrees. They tend to overshoot, and if overshooting, depend on throwing the stick forward to crash down on their target. If they are off the target, forward or aft, they will try a wing-over to crash down on their target.

B. This Command is of the opinion that while in engagement with enemy air forces, it is best to cruise at standard speed, until directly under attack by aircraft in a dive. If unable to shoot [the] plane down while [he is] making his turn into the dive, then as [the] plane starts down, increase speed to flank, and turn toward the plane with full rudder, thus leaving the plane on the bow, where all guns can bear. If it is seen that the plane will come right at the vessel, then as the plane gets near, either turn toward it, presenting the bow, as a narrow, but rather high target, or turn so as to be at right angles to the plane's line of descent, thus presenting the narrow beam and low freeboard as a more difficult target. Judging that the attacked vessel has already closed toward the plane, it will be more apt to overshoot, than to undershoot. This latter method was followed by subject vessel during both attacks. It may be of worth to note that the subject vessel was the only vessel so attacked

that did not suffer a hit or major damage. It may also be noted, that in
the opinion of aviators, the Val, due to the possession of diving flaps, is
probably the hardest of single engine planes to avoid (*LCS(L) 115 Action
Report 16Apr45 5*).

On patrol that day at RP 12, were the *LCS(L)s 11, 13* and the destroyer-
minesweeper *U.S.S. Jeffers* (*DMS 27*). At 1325 the ships were attacked by two *Vals*.
One narrowly missed the *Jeffers* and the other was shot down by *LCS(L) 11*.

That same day, the *LCS(L)s 32, 51* and *116* patrolled on Radar Picket Station
2 along with *U.S.S. Lang* (*DD 399*) and *U.S.S. Stanly* (*DD 478*). At 1310 the ships
went to general quarters. Seven bombers came over at a high altitude and dropped
their cargo on the ships. Fortunately they missed. A *Val* made a dive bombing run
on the *Stanly* and scored a near miss, damaging the ship. Following that, a *Tony*
made a suicide dive on the destroyer and was shot down by the guns of the *32*.
Many of the other planes were shot down by the Combat Air Patrol. The *Stanley*,
in need of minor repairs, left the formation the next day and was replaced by the
U.S.S. Bryant (*DD 665*). The *LCS(L)s 51* and *116* rotated over to Radar Picket
Station 1.

On 12 April, the *Mannert L. Abele* (*DD 733*), *LSM(R)s 189* and *190* were
patrolling on Radar Picket Station 3. They were attacked about 1328 and were
under constant attack for the next hour. *LSM(R) 189* was hit by a *kamikaze* but did
not suffer serious damage. Her score for the day was two *Kates* and one *Val*, with
another assist. The destroyer was not so fortunate, she was hit by a suicide plane
and shortly thereafter by the *Oka* which broke her in two. She went to the bottom
within minutes. *LSM(R)s 189* and *190* patrolled the area fighting off Japanese
planes and picking up survivors. As they went about their task, another Japanese
plane dropped a bomb in the middle of the survivors, killing and wounding a
number.

The appearance of the *Oka* signaled a new turn of events in the performance
of picket duty. With a terminal dive velocity estimated at approximately 575
miles per hour, the weapon seemed to be unstoppable. Existing shipboard
weapons seemed to be inadequate, and the Commanding Officer of the *LSM(R)
189*, Lt. J. M. Stewart suggested that new ordinance be developed to combat the
Oka:

If the ordnance department could develop a projectile that was frangible
and suitable for use in 5"/38 guns and that would have a coverage of about
twenty (20) foot diameter, at 500 yards, it is felt that the ships would not be
so helpless against suicide attacks. What I am suggesting is something on

the shot-gun principle. It will have to be used at a range of from 400 to 800 yards and cover as large an area as possible. Our present VT fuses cannot operate at this range and when these jet propelled planes hit at better than 300 yards-a-second, fuse setting or tracking is hopeless. . . . It would also be helpful in repelling these suicide boats. . . . They close in so near and are so openly exposed that a fragmentation shell, such as the projectile suggested, would be of great help with their disposal (*Report of anti-aircraft action -— LSM(R) 189* 1May45 4).

LCS(L)(3) 116 **under way. Official U.S. Navy Photograph courtesy of Phillip E. Peterson.**

While life on the picket lines was extremely hazardous, the anchorage was not free from attack either. Protecting an anchorage of fully loaded LCTs at Blue Beach in the Hagushi area, were *LCS(L) 35*, the *U.S.S. Clamp (ARS 33)*, a minesweeper, and a PC. At about 0345 on 12 April, the anchorage came under attack by enemy planes. *LCS(L) 35* had a lucky night. A Japanese bomber, approaching from shore, dropped a string of six bombs on the *35*, bracketing her aft section. Fortunately, none came close enough to damage the ship, and the only experience the crew had was a drenching from the bomb splashes.

TEN-GO 3

The third *Ten-Go* operation lasted from 15 to 16 April and involved a total of 165 planes. Of this number, 120 were naval aircraft and 45 army. *LCS(L)s 12, 39, 40* and *119*, along with the *U.S.S. Wickes* (DD 578) and *U.S.S. Ellyson* (DMS 19), were on patrol at Radar Picket Station 4. Two enemy *Vals* approached at about 1900. Since the *Vals* were being chased by the C.A.P., the ships held fire. One of the planes made a run on the *Wickes*, passing over her from bow to stern. She then circled around and was hit by fire from the LCS(L)s and the destroyer. The Japanese plane went down in flames.

Radar Picket Station 1 continued to be the most dangerous. Patrolling on 16 April were the *LCS(L)s 51, 116* and the *U.S.S. Laffey* (*DD 724*). Attacked by 26 Japanese planes, the picket ships had their hands full. *LCS(L) 116* was hit and had to be abandoned. Her casualties were twelve dead and twelve wounded. The *Laffey* was hit by several of the suicide planes. Her batteries put out of order and on fire, she was aided in her fire fighting efforts by the damaged *51*. The Log of the *LCS(L)(3) 51* details the action:

At General Quarters and taking enemy Val dive-bombers under fire, in vicinity of Radar Picket station # 1. DD 724, USS Laffey and LCS(L) 116 in same general area also taking enemy planes under fire. About one dozen friendly Corsairs overhead locked in dog fights. 0815 First enemy plane a Val, shot down by fire from all 40mms and starboard side 20mm s and 50 cals, about 300 yards on starboard beam while flying abut 100 ft. off water and apparently intending to crash dive ship amidships. 0850 Splashed second Val off starboard quarter as plane headed to crash dive DD 724. 0945 Splashed enemy Val diving on us from port bow. *1010 Splashed fifth Val l25 ft. off port beam that exploded and sent its engine into our port side a few inches above the waterline, where it wedged itself securely against the number 42 frame. Some water shipped hereafter when turns are made. Fired at suicide planes attempting to crash dive USS Laffey (DD 724). 1030 Shot down sixth plane, a Zeke crossing our bow port to starboard and heading towards Laffey. For about one-half to three quarters hours Laffey's complete starboard battery seemed to be out of working condition. 1100 Went alongside Laffey's starboard quarter to fight fire raging in her magazine and after compartments. 1130. Pulled away from USS Laffey to pick up three of her survivors nearby . . . 1145 Headed towards vicinity where Corsair pilot was seen to have lighted after parachuting from his plane but discovered his life raft intact leading us to believe he had been rescued by another ship seen in the area. . .1150 Headed towards Point Bolo after obtaining permission from O.T.C. USS Laffey. *0955 Splashed fourth plane, a Jap Val, crossing our stern from port to starboard abut 900 yards from ship.

Richard C. Wessell
Ensign, USNR (218)

The *LCS(L)(3) 51* was awarded a Presidential Unit Citation for this action and its Commanding Officer, Lieutenant Howell D. Chickering, received the Navy Cross

Into this fray, newly arrived from the states via the islands, steamed the *LCS(L)s 61, 63, 81, 82, 83, 85, 86* and *88*, adding to the already large number of these vessels operating around Okinawa. On Monday, 16 April, as the ships entered Kerama Retto they saw their first *kamikaze* attack as two Japanese planes tried to dive into the *U.S.S. Wilson* (*DD 414*). The *Wilson* was able to shoot down both and escape damage. Walter Longhurst, a Gunner's Mate on the *61*, described the situation:

> . . . we saw a destroyer [*Wilson* DD 414] that was patrolling outside the harbor open fire, we were sightseeing. Finally I turned around and there was a flag on the command ship in front of us —- General Quarters flag. We yelled on the phones for General Quarters but no one was on the phones and we had to yell up to the Conn "check the flags." Then we went to General Quarters. The suicide planes dove on that ship and just missed it. Then we pulled into the graveyard [Kerama Retto] and we saw all the ships that had been hit by suicide planes, there were a lot of damaged destroyers (Longhurst interview).

This had been a close call for the *Wilson*, however, she did not escape unscathed. Shrapnel and flying debris killed four men and wounded several others. This attack injected a sense of reality into the minds of the gunboat crews and caused a general lowering of morale. When the immediate action was over, they secured from general quarters and anchored in 20 fathoms of water at 0915. According to Lt. (jg) Powell Pierpoint, Executive Officer of the *LCS(L) 61*, the rest of the day was spent "whiling away the time by looking at all the damaged destroyers scattered here and there about the harbor, and firing at a little grass shack on the beach" (Pierpoint 3). In time, Kerama Retto would have so many damaged ships under repair that she would resemble a naval graveyard. That night the first of many deck gun watches took place as the crews of the newly arrived LCS(L)s prepared to defend themselves against suicide planes, boats and swimmers.

Damaged ships awaiting repair in the Kerama Retto anchorage. Photo courtesy of the National Archives.

At 0746, the *LCS(L)s 32* and *35*, along with the *U.S.S. Bryant* (*DD 665*) came under fire at Radar Picket Station 2. Overhead a number of dogfights were taking place and many Japanese planes were shot down near the ships.

At about 0925 three Vals were observed approaching from the North directly toward the group. At about two miles they separated, one of them continuing directly at the LCS 35 at about 400 feet altitude. When the enemy was 1000 yards off the starboard beam . . . this vessel opened fire and he veered sharply to the West and toward the Bryant now 4000 yards . . . Both LCSs continued firing until the Bryant was in the line of fire. The enemy continued toward the Bryant and when 1000 yards from his target was shot down by a Corsair. Meanwhile the second enemy plane had approached unobserved from the sun, out of our range, and crashed into the destroyer just aft of the bridge causing a large fire. Number three plane was then observed coming in on the starboard beam followed by two Corsairs. The Corsairs veered off and this vessel opened fire and continued to fire until the enemy veered to 090(T) and passed out of range (*LCS(L) 35 Action Report 24Apr45* 1).

The *Val* that struck the destroyer was hit by 40mm fire from the *32* prior to crashing into the *Bryant*. Fires started by the plane caused a number of men to go over the side in order to escape the flames. Within a short period of time, the fire was under control and the *32* and the destroyer were ordered to Radar Picket Station 1 to assist other ships which were under attack. *LCS(L) 35* was left alone to circle the area, picking up four dead and four wounded men. The *32* was credited with an assist.

Nearby, on Radar Picket Station 1, the *U.S.S. Laffey* (*DD 724*) and the *LCS(L)s 51, 114, 115* and *116* were under attack by a large number of suicide *Vals*. Overhead, *Corsairs* of the C.A.P. shot down four of the enemy planes. The *Laffey* was hit by two planes and the *116* by one. The *LCS(L) 32* and the *Bryant* went to their aid. As they went to assist their comrades, the superstructure of the *Bryant* was hit by a suicide *Val* at 0929, causing her to lose steering capability for about ten minutes. After regaining control, she departed for Hagushi and repairs. In the midst of all this, the *51* fired on the attacking planes continually, and by the end of the fray had shot down five *Vals* and one *Zeke*. Unfortunately for her, the *Zeke* exploded only about 25 feet from the ship and the engine struck the gunboat amidships, holing her just below the main deck. The *116* had been

> simultaneously attacked by three Japanese suicide planes. Two of the planes were driven off but the third effected a suicide bombing by crashing into the 40mm gun on the fantail. An explosion followed the crash and fire broke out on the fantail and in the spaces below. While fighting fire and caring for wounded, *LCS 116* was attacked by two other Vals, which also attempted to crash the ship. The first of these was brought down by the LCS(L). The second plane was also brought down by gunfire from the *116*. It crashed into the water approximately 100 yards to starboard. Flotilla Four had suffered its first battle casualty (*War Hist. Flot. Four* 5).

With twelve killed and twelve wounded, it was a disastrous morning for the *116*. The ship was sent to the anchorage for repairs.

At 0850 on 16 April, *LCS(L) 34* and *LSM(R) 191* were sent to aid the *U.S.S. Pringle* (*DD 477*) and the *U.S.S. Hobson* (*DMS 26*) at Radar Picket Station 14. Both destroyers had shot down enemy planes, but the formation was in peril. At

0945 the *34* came under attack by three *Vals* and scored one splash, one probable and one additional, which was damaged. Things did not go as well for the *Pringle* and she was sunk by *kamikazes*. Shortly thereafter, *LCS(L) 34* circled the area and picked up 87 survivors who were then transferred back to Okinawa.

Damage to *LCS(L) 116*, sustained on 16 April, 1945. She was hit by a *kamikaze* while on patrol at Radar Picket Station 1. Photo courtesy of the National Archives.

Early in the morning of 17 April, 1945, the *61* headed northeast towards Hagushi anchorage. Hagushi had been the sight of the initial landings on Okinawa and the bay was loaded with supply ships and warships firing inland to weaken Japanese resistance. As the *61* steamed into the harbor, she was greeted by the sight of battleships, cruisers and destroyers lobbing salvo after salvo of high explosive shells into the hills of Okinawa in support of the ground troops. An ominous sign was a charred LCS(L) under tow by a fleet tug. Mooring next to the *LCS(L) 84*, they met with their Group Commander, Lt. Commander Clifford Montgomery, and were told that they would be assigned to radar picket duty. Further indoctrination of the crew was accomplished as they were told to be on the lookout for suicide boats, swimmers, and planes. They were filled in on the duties that LCS(L)s had been performing, assisting on radar picket duty, aiding damaged ships and protecting the anchorage. *LCS(L) 34* had just returned from picket duty with the rescued survivors of the *Pringle*. The gruesome details gave the crew of the *61* a hint of what was to come. By 1935 hours, the ship was anchored off the southwest side of Okinawa. However, it was not to be a restful night. As Walter Longhurst remembers, "We got to fire at our first plane that night, it came in from the fantail from Okinawa. We were close to the beach and it came off the beach and headed towards us and we started firing and he veered away. We didn't hit him I guess, but we came close" (Longhurst interview).

One of the main duties in the anchorage involved producing a smoke screen so that the anchored ships would be harder to spot by the suicide planes and boats. That night the LCS(L)s used their smoke generators to cover the harbor. This was an advantage for many of the anchored ships. As they kept watch over the anchorage, another plane came out of the smoke that they had laid astern, flew directly over the ship, and was gone before they had a chance to fire on it. Their smoke probably protected them from attack by that plane. This was a prelude of things to come, with much of the action seen by the ships taking place at night under difficult conditions. After securing for the night at 2240 hours, the *61* received its orders for the following day assigning it to Radar Picket Station 2, known among the fleet members as Suicide Gulch.

Normal assignments for the radar picket stations at that point included two destroyers and from two to four LCS(L) ships. Radar Picket Stations 1 through 5 were to the north of Okinawa and stood between it and the main islands of Japan. As a result, any planes flying from Japan proper had to come through that area, making it a virtual hot spot. On the night of 18 April, RP 2 was active with a number of sightings of enemy planes and continual firing by the destroyers. The assembled ships, *LCS(L)s 12, 25* and *61*, along with the destroyers *U.S.S. Luce (DD 522)* and *U.S.S. Twiggs (DD 591)*, went to general quarters at 1840 hours with destroyers picking up planes on radar and firing on them. At 1945 hours, the ships secured from general quarters and continued steaming on station.

The *LCS(L)s 24* and *35* had been assigned to Radar Picket Station 1 along with the *U.S.S. Cowell (DD 547)*, *U.S.S. Little (DD 803)*, *LSM(R) 191* and *PGM 9*. On 20 April a Japanese plane, flying at a very low altitude, slipped past the radar defenses. The gunboat fired on the plane but it did not go down. *LCS(L) 24* remained on station for 20 days, however, no other planes came within range during her time there.

One of the many tasks performed by the LCS(L)s was providing a smoke coverage for the anchored ships. Here three *Mighty Midgets* perform the task. Photo courtesy of the National Archives.

Camaraderie between the ships on radar picket duty was great and an interesting exchange of information continually flowed.

Aside from the main drama of attack and maneuver, Radar Picket Duty brought with it a minor show that was played out on the Voice Radio circuits day and night. The Destroyers we worked with we knew only by their voice calls. Their names were for the log only. Each ship and station took on the personality of its radio talker. In the case of the CCs, there were two of them, one on the I.F.D. circuit and one on the private circuit for the station. If the talkers were hesitant, or didn't speak well, the Destroyers went down in our estimation. If they spoke well and had a sense of humor, it went up. The I.F.D. circuit was fascinating. It was the life-line of the Picket Stations and it lived up to the drama of its task. Over it passed the orders, instructions, and information which implemented the coordination of plane and ship, picket and anchorage. Through it we heard of friends in triumph or trouble and were warned of trouble to come to us (Pierpoint 4).

Screening of the anchorages continued to be hazardous. On the night of 21 April, the *LCS(L) 31* shot down its first plane at Nago Wan. It would finish off seven others during its tour at Okinawa.

Late in the afternoon of 22 April, Radar Picket Station 14 was patrolled by *LCS(L)s 15, 37* and *83*, along with the destroyers *U.S.S. Van Valkenburgh* (*DD 656*), *U.S.S. Wickes* (*DD 578*) and the *LSM(R) 195*. It was to be the first picket duty for the newly arrived *83* and it would prove to be a baptism of fire. For the *LCS(L) 15*, however, it was the end of a very short battle history. The *15*, a Lawley built ship, was a participant in the initial landings at Hagushi and had spent the following weeks on patrol and picket duty. Her total life in battle would last a scant 22 days. On the evening of the 22 April, the formation was jumped by 37 *kamikazes*. One of the planes, a *Val*, targeted the *Wickes*, but abruptly changed as he closed in. After making it through a hail of anti-aircraft fire he crashed into the port side of the *LCS(L) 15*, near the number 5 gun. The bomb carried by the Japanese plane exploded and within a short time, fires raged uncontrollably in the aft section of the ship. The damage was so severe that no possibility of saving her existed. Only a few minutes elapsed from the initial hit to the ship's demise. Filling rapidly from the stern through a massive hole in her hull, the *15* pointed her bow at the sky and slid beneath the waves. Fifteen men had been killed and eleven wounded. *The Log of the U.S.S. Wickes* describes the action:

> . . . 1828 Sighted Japanese dive bomber at 280 degrees True, making run on this ship, distance about 6 miles. Commenced firing. 1830 Enemy plane changed course radically at 1500 yards and ran down the port side of this vessel. 40mm Shells were observed bursting in the fuselage of the plane. Plane crashed into side of LCS-15. LCS immediately began to sink and disappeared below the surface in about 3 minutes. All other ships maneuvered to pick up survivors while Wickes circled formation. 1928 All survivors recovered (*Log Wickes 22Apr45* 24).

The remaining picket ships rescued survivors, transferring them to the *U.S.S. Van Valkenburgh* (*DD 656*) for transport back to safety. After the transfer of survivors, normal picket duty on Radar Picket Station 14 resumed. Early in the afternoon of the 23 April, the *Van Valkenburgh* was replaced by the *U.S.S. Bache* (*DD 470*). The following day, the ships practiced interception techniques along with their accompanying *Corsairs*.

> . . . CAP assigned to this station, 2 F4U [Corsairs], make simulated bombing and strafing runs on formation to afford tracking practice for gun crews. 1045 ceased tracking practice . . . 1444 2 CAP began making simulated bombing and strafing runs on formation for tracking practice. 1515 ceased tracking practice. 2 Corsairs joined CAP. Carried out routine watch (*Log LCS(L) 37* 350).

This type of training was invaluable. In many cases LCS(L) skippers noted in their recommendation sections of action reports that this type of training be increased as it kept the crews in the best condition to fight off the suicide attacks.

Ships operating around Okinawa frequently faced an unpleasant task, the inspection of floating bodies. On 19 April the crew of the *61* saw their first dead Japanese pilot floating in the water. He was not in good condition, having been partially eaten by sharks. A few days later on 22 April another body was sighted. This time the crew took the body on board with the hope of finding intelligence information, but the body had nothing of value. After some of the crew members removed a few buttons from the dead pilot's coat and some Japanese paper money as souvenirs, the body was unceremoniously dumped back into the ocean. Cook Joe Staigar noted that "he stunk like all hell so we didn't keep him long" (Staigar letter) and Radio Man Larry Katz wrote that "A lot of guys didn't eat chow tonight" (Katz 8).

Much of the action that the ships saw took place at night. That evening, as the *LCS(L)s 12, 25* and *61*, along with *LSM(R) 199* and the destroyers *U.S.S. Dyson (DD 572)* and *U.S.S. Twiggs (DD 591)* patrolled on Radar Picket Station 2, a Japanese plane came out of the gloom and passed by before the ships could open fire. Radar on the ships picked up a small craft nearby and the LCS(L)s tried to intercept it. However the small craft was traveling at 20 knots and easily outdistanced the gunboats whose top speed was only 14½ knots. This type of action was frequent and frustrating for the ships' crews.

By the end of the day, the some of the ships at RP 2 had been replaced. On patrol there were the *U.S.S. Wilson (DD 414)*, *U.S.S. Bennion (DD 662)*, *LSM(R) 199* and *LCS(L)s 25* and *61.* Shortly after the *Bennion* arrived on station she came under attack by a *kamikaze*. It came so close that its wingtip smashed the starboard motor whaleboat of the destroyer. Fortunately no one was injured.

Although only a little over three weeks had elapsed since the invasion began, the contribution of the picket ships was obvious. They received the following communique on 24 April:

THE FOLLOWING MESSAGE FROM COMGENTEN IS PASSED TO ALL HANDS WITH CONCURRENCE AND CONGRATULATIONS TO CTF51: "ON BEHALF OF ALL MEMBERS OF TENTH ARMY I DESIRE TO EXPRESS APPRECIATION OF THE SPLENDID SERVICES RENDERED BY CREWS OF RADAR PICKET BOATS OF CTF51 IN CONTRIBUTING TO THE ANTI-AIRCRAFT PROTECTION OF OUR FORCES AT OKINAWA X WITHOUT THEIR SKILL IN WARNING AND GUIDING YOUR PLANES OUR FORCES WOULD HAVE SUFFERED HEAVILY IN LIFE AND

EQUIPMENT X ALTHOUGH THE BULK OF ENEMY AIR ATTACK WAS DIRECTED AT THEM RESULTING IN THEIR SUFFERING SERIOUS CASUALTIES, THEY PERFORMED THEIR HAZARDOUS DUTIES WITH EFFICIENCY AND DISPLAYED A HEROIC DEGREE OF COURAGE X THEY ARE FULL DESERVING OF THE HIGHEST COMMENDATION" S.B. BUCKNER, LT. GEN. USA (*CTG51 to TF51 2220 24Apr45*).

A *Japanese Aichi D3A1* dive bomber. Code named *Val*, these planes were responsible for sinking more allied shipping than any other Japanese aircraft. Photo courtesy of the National Archives.

General quarters was sounded whenever the threat of attack was possible. During daylight hours, when most of the men were at their regular duties, it simply involved taking their assigned positions. However, at night, when many were asleep in their bunks, the sound of the general quarters klaxon going off was nightmarish. Gun crewman William Scrom, of the *61*, described the feeling:

When general quarters went off when we were asleep, we were scared as hell. We got up in the dark except for the red lights that were on down in the crew's quarters. You fought your way up the ladder with 20 other guys and ran down the passageways with people going in all directions. Of course, when the hatches were opened to the outside, the lights went out in the passageways. It was total confusion, you were tripping over people trying to get to your guns. Once you got the cover off the gun, you got strapped into it. You had your earphones on. You stood there in total darkness just waiting for something to happen (Scrom interview).

During daylight hours, the *kamikazes* could easily spot the ships below, unless they were covered by smoke screens. Ship's gunners could just as easily see the planes and the balance sheet was even. However, at night, the Japanese planes frequently had an advantage. As the ships passed through the water, their wake stirred up microscopic plankton which reflected moonlight and produced a phosphorescent glow. To a *kamikaze* flying overhead on a moonlight night, this phosphorescent trail was highly visible and gave them a distinct advantage over the gun crews below. Scrom recalls, "I used to like dark nights, I hated moonlit nights and I stood there in that gun waiting for something to happen and I looked out at that phosphorus and it looked like an arrow pointing to the stern of the ship" (Scrom letter).

Although gunners were at their usual stations, many other crewmen were not. On the *61*, Quartermaster Bob Rielly's position was in the pilot house steering the ship. Below him in the radio shack was the Executive Officer, Mark Sellis. Limited in his actions at that location, Sellis was near enough to the conning tower to take immediate control in case Commanding Officer James Kelley was incapacitated. The other Quartermaster, Ed Robinson, along with Electrician's Mate, Al Jensen, was assigned to the emergency steering compartment at the aft end of the ship. If the main wheel in the pilot house lost control, the ship could be steered manually from there. Jensen describes the post:

This was a real hell-hole, it was 4' by 5' and I'm 6'4" so we were squeezed in there . . . we had to batten down the hatch because the twin 40 was near us. When those things were going off we were just shuddering down there. We couldn't see anything, all we had were the phones on us that were tied in to Captain Kelley's people topside to tell us what to do in case we were hit. So it wasn't great duty, being 6'4" and squeezed into that area wasn't much fun, especially when you had to close the hatch down, it was damn frightening (Jensen interview).

For crewmen stationed below during general quarters, in the engine room, steering engine room, and the numerous compartments sealed by watertight doors, the speculation and anticipation were terrible. They were unable to see what was going on and whether or not they were in imminent danger. For those stationed above, the danger was obvious and the psychological pressure even greater. In *LCS(L) 114 Action Report of 16 April 1945*, the Commanding Officer, Lt. A.P. Glienke noted:

> The psychological effect of this method of attack [*kamikaze*] is the hardest problem to solve. With a complement of 70 men, only 15 men are inside the ship, where they are unable to see the plane diving directly at them. Since the time of the attack [12 April], two men on this vessel who were topside during the attack, have broken down as psycho-neurotic cases and two other border line cases were observed (5).

On 25 April, *LCS(L)s 24, 61, U.S.S. Aaron Ward (DM 34), U.S.S Russell (DD 413), U.S.S. PGM 9*, and *LSM(R) 198* patrolled at Radar Picket Station 2. They were under the constant threat of attack and went to general quarters five times in the space of two days, but fortunately saw no action.

TEN-GO 4

Ten-Go 4 began the evening of 27 to 28 April. One hundred and fifteen Japanese planes, consisting of 65 from the navy and 50 from the army headed towards the pickets and the anchorage at Hagushi. *LCS(L) 53, LSM(R) 195, U.S.S. Brown (DD 546)*, and *U.S.S. J. William Ditter (DMS 31)* were on patrol at Radar Picket Station 10. *The Log of the LCS(L)(3) 53* describes the action:

> 2130 While steaming on course . . . intervals of 1500 yards from *LSM (R) 195* to port of DDs and *LSM (R) 195*. DDs opened fire on plane bearing 160 degrees T at distance of 5000 yards from us. In the meantime enemy aircraft attacked us from 300 degrees T coming in at altitude of 500 feet. Enemy plane peeled off on left wing and headed straight for conn. Immediately upon sighting plane all guns opened fire and speed was increased to full. Plane passed aft of conn approximately 30 feet. While flying over ship starboard wing fell from plane by our AA fire and hit water in wake of ship. Believe two bombs fell 20 to 30 feet aft of fantail but did not explode. Scrap from plane fell on deck. Enemy plane landed 25 feet off starboard beam showering decks with spray. Plane sunk instantaneously. Immediately after plane crashed destroyer fire fell in pattern around ship most of which fell in line across bow from 30 feet to 175 yards. Captain ordered hard left rudder and flank speed to swing and avoid line of fire. Radio report was sent immediately to SOPA informing him of shellfire and splashing plane. DD fire ceased immediately. Plane splashed believed to be Hamp (56).

A *Mitsubishi A6M3* fighter. Originally code named *Hamp*, the designation was later changed to *Zeke*, but the plane was most commonly known as the *Zero*. This clipped wing version was captured towards the end of the war and displays American insignia. Photo courtesy of the National Archives.

The last incident was not unusual. In the melee that surrounded these attacks, ships fired at will on numerous targets and sometimes placed one another in jeopardy.

At the same time, Radar Picket Station 1 was also under attack. Patrolling there were the *LCS(L)s 11, 31* and *61*, along with the *U.S.S. Mustin (DD 413)*, and the *U.S.S. Aaron Ward (DM 34)*. The *61* recorded the activity:

Steaming on station 17 miles south of Radar Picket Station 1, on courses 270(T) and 090(T) using two engines per quad at standard speed of 9.5 knots. Ship is darkened. Material condition Baker and condition of readiness II set. 0210 Sounded general quarters. Enemy aircraft reported bearing 045(T) and range 4500 yards. 0255 Opened fire on enemy aircraft . . . 0400 Secured from general quarters . . . (*Log LCS(L) 61* 233).

It was a close call for the *61*. According to Pierpoint, "a bogey made a run on us from dead ahead. He passed over the ship and was driven off by the after 40mm gun but the whole thing was over so quickly we could not tell whether we had hit him or not" (Pierpoint 4). Reports from other ships indicated that the plane, a *Kate*, had been downed by the *61's* guns. This was the type of action that many ships experienced on picket duty. General quarters would sound in the middle of the night, waking everyone with a shrill, penetrating klaxon. Men would jump out of their bunks half-dressed, race to battle stations and strain to spot incoming *kamikazes* through the dark of night. Shooting in these cases was inconclusive, with the aircraft disappearing into the gloom, possibly to go down or to be shot down by another ship. All that was certain in this event was that the *61* had escaped harm.

The *Nakajima B5N2*, code named *Kate*, was the best of the Japanese torpedo bombers. Powered by a 1,000 h.p. engine, the plane had a maximum speed of only 235 m.p.h., making it one of the easier *kamikazes* to hit. Photo courtesy of the National Archives.

In the early evening of 28 April, things warmed up again for the ships at RP 1, which included *LCS(L)s 11, 31, 61* and the destroyers *U.S.S. Bennion (DD 662)* and *U.S.S. Mustin (DD 527)*. A tragedy almost occurred when the 61's conn reported to the gunners that a friendly plane was about to fly across the bow from the starboard to the port side, however, the gunners didn't get the message. Nighttime identification was difficult, and as the Marine *Corsair* crossed the bow and came down the port side, the gunners opened fire. Fortunately, they were told to cease firing before they scored a hit on one of their own planes (Longhurst interview). Such incidents were common throughout the war, particularly in the confusion of combat conditions. Marine and Navy planes were continually in the area of the radar picket stations as part of the Combat Air Patrol. One of the functions of the ships on radar picket duty was to identify incoming enemy aircraft and guide the American planes towards them so that they might be intercepted before they could get to the ships in Hagushi anchorage and other locations near Okinawa.

Within a few minutes after the *Corsair* passed over, a Japanese plane came through on the the same path as the *Corsair*, however, Fire Control Director Larry Fabroni picked him up and began tracking him as he came across the bow from starboard to port. After he crossed the bow and was clear of the ship in front, Fabroni opened fire with the forward twin 40s. "As soon as he realized that he was being fired on, the Jap turned in toward the *61* but he was much, much too late" (Pierpoint 5). The plane burst into flames and crashed about a 100 yards off the port beam. He remained on fire for some time and slowly sank to the bottom as the ships continued on their patrol (*Log 61* 233). Several weeks later, the LCS(L)s received the following message:

28 MAY 1945 - A - M834 - 280245 - W T8031 T8011 T8061 [Call letters for the LCS (L)s were T8031, 8011, 8061] BT FOLLOWING FROM - CTF 51 - TO AARON WARD AND SUPPORTING VESSELS QUOTE - THROUGHOUT NIGHT OF 27 AND 28 APRIL WHILE ON RADAR PICKET STATION ONE YOU AND YOUR SUPPORTING GROUP WERE UNDER CONSTANT AIR ATTACK SPLASHING TWO X THE PERFORMANCE OF THIS TEAM WAS SUPER X PASS ON TO YOUR JAP EXTERMINATING GANG BT (CTF51 28 May 1945).

LCS(L) 61 **cruises off Okinawa. Photo courtesy of William Mason.**

Unofficial reports that day indicated that 105 planes were shot down in the area around Radar Picket Station 1 (Katz 8). The constant firing had caused a number of problems, particularly with rounds falling on friendly ships. Commander Task Force 51 sent the following message:

BT NUMBER OF SHIPS HAVE BEEN HIT BY INDISCRIMINATE FIRING TONIGHT X MEN HAVE BEEN INJURED X DON'T FIRE UNLESS YOU CAN SEE BY EYE OR RADAR X DON'T FIRE WHEN IN SMOKE BT OUT (CTF51 28 April, 1945).

This was a recurring problem in the war zone. Only a few weeks earlier, on 6 April, the Hagushi area had suffered greatly. During that battle, "friendly fire killed four Americans and wounded 34 others in the XXIV Corps zone, ignited an ammunition dump near Kadena, destroyed an oil barge, and in the late afternoon shot down two American planes over the beaches. Some ships also suffered damage and casualties" (Appleman 99).

In spite of the friendly fire problems, the picket ships had performed admirably. On the morning of 29 April, they received the following message from Commander Task Force 51:

REQUEST YOU PASS MY HEARTY CONGRATULATIONS TO ALL PILOTS OF CAP AND RADAR PICKET GROUPS CONCERNED IN YESTERDAY'S SUPERB DEFENSE OF OUR SURFACE FORCES IN THE OKINAWA AREA X WELL DONE. (CTG51.5 Dispatch 1230 29 April, 1945).

Patrolling off Okinawa on 28 April, the crew of the *LCS(L) 63* saw two LCI(L)s firing on an object in the water. It turned out to be a suicide boat, however, the LCI(L) guns could not depress sufficiently and they were having difficulty hitting the small craft. They stood by as the *63* took the boat under fire. She opened up with her 40mm guns at a range of 800 yards and continued firing until the boat capsized and sank when it was only 200 yards off.

Other ships continued support duty for the anchorages. On 30 April, while covering the ships in Nago Wan, the *LCS(L) 32* went to the aid of a merchant vessel that had been hit by a *kamikaze*. At 0337, the *32* observed a bomb hit on the *S.S. Hall Young*, which was carrying gasoline and ammunition for the invasion force. The *32* received permission from CTU 52.19.2 to go to her aid. When they arrived at the side of the ship they found that she had been hit a few feet above the waterline, portside aft. Two of her holds were ablaze and a large hole was present in her port side. Using their fire-fighting expertise, the crew of the *32* extinguished the fires and saved the ship. Lt. Jewel M. Evans, the Commanding Officer of the *32*, received the Bronze Star for his ship's work that day.

Not all the action took place at the radar picket stations. A TBF *Avenger* torpedo bomber had been shot down on the southeastern side of Okinawa near Yonibara Bay. *LCS(L)s 114, 118* and *119* were sent into the hostile bay area to find the fliers who were believed to have bailed out of their damaged plane. As the *114* patrolled to within 500 yards of the head of the bay, she encountered a mine, which she promptly took under fire and sank. Finding no survivors of the aircraft, she came under mortar and machine gun fire from the shore as she tried to exit the bay. *LCS(L) 119*, which had been covering her, returned fire. After identifying the machine gun emplacements and the source of the mortars, the two ships opened fire on a small house. A huge explosion took place as the rounds from the *Mighty Midgets* struck home. They had taken out an enemy ammunition dump. The three LCS(L)s went back to their regular patrol area.

The month ended with action on Radar Picket Station 3. On patrol there on 30 April were the *LCS(L)s 18, 52, 110, U.S.S. Henry A. Wiley* (*DD 597*), *U.S.S. Sproston* (*DD 577*) and *LSM(R) 195*. At 0308 a Japanese *Helen* bomber approached the ships and was taken under fire by the *18* and nearby destroyers. It reversed course and passed over the LCS(L)s. All three took it under fire and it crashed in flames 3,000 yards off the starboard bow of the *52* (*LCS(L) 52 Action Report 1May45* 1). The *18* got credit for the plane with assists credited to the *52* and *110*.

The opening month of the invasion of Okinawa was over. Throughout April, the LCS(L)s had proven their worth. In addition to the above-mentioned actions, numerous other events occurred. Virtually every ship in the LCS(L) fleet fired its guns at the enemy. In some cases they were brief, isolated encounters, and in others they were intense. In addition to fights with enemy aircraft, the *Mighty Midgets* had also encountered numerous skunk boats, sinking many and driving others off. Shore installations had been strafed repeatedly, destroying much valuable real estate and its accompanying structures, thereby depriving the enemy of observation posts, communications centers and ammunition and material supplies. However, it was not all one-sided, the ships had suffered many casualties and some had been sunk or damaged. There would be no respite for the next two months, until the enemy was defeated.

The rigors of naval warfare required regular ship maintenance and repair. Here the *LCS(L) 126* is drydocked for some work. Photo courtesy of Ray Baumler.

CHAPTER V

PICKET DUTY AND SKUNK PATROL

By the end of April, 1945, the invasion force had secured the beaches and moved well inland in the face of stiff Japanese resistance. The pattern of action off shore had been established, with regular patrols in the Hagushi anchorage to protect the assembled ships against Japanese suicide boats and aircraft. Where Japanese resistance could be identified, ships of the fleet patrolled off the beaches firing on targets of opportunity.

TEN-GO 5

The fifth of the *Ten-Go* operations took place from 3 to 4 May. During this action 75 navy and 50 army planes attacked the American ships. Cruising on Radar Picket Station 10 on 3 May were *LCS(L)s 14, 25, 83, LSM(R) 195, U.S.S. Little (DD 803)* and *U.S.S. Aaron Ward (DM 34)*. The ships came under attack at 0827 by approximately 25 Japanese planes. This was to be a disaster for the picket ships which sustained serious losses. Recounted in the *Log of the USS LCS(L)(3) 83* is a part of the story:

> 1827 Sounded General Quarters. 1826 DM 34 AARON WARD has enemy plane under fire. 1830 Plane crashed into DM 34. 1832 Planes crashed into both DM 34 and DD 803 LITTLE. Proceeding independently to the stricken ships. 1845 Both ships burning and out of control. LSM 195 fell behind because of engine trouble. 1848 DD 803 burning. 1855 DD 803 appears to be broken amidships. 1902 DD 803 sunk bearing 025(t). 1906 Opened fire on plane attacking LSM 195. Plane hit LSM 195. 1910 Plane took mast off LCS 25 in suicide dive. 1912 Plane missed DM 34 after another hit it

amidships. 1915 Picking up survivors. Plane attacked us from port side. All guns to port firing. Plane out of control crashed in water about 50 ft. over our bow. LSM burning furiously. Plane coming in on our stern shot down, fired at us as it hit the water. 1920 Lowered life rafts. Men on them to pick up survivors. LSM exploding. 1926 Another plane crashed into the DM 34. 1942 LSM 195 sank bearing 190(t). Still picking up survivors from DD LITTLE. LCSs 25 and 14 with DM 34. 1959 still picking up survivors . . . 2000 to 2400 Picking up survivors from DD 803, Underway to aid of DM AARON WARD . . . (6).

The *Little,* cruising about eight miles to the east, had been too far from her support ships to make use of their firepower. Coming along the port side of the *Aaron Ward* was the *LCS(L) 14.* Some of her men transferred on board the destroyer to help fight the unabated fires in the forward section of the destroyer. *LCS(L) 14* moved forward to fight them. As she neared the flames, ammunition from one of the 40mm magazines exploded, causing the fire-fighting crew to dive for cover. Lieutenant Ralph Todd, the Commanding Officer, rallied his crew and they resumed their battle. *LCS(L) 83* lined up on the starboard side of the *Aaron Ward.* As her sister ship was doing, she commenced pumping operations. The serious nature of the situation called for extra relief and the *U.S.S. Shannon (DM 25)* was sent out from Nago Wan to assist in picking up survivors. She arrived at 2120 and began to tow the *Aaron Ward* back to safety. *LCS(L) 25* had shot down two of the planes, but parts of one had struck her causing some minor damage. She rescued 57 survivors from the *Little* and one from the *Aaron Ward.* Her own losses were one killed and ten wounded. With the *Little* and the *LSM(R) 195* sunk, the *Aaron Ward* badly damaged, and the LCS(L)s roughed up, the gunboats spent the remainder of 3 May picking up survivors and transferring the dead and wounded to *PCE(R) 853* where they received medical aid.

At the same time, the ships at RP 9 also were attacked. Present were *LCS(L)s 89, 111* and *117,* along with the *U.S.S. Bache (DD 470)* and the *U.S.S. Macomb (DMS 23).* At 1826, two *Judys* came in from the east and started a suicide run on the destroyers. They were taken under fire by the destroyers but one hit the *Macomb* on the fantail. The explosion threw men overboard and started a fire. An American plane from the *U.S.S. Rudyard Bay (CVE 81)* was chasing the *Judys* and was hit by fire from one of the destroyers and the *LCS(L) 111.* Lt. (jg) C.M. Harper, the pilot, crashed his plane into the stern of the *111.* Fortunately there were no casualties from the crash, and Harper was picked up and transferred back to his ship. The mistake occurred because the American plane had its landing gear down, which made it resemble a *Val* and caused the ships to open fire.

Photo showing damage to the deck area of the *Aaron Ward* (*DM 34*) after being struck by *kamikazes* at RP 10 on 3 May, 1945. Photo courtesy of the National Archives.

Early on 4 May, as the ships on Radar Picket Station 10 were licking their wounds, activity at Radar Picket Station 1 picked up. At 0730 *LCS(L)s 21, 23, 31, LSM (R) 194* and the destroyers *U.S.S. Ingraham* (*DD 694*) and *U.S.S. Morrison* (*DD 560*) came under attack by a combination of 58 planes comprised of *Zekes*, *Sams*, *Petes* and *Kates*. As the first wave of planes attacked, three were shot down by the *LCS(L) 21*. The *31* got two but the second was too close and struck the ship, killing 14 men and wounding others. Actual damage to the ship was not great and her performance under fire won her a Presidential Unit Citation which read:

> . . . LCS 31 promptly opened fire on an overwhelming force of suicide planes and maintained a steady barrage from her anti-aircraft guns, scoring repeated hits on two of the targets, but failing to stop the terrific momentum of the craft which crashed, between the conning tower and forward 40mm gun and the other across the main deck aft. Perilously crippled by the

resultant fires, extensive damage and personnel casualties, the *LCS 31* quickly shifted to emergency steering and remained in action, she responded gallantly to the determined and aggressive efforts of the officers and men who controlled her fire; she continued the desperate fight, destroying the third and fourth attackers close aboard and, despite severely reduced fire power, scored two more hits at longer ranges. Returning to pick up men blown overboard by the crashes, *LCS 31* completed a record of heroic achievement against overwhelming odds (*War Hist. LCS(L) 31* 2).

Struck by a suicide plane and down by the bow, the *Ingraham* limped back to Kerama Retto for repairs. The *Morrison* did not fare as well. She was hit near the forward stack by a *Zero* and exploded. Within a few minutes, two *Pete* float-biplanes crashed into her. From her first hit to her sinking, only four minutes elapsed. A *Val* made a run on the *LCS(L) 21* and she opened fire at 2,000 yards, setting the plane on fire. The plane veered into the stern of *LSM(R) 194*, exploding her magazine and throwing many of her crew into the water. Those not blown overboard abandoned ship as she sank.

Overhead, the C.A.P. had a field day with the enemy planes. The Commanding Officer of the *LCS(L) 21* estimated "that they accounted for 20 to 30 planes during the attack" (*LCS(L) 21 Action Report 6May45* 2). Their enthusiasm did cause problems, however. They frequently followed the *kamikazes* into their suicide dives, attempting to shoot them down and making it difficult for the ships to fire on the planes for fear of hitting their own.

Maneuvering through the area, the *LCS (L) 21*, after shooting down a total of five planes, picked up oil-covered survivors from the two ships. A total of 236 were rescued by this vessel and she received the Navy Unit Commendation. *LCS(L) 23* shot down four planes and recorded two assists. In all, the *Mighty Midgets* had given a good account of themselves.

RP 12 came under attack at 0807. Ships patrolling there were the *LCS(L)s 81, 84, 118, LSM(R) 190* and the *U.S.S. Luce (DD 522)*. They were attacked by 21 *kamikazes*. Although they were assisted by the Combat Air Patrol, which shot down several of the enemy planes, some got through. The *Luce* was attacked by one plane which missed her but knocked out her power supply. A second hit her amidships to port and exploded violently. The destroyer began to list as the LCS(L)s tried to aid her. Within ten minutes, the *Luce* went to the bottom. *LCS(L) 118* picked up 114 survivors, including ten officers and the Captain. As the destroyer was in her last minutes, other Japanese planes were striking at the *LSM(R) 190*.

The attack on the LSM(R) 190 began with a Dinah flying in over the stern and dropping a bomb which missed. This plane was hit by our automatic weapons. Thereupon the plane turned over, returned and dived into the 5/38 mount, setting it on fire. Shrapnel resulting from the plane crash severely injured the Commanding Officer, rendering him prostrate and immediately killed the Gunnery Officer. The fire . . . spread to the powder and handling rooms . . . a second plane (Val) came in on the port beam very low and crashed into the upper level of the engine room . . . Fires immediately broke out in the engine room and shortly smoke was so thick that it was impossible to see the controls. This second attack disabled the auxiliary fire pump . . . a third plane (Dinah) crossing from port to starboard at masthead height dropped a bomb which missed by 700 yards. By this time all guns except the starboard 20mm were inoperative as a result of material and personnel casualties. A fourth plane attacked in "sneak" fashion releasing a bomb which hit in the area of the Mk. 51 Director tub (*LSM(R) 190 Action Report 18Aug45* 2-3).

After vainly attempting to fight the fires which had grown beyond control, the order was given to abandon ship at about 0830. Within a half-hour, at approximately 0905, the *LSM(R) 190* went to the bottom.

LCS(L) 84 patrolled the area, picking up survivors from the LSM(R) while *LCS(L) 81* picked up 47 more survivors from the *Luce*. Many of the wounded from the ships were in bad condition. They were covered with oil and a number had second or third degree burns caused by the fires and explosions. So many of the survivors were in serious condition that the *Henry A. Wiley* (*DD 597*) was sent out to take the worst cases from the picket ships. The *Kilty* (*APD 15*) took the remainder (*Log LCS(L)(3) 118* 325). Having transferred the rescued men, the *LCS(L)s 81, 84* and *118* resumed patrolling the station. They were soon joined by the *U.S.S. Wilkes* (*DD 441*) and *LSM(R) 199*.

Shortly after RP 9 was attacked, Radar Picket Station 1 again became a target. Ships present at that time included *LCS(L)s 23, 56, 87, LSM(R) 197*, the *U.S.S. Ingraham* (*DD 694*) and the *U.S.S. Bache* (*DD 470*). At about 1900, 30 Japanese planes came over, consisting of a combination of *Vals, Petes* and *Zekes*. A number of them dove on the destroyers and one hit the *Bache* amidships, setting her afire. The *LCS(L) 23* went to her aid, firing on various targets as they came into range. A *Val* went down and then a *Betty*. Five planes went after the *23*, and she drove them off. By the end of the engagement the *23* had four kills and three assists.

A *Mitsubishi A6M5 Reisen* **fighter. Known to the allies as the** *Hamp, Zero* **or** *Zeke,*
it was one of Japan's most successful fighters. This version, powered by a Nakajima
1,130 h.p. engine, was capable of speeds to 350 m.p.h. Photo courtesy of the
National Archives.

About the same time, Radar Picket Station 10 was attacked. Cruising at that
station, which was near Kuma Shima Island, were *LCS(L)s 54, 55, 110 and LSM(R)*
192 along with the *U.S.S. Cowell (DD 547)* and the *U.S.S. Gwin (DM 33)*. At 1920
the formation was attacked by six Japanese planes. The *55* scored a direct hit on one
of them with its twin 40mm guns and it went down in flames. The *55* and the *110*
both fired on a *Zeke* and knocked it out of the sky. Shortly thereafter, *Oscars* dove
on both the *54* and the *55* and were shot down. Another *Oscar* dove on the *LSM(R)*
192 from dead ahead and was destroyed. It was a near miss. Three other planes
headed for the *Gwin*. Two were shot down and the *Gwin* took a hit from the third.

Suicide boats continued to plague the anchorages. In Buckner Bay, the *LCS(L)*
24 was on patrol overnight from 3 to 4 May, when Japanese small boat activity was
observed. Of 15 small boats in the area, 14 were destroyed by the LCS(L)s on
patrol.

May 4 proved to be one of the most dangerous for the ships at Radar Picket Station 7 as they were near the escort carrier *U.S.S. Sangamon* (*CVE 26*) when she was hit by a *kamikaze*. *LCS(L)s 13, 16, 61* and the destroyers *U.S.S. Fullam* (*DD 474*) and *U.S.S. Hudson* (*DD 475*) were on patrol there and went to her aid.

The *Sangamon* had originally been built as an oiler (*AO 28*) and had been used as such from 1940 through 1941. In 1942, she was converted to a carrier along with three other oilers. The *Log of the LCS(L) 61* tells part of the story:

Steaming as before. 1900 Sounded general quarters: enemy aircraft bearing 270(T) and range 5 miles . . . 1930 Sounded general quarters: enemy aircraft bearing 050(T) and range 32 miles . . . Steaming as before. 2005 Japanese aircraft hit USS Sangamon bearing 350(T) and range 5 miles. 2010 Steaming with USS LCS(L) 13 and USS LCS(L) 16 at full speed (14 knots), proceeding to USS Sangamon (CVE 26). 2015 Changed speed to flank (15 knots). 2020 Jettisoned 127 rockets and one gasoline drum. USS LCS(L) 13 went alongside port side of carrier and suffered broken mast which fell over conn. USS Sangamon was blazing furiously amidships on flight deck, and hanger deck. Ammunition and gasoline was continuously exploding, rocking whole ship. 2035 Came along starboard side of USS Sangamon with all fire lines streaming but unable to give her any water due to planes she was pushing over side. One plane landing on fantail of destroyer who went alongside ahead of us. 2045 Attempted to come along port side of USS Sangamon but was ordered to try starboard side again as USS *LCS(L) 13* was coming along port side. 2050 Came along starboard side again as USS *LCS(L) 13* was coming along port side. 2050 Came along starboard side of fantail of USS Sangamon. No water needed. Requested to report to bow of carrier as communications with fantail was out. 2052 Alongside starboard bow and was told to put water under superstructure or standby if unable to do so. 2100 Proceeded along starboard side. Unable to put water over due to smoke which made it impossible to see carrier even when close aboard. 2145 Fires aboard USS Sangamon under control . . . 2330 secured from general quarters. 2345 Proceeded with USS LCS(L) 16 to original station in Roger Peter 7 (246).

Quick action by the ships of Radar Picket 7 were, in large part, responsible for saving the carrier. Gunner's Mate Walter Longhurst of the *61* described the event:

We were out on Radar Picket 7 and the Sangamon was operating about a mile from us. We went to general quarters and we could see them get planes off, they got about 2 planes off and we saw two suicide planes diving on them. One hit her amidships around the hangar deck and the other one hit her in about the same place. We were ordered to go alongside and put hoses on her since we had quite a bit of fire equipment. . . . We came up alongside and the ammunition was going off in the gun tubs as we were pulling up and of course, being a small ship, we were looking up at the gun tubs and the flight deck of the carrier . . . (Longhurst interview).

A *kamikaze* makes a suicide dive on the carrier *U.S.S. Sangamon* (*CVE 26*), 4 May, 1945. Photo courtesy of the National Archives.

The situation on the carrier was grave, with munitions and aviation gas exploding continuously "it was a pretty hot place to be. A lot of guys were blown overboard or burned to death. All the *Wildcats* and *Corsairs* were thrown overboard. One just missed our bow" (Katz 9). Up on the forward end of the carrier, crewmen had formed a line and were passing bombs forward to be jettisoned. As the gunboats arrived on the scene, they could hear cheers from the crew of the carrier. Men had already jumped overboard, but with the arrival of the LCS(L)s and the destroyer, they kept to their station and worked to save their ship. Crewmen who had jumped over the side faced an uncertain fate. Captain Kelley later wrote: "Prior to our coming alongside some men had started to jump off the fantail, but our arrival was marked by cheers by the men on the carrier and no further cases of men abandoning the ship were observed" (*CO LCS(L)(3) 61 letter 11 July, 1945*).

Damage to the *U.S.S. Sangamon* (*CVE 26*) after *kamikaze* attack near RP 7 on 4 May, 1945. Photo courtesy of the National Archives.

The following day, the picket ships received this message:

THE SUPPORT SHIPS OF ROGER PETER SEVEN ARE TO BE CONGRATULATED FOR A SUPERB JOB LAST NIGHT X YOU WERE CERTAINLY RESPONSIBLE TO A LARGE DEGREE IN SAVING THE CARRIER X REQUEST DUNGEON SIX SUBMIT NAMES OF ALL COMMANDING OFFICERS INCLUDING DUNGEON THREE AND ALBERT FOURTEEN BT K (DD475 Dispatch 5 June, 1945).

LCS(L) 16 **was one of the** *Mighty Midgets* **that aided the carrier** *U.S.S. Sangamon* **(***CVE 26***) after she was hit by a** *kamikaze* **on 4 May, 1945 off Okinawa. Photo courtesy of the National Archives.**

The hazards of the mission were great and ultimately generated Silver Star awards for the commanding officers of the LCS(L)s. Lieutenants James W. Kelley of the *61*, Homer O. White, Jr. of the *16* and Lieutenant (jg) Billy R. Hart of the *13* all received the awards.

Not all of the danger to the *Mighty Midgets* came from the sky. *LCS(L)s 24, 37, 38, 39* and *40* had been ordered to patrol Nakagusuku Wan on 27 April. In that capacity the ships encountered and destroyed many enemy suicide boats. *LCS(L) 40* destroyed 13 of the craft between the beginning of the patrol and 4 May. At 0608, on 4 May, they

> sighted an enemy swimmer about 600 yards northwest of Chinen Misaki. Closed him and attempted to bring him aboard, but when alongside he drew a hand grenade from out of his shirt and attempted to throw it at the men rescuing him. He was dispatched with small arms fire. This man was in full uniform less helmet and a life jacket. He spoke English and on our approach asked us to help him (*LCS(L) 40 Action Report 8Aug45* 7).

A half-hour later a second swimmer was spotted 1600 yards east of Yonibaru clad in a full uniform and wearing a life jacket and helmet, but no shoes. Having had their first experience with a suicide swimmer, the crew took no chances. He was killed by small arms fire before he could get near the ship. The LCS(L)s would continue on this duty until the 20 May, destroying many suicide boats on the water and ashore.

On the west side of the island, at the southern end of the Hagushi anchorage, the *LCS(L) 12* was also on skunk patrol. At about 0235 she encountered two of the craft, which made a run on her. She fired on both and then lost contact with them. In all probability her actions saved her from attack. Fifteen minutes later, a damaged boat was found and sunk by one of the other LCS(L)s. Thus ended 4 May, which would go down as one of the bloodiest days for the radar picket ships at Okinawa.

LCS(L)s 14, 61, 115, LSM(R) 196, U.S.S. Gainard (DD 706), and *U.S.S. J.W. Ditter (DM 31)* spent several days of picket duty at RP 7, with continual calls to general quarters and sightings of enemy planes. At 1935 hours on 9 May, 1945, a *Betty* passed low over the bow of the *61* and was taken under fire by both the *61* and the *14*. A number of hits were observed and the plane flew out of sight. Within minutes a large underwater explosion was felt and the plane did not reappear. The Combat Air Patrol sighted the wreckage and confirmed that the ships had made a kill. On 10 May, 1945 the *61* left formation to pick up survivors of a downed *PBM* aircraft.

On 10 May *LCS(L)s 65, 66, 67, 90, 92, 93, 94, 112, 121, 122* and *123* arrived from Saipan, having convoyed other vessels to Okinawa. Accompanying them was *LC(FF) 1082* with Captain Neill Phillips aboard. He would serve as the Commander of Flotilla Four. Their introduction to the Hagushi Anchorage came amidst the shelling of enemy positions by the larger ships in the area.

The *LCS(L) 83* also saw action on 11 May. Along with the other ships at Radar Picket Station 15, usually referred to as "Suicide Alley," the *LCS(L)s 82, 84, LSM(R) 193*, and the destroyers *U.S.S. Evans (DD 552)* and the *U.S.S. Hugh W. Hadley (DD 774)*, the *83* came under attack. At about 0755, the Fighter Director Officer in the Combat Information Center reported a large number of planes headed towards the station. He "estimated that the total number of enemy planes was 156, coming in at different heights in groups as follows: Raid One 36, Raid Two 50, Raid Three 20, Raid Four 20 to 30, Raid Five 20" (*CO DD 774 15 May 1945*). At 0805 the first enemy plane was spotted by the *LCS(L) 83*. A formation of nearly 50 Japanese planes, consisting of *Vals, Jills, Tonys* and *Oscars* was approaching the fleet. The *Log of the LCS(L)(3) 82* recorded the action:

Underway in formation as before on course 230(T) with standard speed 10 knots, all hands at battle stations. 0814 CAP splashed twin engine aircraft 25 miles North. 0825 DD 774 reported many bogies coming in from North, at about 50 miles, CAP intercepting. 0831 two low fliers approaching formation, now on course 140(T) again from port quarter. DDs opening fire. 0836 one Val splashed about one mile from *DD 552*, but second plane dived into *DD 552*. Three Jills now appeared from same direction, veered right and started across stern of formation, range about three miles. First passed clear, came up stb'd and was splashed by LCS(L) (3) 84. Second was splashed by fire from DDs. Third, carrying torpedo, turned back to port and started run on DD 552. 0837 opened fire on this plane at about 3500 yards and full deflection. Tracking was excellent, and several hits were made. Jill wobbled and missed DD 552, and dropped torpedo. 0838 Jill wavered into water about a half mile past DD 552, sank slowly with no explosion. 0845 opened fire on Tony loaded with bombs in wing racks, coming in on port quarter, we and others apparently hitting him. 0846 Tony splashed. 0900 opened fire on lone Oscar coming in from our stb'd and exposed quarter. Firing ragged, plane passed overhead with little damage. Began hitting plane repeatedly as he passed over to our port side, and started to dive on LCS(L)(3) 84. Tore two large sections out of wings. Man overboard from LCS(L)(3) 84 a little before this. 0904 Oscar splashed very close aboard LCS(L)(3) 84. Another plane diving into water close to DD 774. 0905 DD 774 hit by suicide plane. 0910 LCS(L)(3) 83 splashed plane in dive very close aboard her. Second plane, an Oscar, coming down towards us from stbd. bow. Opened fire on Oscar leveling off at about 1000 feet and heading directly at us, hitting plane repeatedly. Aircraft broke in half directly overhead, wings and engine falling straight at this ship. 0915 all engines ahead flank to avoid falling Oscar, which crashed into our wake, about 100 yards astern, a moment later. 0918 came to course 070(T), proceeding at maximum speed to aid of DD 552, previously reported abandoning ship and now out of communication with us. 0920 rigged ship's hose and both Hale pumps to fight fires aboard DD 552. Boarding party standing by. LCS(L)(3) 83 and LSM 193 proceeding towards DD 774, then reportedly abandoning ship; LCS(L)(3) 84 accompanying us. 0928 Secured to stb'd side of *DD 552*, Chinese gangway. DD was firing torpedoes to port at this time. 0930 passed hoses to DD; began taking aboard survivors who were casualties. 0940 Val making run at us from our stern, chased by CAP. Opened fire with after gun, securing first hits at about 400 yards. Val tail chopped up and prop shot off, veered right, missed DD by narrow margin and splashed about 200 yards dead ahead of us. We put several shots through the bow of the DD by accident, and probably started the forecastle fire. 0945 emergency burning outfit put over to cut hole in fwd. deck. Now fighting fires in forward fire room superstructure amidships, and forecastle. Fires were soon put out, and pumping commenced (345).

Both of the destroyers survived the attacks after being hit by the *kamikazes*. In addition, the *Hadley* had also been hit by an *Oka*. The number of Japanese planes destroyed was amazing, with the *Hadley* downing 23 and the *Evans* 19. *LCS(L) 82* shot down three and recorded two assists as did *LCS(L)s 83*. Number *84* shot down one and had one assist. Later, the *82, 83* and *84* received the Navy Unit Commendation and the Commanding Officer of the *82*, Peter Beierl, was awarded a Bronze Star.

This attack reinforced the opinion of the LCS(L) skippers that they needed better coordination with the destroyers if they were to be of assistance to them. In this case the LCS(L)s had been steaming in a diamond formation and were close enough to support each other with their firepower. The destroyers had been circling the formation and once under attack took off at flank speed, leaving the LCS(L)s too far away to be of use. As a result the destroyers were basically on their own in defending themselves. Lt. P.G. Beierl, Commanding Officer of the *LCS(L) 82* summed it up:

> It was noted that the DDs, during the action, as during all previous alerts, operate at high speed and without much consideration to remaining close to their AA support. All hits scored on DDs by enemy aircraft were pressed home without interference from the support units, which were out of range during most of the action. The smaller ships, which stayed together in close formation, were able to help each other, and scored highly against the enemy without damage to themselves (*LCS(L) 82 Action Report 12May45* 5).

The same day, 11 May, at Radar Picket Station 5, *LCS(L)s 52, 88, 109, 114, PGM 20*, and the destroyers *U.S.S. Douglas H. Fox (DD 779)* and *U.S.S. Harry F. Bauer (DM 26)* came under attack by a combination of planes, including two *Kates*, two *Zekes*, two *Oscars* and one *Sally* at approximately 0800. Action began when both destroyers opened fire on the *Sally*. *LCS(L) 88* sighted two enemy planes which approached and headed for the destroyers. She opened fire with all three 40mm guns. One of the planes continued on its course, the other turned and circled astern of the column of support craft. The first plane was hit repeatedly and splashed into the water near the *Bauer.*

During the time that the first plane was under fire, the second Oscar continued around the stern of the support column and approached the LCS(L) 88 at 270 degrees relative, speed 200 knots, altitude 150 feet. The plane headed for the conn but sheared to the right as it closed in. Both twin 40mm guns and both port 20mm guns were directing a very accurate stream of fire at the plane. When it was approximately 100 yards from the ship it dropped its bomb. An instant after this the aircraft burst into flames and fell on the starboard side of the ship. The bomb hit the *88* on the fantail at approximately . . . four feet from the port side. A fire was started . . . The captain, Lieut. Casimir L. Bigos, USNR, and a number of personnel were killed as a result of the explosion (Phillips, *War Hist. Flot. Four 6-7*).

As this was going on, the other LCS(L)s steamed in a circular pattern about 1500 yards in diameter around the *88*, firing on other planes and protecting their sister ship from further damage. Three of the aft compartments on the *88* had been flooded, and the fires started by the attack were quickly put out by the fire control teams. Her rudder was jammed by the force of the bomb and she was unable to continue on patrol. *LCS(L) 114* began to tow her back to Kerama Retto for repairs, but the jammed rudder made it too difficult and the task had to be completed by a fleet tug. The Executive Officer, Ensign James W. Howard, took over command as the ship underwent repairs which ultimately required that she be sent stateside.

Other tasks were assigned to the *Mighty Midgets*. Between 11 and 13 May, 1945, six LCS(L)s, the *11, 12, 20, 21, 85* and the *89*, were assigned to support a landing on Tori Shima. Accompanied by the destroyers *U.S.S. Drexler* (*DD 741*), the *U.S.S. Shubrick* (*DD 639*), and the *LST 620*, the ships comprised Task Group 51.24. At 0630 on 12 May, the destroyers began to bombard the beaches with their 5 inch guns. A few minutes later, the gunboats worked over the beaches and then patrolled the shoreline searching out targets of opportunity. As this was being accomplished, the LVTs were unloaded from the LST and headed in to the beach. Some concern was voiced over the possibility of gun emplacements in caves near the base of cliffs on the southwest beach area. Fortunately, no opposition was encountered and the landing went smoothly. *LST 620* landed its troops and equipment. With the beaches secured and no opposition above or on the ground, the ships turned to other duties. *LCS(L)s 21* and *85*, along with the *Drexler*, remained in the area for anti-aircraft protection. The other gunboats left for the Hagushi anchorage at about 1737 in the company of the *Shubrick*. Half-way back to the anchorage, they had an air alert. A nearby destroyer, the *U.S.S. Compton* (*DD 705*) and the *LCS(L) 12* shot down a *Betty* at 1915.

LCS(L)s 19, 52, 82, 83, 84, 86 and *111* had been assigned skunk patrol in the southwest sector of the Hagushi anchorage. In the evening of 12 May, the *19* discovered two skunk boats and sent both to the bottom. Problems in observing the boats at night were identified in the ship's *Action Report (18May45)*, and it was noted that the standard ship's blinker light was of little use as a searchlight. This deficiency was noted by other ships and within a month a request by Captain T. C. Aylward, Commanding Officer of Flotilla Three had reached the Chief of Naval Operations. By July, searchlight improvements were being planned, however the end of the war made it unnecessary (*COMSERVPAC 30Jun45*). Fortunately for many of the ships on patrol, there were larger ships nearby with arc lights that were able to do a satisfactory job of illuminating the suicide boats. Just to the north, the *LCS(L)s 82* and *84* were also on patrol. The *Log of the LCS(L)(3) 82* describes the action:

> 2330 sounded General Quarters, skunk reported in vicinity. LCS(L) 84 reported contact and requested illumination in our area. . . . 2353 illumination stopped, visibility poor due to haze from smoke screening operations and night blindness from recent starshells, when boat, dead in water, and about 75 five yards ahead flank, on relative bearing 010, was sighted by captain through binoculars. All engines ahead flank, left hard rudder to expose battery and heel ship towards boat in order to bring our guns to bear. Illumination with 12 inch signal search light and opened fire with fwd and stbd guns as small craft got underway and charged our stbd bow. Gunfire was thick and close enough to obscure target completely for a moment, and apparently confused or blinded the operators. Target passed within 15 feet of bow, veering out to our stbd, then turned directly towards stbd quarter, at no time exceeding range of about 50 feet. After stbd 20MM and 40MM were able to continue firing as target closed and passed close under our stern, about ten feet away at closest. . . . Underway at various courses and speeds to track down enemy small craft. . . . 0018 arc light from ship believed to be APD picked up our target from our stbd, illuminating it very well. . . . 0019 target hit several times, going dead in water. 0022 target well illuminated, disappeared without explosion (349,351).

The immediate danger over, the LCS(L)s resumed their patrol.

On 13 May *LCS(L)s 23, 56, 87* and *LSM(R) 197* were on patrol at Radar Picket Station 9 along with the *U.S.S. Bache (DD 470)*, and the *U.S.S. Porter (DD 579)*. A suicide *Val* struck the destroyer amidships setting her afire. The *LCS(L) 87* went to her aid. Mooring to the port side of the destroyer, she sent in a boarding party and six hoses and the fires were soon extinguished. *LCS(L) 87* took eleven wounded men aboard and treated them.

Skunks continued to be a problem on the eastern side of the island as well. *LCS(L) 113* was assigned patrol duty along the southwest shore of Kutaka Shima in Nakagusuku Wan. Recently arrived from the states, it was to be her first combat activity. From 0840 to 0930 she found and destroyed six suicide boats hidden along the beach. This was apparently not an easy task as the boats were well-hidden. The Commanding Officer of the *113* reported that the:

> Boats are cleverly concealed. It is necessary to gaze intently at one spot for some time before a boat can be detected. They are generally hidden along a sandy beach. Small sand dunes are made use of and you may be able to just see a small part of the boat sticking up from behind a small rise in the sand. Most of the boats were placed with the bows headed towards the beach. The enemy cuts off palmetto and fills the boat up with it as well as pushing it into a palmetto clump. If you see a low row of palmetto within a palmetto clump you must keep looking for some time before you can suspect that a boat is hidden there. If you suspect the presence of a boat or have any doubts you had best open fire and clear some of the palmetto away with gun fire. . . . Enemy generally places a number of boats in one place. When approaching a sandy beach it is a good idea to look for paths leading down to the beach and notice grass to see if it is well worn and scuffed. If it is then this is likely a skunk nest (*LCS(L) 113 Action Report 16May45* 3).

Additional LCS(L)s arrived at Okinawa on 17 May. Ships numbered *68, 69, 91, 95, 120* and *124* arrived from Ulithi and were assigned radar picket duty and other patrol chores.

By 16 May, 1945, the installation of shore based radar at Ie Shima and Hedo Saki made it possible to reduce the number of occupied radar picket stations to five. From that point on only stations 5,7, 9,15 and 16 were patrolled (*Action Report Capture of Okinawa Gunto* 9). Reducing the number of active stations made it possible to have three destroyers and four LCS(L)s on each.

Radar Picket Station 9 was patrolled by *LCS(L)s 53, 65, 66, 67* and destroyers *U.S.S. Douglas H. Fox* (*DD 779*), and *U.S.S. Henry A. Wiley* (*DD 597*) on 14 May. The first two days held some action, with one plane fired on the first day and the destroyers shooting down two others on 15 May. On 17 May, at 1945, the station was attacked by a number of planes. Two were shot down by the destroyers and the *Mighty Midgets* shared another kill. At 1936, the *Fox* was hit in the forward gun turret by a *kamikaze* and set afire. Continuing attacks by Japanese planes plagued the picket ships. Fighting the fires on the *Fox,* driving off *kamikazes* and picking up survivors occupied most of the day. Damaged and in need of repair, the *Fox* was relieved by the *U.S.S. William D. Porter* (*DD 579*). On the evening of the 18 May, six more planes attacked the station and *LCS(L)s 53* and *67* assisted in shooting down a *Zeke*.

Still other small islands had to be taken to secure the fleet. On the eastern shore, at the entrance to Nakagusuku Wan, stood the small island of Kutaka Shima. Supposedly a Japanese triangulation station was located there and a Marine Reconnaissance unit was to land and capture it. Detailed to support the assault were the *LCS(L)s 25, 40* and *113*, along with the *U.S.S. Willard Keith* (*DD 795*). At 0347, the ships rendezvoused and headed for the beach. The gunboats strafed the beaches as the LVTs made for shore and then cruised the shoreline in search of targets. Only two live Japanese were found on the beach. The Marines completed their mission and were evacuated.

On 21 May, the *LCS(L) 119*, returning to the Hagushi anchorage, came under attack by two *Vals* and a *Nell* near Kiyamu Saki. Her 40mm guns took care of the *Nell*, but one of the *Vals* dove on her and strafed her. The plane missed and crashed into the water off the port bow. Gasoline from the plane started fires on the ship but they were quickly extinguished.

TEN-GO 7

Ten-Go 7 took place from 23 to 25 May, 1945. Down from the north came 165 suicide planes, 65 from the naval forces and 100 from the army. Duty on Radar Picket Station 15 was extremely hazardous. Pierpoint of the *61* stated: "from the time we got there until the time we left we were under almost constant attack during the hours of darkness. It was without a doubt the warmest station we ever inhabited" (Pierpoint 6). On the evening of the 23, things at Radar Picket Station 15 heated up. Manned by *LCS(L)s 61, 85, 89, 121* and four destroyers, the *U.S.S. Bradford* (*DD 545*), *U.S.S. Massey* (*DD 778*), *U.S.S. Foote* (*DD 511*) and the *U.S.S. Watts* (*DD 567*), the station came under attack late in the evening. In all, "sixteen different raids came over during 5 hours of GQ" (Katz 10). The destroyers, which normally alerted the LCS(L)s and other ships on duty of the approach of enemy planes, were simply overwhelmed. According to Gunner's Mate Walter Longhurst of the *61*:

McDonald was the telephone operator, he always relayed the messages. "Fifteen bogeys — don't worry , little boys [nickname for LCS(L) ships] we've got 'em covered." At that time all hell broke loose. Planes started coming in — we were firing at them, they were firing, everyone was firing. I don't know if we hit them but everyone was shooting" (Longhurst interview).

So many planes flew over that it was impossible to identify specific aircraft for the gunners to follow. In the midst of this, the *LCS(L) 61, 85, 89* and *121* steamed in a diamond formation. At 2027, a Japanese plane dove on the *121*, which was at the end of the formation. After strafing the ship, it dropped a fragmentation bomb. Under fire from both the *121* and the *61*, the plane went down in flames. Although the bomb missed, two crewmen on the *121* were killed and four wounded. Her steering mechanism was also damaged and she had to leave formation and head back for repairs.

The 24 and 25 of May were also hazardous days. Under frequent attack by *kamikazes*, the LCS(L)s and their accompanying destroyers found themselves firing continually during the nighttime hours. Pierpoint recalls, "At one time there were seven raids directly above us and the number one director was endeavoring to keep three planes under fire at the same time. . . . a lot of planes were shot down" (Pierpoint 7). When the raid was over, the ships received the following communiqué:

24 MAY 1945 2319 - FROM CTF 51 - ACTION R.P. 15 GANG BT CONGRATULATIONS FOR A GOOD JOB DONE ON R.P. 15 BT (CTF5124 May 1945).

On 25 May, the *U.S.S. Stormes* (*DD 780*) was hit by a *kamikaze*. The *Log of the LCS(L) 61* recorded the event:

Steaming as before. Enemy plane reported in vicinity. 0801 Sounded general quarters. . . . 0905 Destroyers on station commenced firing. 0907 Destroyers ceased firing. Enemy plane made suicide crash on fantail of USS Stormes (DD 780). 0915 Secured from general quarters. 1058 Sounded general quarters: enemy plane in vicinity. 1130 Secured from general quarters (288).

Fortunately, the *Stormes* did not suffer serious damage, and the fire started by the Japanese plane was quickly extinguished. Her accompanying gunboats, the *LCS(L)s 61, 85, 89* and *121* had taken the plane under fire, but unfortunately not in time.

As *Ten-Go 7* was underway, patrolling of the anchorages continued. Early in the evening of 23 May, about 0540, the *LCS(L) 69* was returning from skunk patrol. As she approached the southern end of Mae Shima, she spotted a small boat on shore. Opening fire with her 40mm guns, she blew holes in the boat, rendering it unserviceable. Still another of the suicide boats was sent to the bottom near Radar Picket Station 16 by the *LCS(L) 63* around 1300.

TEN-GO 8

Ten-Go 8 lasted from 27 to 29 May and consisted of 110 planes, 60 from the navy and 50 from the army. At RP 5, *LCS(L)s 12, 82, 86* and *123* patrolled along with the *U.S.S. Anthony* (*DD 515*) and the *U.S.S. Braine* (*DD 630*). At around 0730, the destroyers picked up bogies coming in on the formation and alerted the gunboats. Three *Vals* attacked the formation around 0806. One was shot down by the *86*. After avoiding fire from the other picket ships, the remaining two crashed into the *Braine*, one just forward of the superstructure and the second just forward of the number two smokestack at the level of the main deck. Prior to the actual crashes, the Captain had ordered hard right rudder. Damage from the two planes disrupted the steering capabilities of the destroyer, and as her crew fought the blazes caused by the attack, she steamed out of control in large circles for more than an hour before the other ships could come to her aid. Seriously wounded men were dropped over the side in life jackets so that they could be picked up by the accompanying destroyer and the LCS(L)s. Many of the destroyer's crew, trapped in the center of the ship by the flames, were ordered to abandon ship in order to save themselves. Finally, after the *Braine* was brought under control, the *Mighty Midgets* were able to demonstrate their fire fighting capabilities, and aided the destroyer's crew in putting out the fires. In all, 67 crewmen on the *Braine* were killed and 103 wounded. However, the destroyer survived.

At the southern end of Okinawa lay Katchin Wan (bay). A number of ships (APAs, AKAs and other cargo ships) were unloading in the area on 25 May when they were attacked by a *Tony*. Gunners on the *LCS(L) 112* spotted the plane as she passed to her starboard over Tsuken Shima. The *112* and her sister ships took the plane under fire and splashed her.

Two more days went by with the picket ships under continual attack from Japanese suicide planes. Four LCS(L)s, the *52, 55, 56* and *61*, were on patrol with the *U.S.S. Ammen (DD 527)*, and *U.S.S. Boyd (DD 544)* at RP 15 when they came under attack at about 2220 hours on 27 May, 1945 A Japanese plane dropped a bomb alongside the *52* and one officer and ten enlisted men were killed. It continued its attack and was shot down by the combined efforts of the *52* and *61*. Her gyro repeater rendered inoperable, the 52 was ordered back to Hagushi for repairs with the *LCS(L) 61* as her escort.

Steaming in company with USS LCS(L)(3) 52 en route to Hagushi anchorage on course 180(T) 183(pgc) at 12.5 knots. Ship is darkened. Ship is at general quarters. Captain is at conn. 0140 Commenced firing on enemy plane Betty bearing 180(R) and destroyed him. 0141 Plane fell in wake approximately 20 feet dead ahead after attempting to crash into this ship. Columbus, Joe . . . was struck by fragments of the plane (*Log LCS (L) 61* 293).

This was probably the closest call that the *61* had during the war. Longhurst describes the event:

We were escorting them [LCS(L)(3) 52] back to harbor and picked up another bogey off the bow. We were steaming in the lead and they were behind us. The plane circled around us and turned and we turned towards her since the second ship didn't have her aft guns working. She circled around and came in back of us and we opened fire and one gun jammed on my gun. We unjammed it, it lasted about a minute and this plane coming in . . . looked like it was going to land right on top of us. The gun kept firing and the plane came in and the concussion from our gun went up under its wings and lifted it up a bit (Longhurst interview).

Fortunately for the *61*, Captain Jim Kelley made the right move. Quartermaster Bob Rielly was at the wheel as Kelley watched the Jap *Betty* heading straight for the conning tower. He ordered Rielly "all ahead, flank speed." About five seconds later he called out "Hard left rudder"(Rielly interview). Gunner's Mate Bill Scrom recalls what happened next:

. . . the water came over the main deck in front of the gun tubs and when this thing hit [the Japanese plane] the water filled that gun tub all up. I was wet up over my knees, my back and all . . . I could see the water coming cause I was looking over my shoulder like this and the next thing I knew Alabama [Cardinal] was awash, he was on his knees, he got knocked over and he was trying to grab the gun mount or the shield to hold on and of course I was strapped in — I couldn't go anywhere. The water came over my shoulder and it filled the mouthpiece with water and the ship righted herself. . . . I remember I fired right over Berter's head and I followed it [the Japanese plane] right up into the air (Scrom interview).

The *Betty*, in flames, had slipped past the conning tower and barely cleared the bow of the ship. She crashed twenty feet ahead of the *61*. A huge column of water, gasoline and debris went up in the air and showered the gunboat. A section of the tail bounced back and struck Bosun Joe Columbus, knocking him out. The plane did not sink immediately, and as the *61* passed by, the hull scrapped along the downed aircraft. The pilot's parachute was found draped over the forward running light just in front of the Number 2 gun. Having escaped its closest call, the *61* resumed its trip back to Hagushi. At 0355 it dropped anchor, however, the day was not over.

> Anchored as before. 0800 Sounded general quarters: enemy aircraft in area. 0809 Japanese plane, Hamp, shot down bearing 135(R) and distance 1500 yards. 0858 Secured from general quarters (*Log* 293).

The immediate action over, the *61* secured for the night at her anchorage and proceeded to make smoke for the anchored ships.

A *Kawasaki Ki-61-1 Hien* **fighter. This plane was capable of speeds up to 368 m.p.h. and carried the code name** *Tony*. **Photo courtesy of the National Archives.**

LCS(L) 56 put in a difficult day at RP 15A on 28 May. Along with *LCS(L)s 55, 66, 114* and the destroyers *U.S.S. Lowry* (*DD 770*) and the *U.S.S. Drexler* (*DD 741*) she observed the *Drexler* take hits from two planes, one on her port side at 0655 and one on her starboard side at about 0700. Within seconds large explosions shook the destroyer and within four minutes, she had gone to the bottom. *U.S.S. Watts* (*DD 567*), along with the four LCS(L)s cruised the area, picking up the dead and wounded. The *114* picked up 119 survivors.

On 28 May, the *LCS(L) (3) 119* suffered major damage at Hagushi Bay, while on skunk patrol on the northern flank of the anchorage. Six planes, including two *Bettys*, one *Zeke* and three *Rufes*, went after the gunboat. First attacked by a *Betty* bomber, which she shot down, she was then attacked by a bomb-carrying *Rufe*. The *Rufe* struck her on the starboard quarter near the engine room at 0018. Fires spread through the aft section of the ship, igniting ammunition and forcing the crew to transfer to a tug that was helping fight the fires. At 0105 another *Rufe* flew over the stern, dropping two depth charges in the water. Fortunately the explosion caused no further damage to the ship. This attack caused the deaths of 14 men and the wounding of 18 others. *LCS(L) 67* was engaged in laying a smoke cover for the *U.S.S. New Mexico* (*BB 40*) and received orders to aid her sister LCS(L). Moving alongside the *119*, she assisted in putting out the fires, pumping her out and towing her in for repair.

At RP 11A the *LCS(L)s 54, 83, 84* and *115* accompanied the destroyers *U.S.S. Wadsworth* (*DD 516,*) and the *U.S.S. Sproston* (*DD 577*) on patrol. The LCS(L)s were cruising in their standard diamond shaped formation, and the destroyers were maneuvering independently around the gunboats using their speed to full advantage. At about 0040 the formation came under attack and the first plane, a *Betty*, was brought down by the combined firepower of all the ships. The *Sproston* shot down a *Kate* and the *115* splashed another. Fire from the *115* and *84* put a second *Kate* in the water.

In Nakagusuka Bay, a number of merchant ships were unloading supplies. In the early morning of 1 June, the area came under attack by Japanese *Tonys*. *LCS(L) 111* observed a plane flying slowly off her starboard side. Unfortunately the *111* and other support ships in the area mistook her for a friendly plane and did not fire on her. Shortly thereafter, another *Tony* was able to crash into the port side superstructure of the *U.S.S. Sandoval* (*APA 194*). Minutes later a third plane made a run on the cargo ships, which opened up with their three and five inch guns. This drove the plane off course and within range of the *111's* guns, a fatal mistake for the Japanese pilot. He went down in flames. At 0757 still another plane came in on the formation and was splashed astern of the *111*. On the other side of the anchorage, the *Josiah Snelling*, a merchant ship, was not so fortunate. She took a *kamikaze* hit on the forward section of her main deck.

On duty at Radar Picket Station 9 on 29 May were the *LCS(L)s 11, 20, 92*, *U.S.S. Pritchett* (*DD 561*), *U.S.S. Dyson* (*DD 572*), and the *U.S.S. Aulick* (*DD 569*). The Japanese *Zeke* that picked the *92* for a target soon went down in flames behind the ship.

On 29 May 1945, the following dispatch was sent by Commander Task Force 51:

DURING THE RECENT ATTACKS THIS FORCE HAS AGAIN DEMONSTRATED ITS ALERTNESS AND EFFICIENCY BY KNOCKING DOWN THE MAJORITY OF JAP PLANES SENT

AGAINST IT X THE TOTAL FOR THE PAST TWO DAYS IS NOW MORE THAN 115 X <u>AGAINST THE PICKETS, MIGHTY MIDGETS</u> AND SCREEN HAVE BORNE THE BRUNT OF THE ATTACK, AND BY THEIR SHARP SHOOTING AND INTESTINAL FORTITUDE HAVE ADDED TO THE ALREADY GLORIOUS TRADITIONS OF THE OKINAWA CAMPAIGN X ALSO TO THE CAP AND SALVAGE GROUP WE TIP OUR HATS FOR THEIR FINE PERFORMANCES UNDER MOST DIFFICULT CONDITIONS X YOU ARE LICKING THE JAPS AND THEY KNOW IT X A HEARTY WELL DONE TO ALL HANDS (CTF51 29 May 1945).

Also on 29 May, word was received that Radar Picket Station 16 was to be inoperable. A new station, 11A, had been created in an attempt to improve the interception of Japanese planes.

May had been a long and bloody month for the picket ships, but their ordeal was not over. Immersed in a hell with death above, below and on the seas with them, they endeavored to defeat their enemy and remain alive.

LCS*(L) 11* **participated in the initial assault on Okinawa, attacking Yellow Beach 1 on 1 April, 1945. She continued her distinguished service at Okinawa, serving on screen patrol duty and radar picket duty. Photo courtesy of the U.S. Naval Institute.**

CHAPTER VI

OKINAWA SUBDUED AND THE END OF THE WAR

TEN-GO 9

Two months had elapsed since the invasion of Okinawa had begun. The Japanese had lost many planes but were not finished. They launched yet another attack. *Ten-Go 9* lasted from 3 to 7 June, 1945. Attacking the ships at Okinawa were 20 Navy and 30 Army planes.

Among the ships patrolling at Radar Picket Station 9 on 29 May were *LCS(L)s 11, 20, 92* and *122*. The ships were attacked by two planes, which they shot down. The 122 claimed one sure and one assist. For the next few days the station was not attacked, however, on 3 June the Combat Air Patrol shot down six enemy planes nearby. The ships went back to the anchorage for two days under threat of a typhoon and then resumed their picket duty. For several days scattered attacks took place, with the C.A.P. and the accompanying destroyers accounting for another six bogeys.

Additional landings on Okinawa's offshore islands took place on 3 June as well. *LCS(L)s 68, 69, 91, 95, 120, 124* and *LC(FF) 1079*, operating as Task Unit 31.25.41, supported landings on Iheya Shima. As with other landings, the ships led the troop carriers in to shore, launching rockets and then strafing the beaches. At 1014, the LCS(L)s lined up and began the assault. Of particular concern was the beach area, which "was high and rocky and overlooked the landing area" (*LCS(L) 91 Action Report 3Jun45*). The gunboats fired off a salvo of rockets and then turned and strafed the beaches as the landing boats went through their lines. At 1032, the LCS(L)s returned to the transport area as *Corsairs* and *TBMs* worked over the beaches with rockets and machine guns. Fortunately, no enemy opposition was encountered in this landing. The *91* was ordered to the north end of the island where she joined the *U.S.S. Gainard (DD 706)* on anti-aircraft patrol. On 4 June, the ships were ordered to Nago Wan to ride out a typhoon. The storm blew past and they returned to Iheya Shima the following day.

On 3 June, at Radar Picket Station 16A, *LCS(L)s 63, 64, 118* and *121* along with *U.S.S. Harry E. Hubbard (DD 748)*, *U.S.S. Pritchett (DD 561)* and *U.S.S. Knapp (DD 653)* came under attack by several enemy planes. One was shot down by a destroyer and the others were driven away by the combined gunfire of the picket ships (*Log LCS(L)(3) 118* 385). At RP 15A, *LCS(L)s 55, 56, 66* and *114*, along with the *U.S.S. Caperton (DD 650)*, *U.S.S. Cogswell (DD 651)* and the *U.S.S. Wadsworth (DD 516)* patrolled the area looking for enemy aircraft. At 1317, five planes approached the ships, with one *Val* heading for the LCS(L)s and the others heading for the destroyers. The *66* took her under fire and she splashed close to the *56*.

The same day, at RP 11A, *LCS(L)s 16, 54, 83* and *84* were on patrol with the *U.S.S. Robert H. Smith (DM 23)*, the *U.S.S. Cassin Young (DD 793)* and the *U.S.S. Thomas E. Fraser (DM 24)*. Overhead flew the C.A.P., directed by the *Cassin Young*. At 1325, several enemy planes were reported approaching the picket station from the north. Three miles separated the diamond formation of the LCS(L)s and the column of destroyers. Within a few minutes, the *Corsairs* of the C.A.P. had shot down one plane and chased off another. An *Oscar* dove on the *16*. She took it under fire and it crashed 50 feet off her port beam. A second *Oscar* approached the ships but was driven off by fire from the LCS(L)s.

Suicide boats and swimmers were a constant threat and on 5 June, about 2230, *LCS(L) 62* encountered a 20 foot enemy canoe carrying six suicide swimmers and a lot of equipment. Closing to 100 yards, the gunboat was ordered to take prisoners if possible. Commands were given to the Japanese via bullhorn to surrender , but they jumped into the water. The LCS(L) crew fired on the canoe and the swimmers with small arms, killing five of the men and damaging the canoe. The sixth man was located and tried to swim away, but a burst from the .50 cal. machine gun made him surrender. At 1130 he was hauled aboard and examined.

> Just as he was to be tied up, he changed his mind about capture and leaped over the side again — total time on board about one minute. Every effort possible was made by the ship to entice him back aboard again, but to no avail . . . The erstwhile prisoner, under close surveillance, swam back to the canoe. At 1230, this vessel made a run on the canoe and dropped a Mark 7 anti-tank mine (15 second fuse), within 20 feet of the Jap for experimental purposes. Although the heavy explosion resulting shook up the ship

considerably, the Jap remained unharmed. The LCS 81 made a run on the canoe and the Jap was seen no more (*LCS(L) 62 Action Report 6Jun45*)

LCS(L) 81 destroyed another boat the following day, killing one man and capturing four. Although they were dressed in civilian clothes, they were later identified as Japanese Marines. Their mission was unclear, as one man had a large amount of money and the canoe sank before its contents could be identified. Number *81* experienced continuing action of this sort until the end of the patrol. By 14 June, she had captured three more boats and taken 37 prisoners.

The normal procedure for taking such prisoners on board was to have them strip before allowing them near the ship. This prevented surprise attacks from hidden weapons, which might be grenades, knives or other items. Gunboat crews could never be sure of what they were encountering. On 6 June at 0103, the *LCS(L) 20* approached a small boat which contained three Okinawan fishermen. No weapons or uniforms were found and the men were transferred to the *APA 179*. Shore targets were strafed and destroyed by fire from 40mm and 20mm gunfire from the *LCS(L)s 62* and *82*.

On 1 June, 1945, Task Group 52.19, consisting of *LC(FF) 786, LCS(L)s 61, 62, 65, 81, 82* and *90* left the Hagushi anchorage for a two week patrol assignment at Nakagusuku Wan, which would later be known as Buckner's Bay. It was given that designation on 4 July, 1945 in honor of Army General Simon Bolivar Buckner, who was killed on 18 June, 1945 during the Okinawa campaign. Located on the southeast side of Okinawa, it was near the site of the diversionary landing early in the campaign. The area was relatively calm, and at first the ships did not see any action. However, on 3 June there were enemy planes in the area and the ships went to general quarters five times. One *Zeke* was shot down over the anchorage, and the ships continued to lend anti-aircraft support to the larger vessels assembled there.

On the morning of 4 June, a spotter plane was forced down on Kutaka Shima. The *61* and the *LC(FF) 786* sent men ashore to search for him, but he could not be located. The typhoon that had been reported heading for Okinawa concerned these ships also. Accordingly, they anchored in a safe position in the bay that night, with plans for riding out the storm. Fortunately it passed to the east and they were able to resume patrol duties the next day. Early the next day the enemy sent out more planes, and the ships were forced to general quarters in the morning and again in the evening. No contact with aircraft was made and the ships continued on patrol.

Between 5 and 14 June, the patrol fleet went to general quarters nine times. The most dangerous date during this time was the evening of 6 June.

1611 Went to general quarters: enemy planes in vicinity. 1647 Secured from general quarters . . . 1710 Went to general quarters. 1713 Sighted enemy plane visually bearing 110(T) and range 10,000 yards. 1721 One destroyer hit by a Val....1734 Secured from general quarters....1909 Went to general quarters. Arrived on patrol station . . . took up patrol . . . using two engines in port quad at speed of 6 knots. Secured from general quarters. 1952 Went to general quarters: enemy planes in vicinity . . . Steaming as before. 2032 Secured from general quarters (*Log LCS 61* 314).

Most of the general quarters usually occurred in the late afternoon or at night, making it difficult for the men to get any rest. In addition to the constant overhead flights, there was still a threat from suicide boats. Calls to general quarters occurred regularly in Nakagusuku Wan during this period.

On 6 June, Radar Picket Station 9 was under patrol by *LCS(L)s 12, 85, 117, 123* and the destroyers *U.S.S. Claxton* (*DD 571*), *U.S.S. Stoddard* (*DD 566*), and *U.S.S. Massey* (*DD 778*). One to two miles separated the diamond formation of the gunboats and the column of destroyers. At about 1615, the flash red alert was given and the LCS(L)s maneuvered to close the distance between them and the destroyers. The numbers of the enemy planes were estimated at from six to twelve of the *Tojo* and *Tony* types. As they approached the ship formations, two were shot down by the C.A.P. and the others driven off. A short while later, at 1855, the destroyers opened fire on a plane and brought it down. A few minutes later another plane made a run on the LCS(L)s. They were able to concentrate a great deal of fire power on the plane and it went down in the center of the formation. *LCS(L) 12* was given credit for the splash, with the plane passing directly over her at mast height. At 1901 a twin engine Japanese plane headed past the gunboats in an attempt on the destroyers. It was shot down by combined fire from the *117* and the *85*. Still another *Tojo* passed down the starboard side of the LCS(L) formation and was shot down as it attempted an unsuccessful dive on the *LCS(L) 12*. The day's action ended at 1943 with the destroyers splashing two more planes.

Somewhere in the chain of command an interesting concept was born. Ships struck by *kamikazes* frequently caught fire. This made them easy targets for attacks by additional planes which were out to sink any American ship they could see. The Navy brass determined that it might be possible to trick the Japanese fliers into diving on a decoy. On 8 June this tactic was tested when the *LCS(L) 36* patrolled off of Ie Shima, towing a float behind her. On the float was a mast and a barrel of gasoline and oil. Once night fell, the liquid was set afire and the ship set the burning decoy adrift, hoping to attract a *kamikaze* as a flame might attract a moth. The *31, 36* and *51* sat a couple miles off the side to watch the show. Gradually dawn came, but not the *kamikazes*. This ruse was attempted several other times, and the *63, 64* and *124* played the game again on 18 June, but to no avail.

LCS(L)s 95, 91, 68 and *124* **lead the attack on Blue Beaches 1 and 2 at Aguni Island, 9 June, 1945. Official U.S. Navy Photograph courtesy of the National Archives.**

Another assault was undertaken at Aguni Shima on 9 June. At 0533, the gunboats assembled 3,700 yards from the beach in preparation for the assault. They formed their standard line, with the *95* on the left, followed by the *91, 68, 124, 120, 69* and the *LC(FF) 1079* at the extreme right. At 0540 they began their run to the beach, firing their rockets and then their 40mm and 20mm guns at suspected enemy gun emplacements. At 0606, American planes strafed the beaches as the gunboats slowed to allow the troop carriers through their lines. Again landings were made with no resistance. Other members of the LCS(L) fleet had their hands full also. On 10 June *LCS(L)s 18, 86, 94, 122,* and destroyers *U.S.S. Caperton* (*DD 650*), *U.S.S. Cogswell* (*DD 651*), and the *U.S.S. William D. Porter* (*DD 579*) were patrolling at Radar Picket Station 15A. Under attack by Japanese planes, the *Porter* was crashed by a *Val* at 0825. The plane was fired upon by the *LCS(L) 94*, but she only got off a few rounds before it struck the radar mast of the destroyer and hit the water near the stern. A 500 pound bomb carried by the plane exploded and tore open the hull of the destroyer from "frame 46 aft to the fantail" (*LCS(L)(3) 86 Action Report 10Jun45* 3). LCS(L)s immediately went to her aid. Within a half hour the ship was down by the stern with a heavy starboard list. Placing salvage parties aboard, the LCS(L)s attempted to pump her out. It soon became obvious that the pumps could not keep up with the flooding. Attempts were made to tow the destroyer to port by *LCS(L) 86*, however, the line parted and the extreme listing of the ship made further attempts impossible. By continuing their efforts, the support ships were able to remove all the crew members. The *Log of the LCS(L)(3) 86* recorded the action:

> Patrolling as before. 0825, enemy suicide planes crashed into stern of DD 579. Sounded General Quarters. 0838, proceeding to assistance of DD 579. 0857, moored, starboard side, forward, to DD 579. Also moored to DD 579 were USS(L)(3) 18 starboard side aft, USS LCS (L)(3) 94 to port side, forward and USS LCS(L)(3) 122 port side aft. DD 579 was down by the stern and had a heavy starboard list. 0900, Salvage party boarded DD 579 with equipment to aid in pumping her out. 0919, depth charge exploded under us. No casualties reported as result of explosion. 0925, received 29 injured men from DD 579. 1000, made preparations to tow. 1023, commenced towing, swinging DD 579 around to base course 195 degrees (T). 1026, number one line reported breaking. 1030, ceased towing operations. 1055, DD 579 now listing badly to starboard and down badly by the stern. 1106, engine rooms on DD 579 ordered abandoned. Pumps reported rapidly losing ground. 1109, USS LCS(L)(3) 18 cast off from DD 579 and cleared her wreckage. 1110, DD 579 ordered abandoned. Last of survivors came aboard. 1113, cast off last lines from DD 579 and backed off clear of wreckage. 1119, DD 579 sunk. 1147, USS LCS(L)(3) 18 came alongside and moored to our starboard. 2 stanchions supporting #3 gun were broken in the operation. Received salvage equipment and crew members who were aboard (182).

The *U.S.S. William D. Porter* was added to the list of destroyers sunk on the picket lines. What is noteworthy is that, through great luck in not sustaining deaths from the initial impact of the plane and the superb rescue work by the LCS(L)s, she became the only ship sunk in the war without loss of life. *LCS(L)s 86* and *122* were awarded the Navy Unit Commendation for their efforts that day.

LCS(L) 122 with survivors of the sinking U.S.S. Porter (DD 579). The masts of LCS(L)s 86 and 18 may be seen behind the destroyer. Official U.S. Navy Photograph courtesy of the National Archives.

Problems leading to the sinking of the *Porter* were identified by the Commanding Officer of the *86*, Lt. H.N. Houston:

We believe our operations were greatly hampered by the fact that so many friendly planes, mostly TBFs and TBMs , were in the area, singly, or occasionally in pairs, without IFF [Identification Friend or Foe] showing. We believe the loss of this destroyer in a large part due to this condition. Times beyond number our CAP was sent off on a Bogey hunt, leaving us without air cover, only to report the bogey as friendly. This establishes an unnecessary drain on our air cover as well as setting up a false sense of security...The friendly's presence here we believe caused the suicide plane to be mistaken for said friendly, or at least to warrant slight attention, hence the disaster. This may be qualified by the fact that the plane had, at least fabric wings, which did not make a marked radar contact (*LCS(L) 86 Action Report 10Jun45* 4).

The LCS(L)s, accompanied by three destroyers, *U.S.S. Caperton* (*DD 650*), *U.S.S. Cogswell* (DD *651*) and *U.S.S. Amen* (*DD 527*) continued on their patrol at Radar Picket Station 15A. On the following day, 11 June, the picket ships were under attack again. At 1901 seven enemy aircraft were sighted. One was shot down by the Combat Air Patrol, but a second got through the hail of fire put up by the gunboats and crashed close by the *LCS(L) 122*. A third had better aim and crashed into her conn. A fourth plane was shot down by *LCS(L) 86*. The *Log of the LCS (L) (3) 122* records the action:

> At 1900 on 11 June 1945 this ship was hit by a Japanese suicide plane, type Val, while on Radar Picket Patrol. Previously there had been one Val shot down and one assist by this ship. In the fire after the plane crash, the quartermaster's note book, Radio logs and rough deck logs were destroyed. Plane hit at the base of the conning tower on the starboard side destroying the radio room, crew's head and part of the conn. Fire and water damage throughout the ship. Bomb passed through ship and exploded on the port side of the ship showering port side of the ship with shrapnel. Eight men were killed in action, three men missing in action and declared dead. Wounded totaled 29 . . . Commanding Officer, Lt. R. M. McCool was wounded in action. Executive Officer R. K. Bruns Lt. (Jg) assumed command of ship (374).

Commanding Officer, Lieutenant Richard M. McCool, although wounded, aided in the rescue of his men. McCool would later write:

> I do not know how long it was before I came to enough to realize what the situation was or if there was anyone else alive then at the conning station. Because of the fires on the starboard side, I scrambled over the port side of the conning station and dropped down to the gun deck and then somehow got to the main deck. My chief concern at the time was to get hoses on the fire to keep it from spreading forward to the rocket launchers and ammunition storage and this is what I tried to get our own damage control people on to plus calling to the other ships to try to get their hoses on that area (McCool letter 1).

For his efforts, he was awarded the Congressional Medal of Honor, the only LCS(L) man to be so honored. His citation read:

> The PRESIDENT OF THE UNITED STATES takes pleasure in presenting the MEDAL OF HONOR to LIEUTENANT RICHARD MILES MCCOOL, JR. United States Navy for service set forth in the following citation:

Lt. Richard M. McCool receives the Congressional Medal of Honor from President Harry Truman. Official U.S. Navy Photograph, courtesy of Richard M. McCool.

For conspicuous gallantry and intrepidity at the risk of his life above and beyond the call of duty as commanding officer of the U.S.S. LCS 122 during operations against enemy Japanese forces in the Ryukyu chain, 10 and 11 June, 1945. Sharply vigilant during hostile air raids against allied ships on radar picket duty off Okinawa on 10 June, Lieutenant McCool aided materially in evacuating all survivors from a sinking destroyer which had sustained mortal damage under the devastating attacks. When his own craft was attacked simultaneously by two of the enemy's suicide squadron early in the evening of 11 June, he instantly hurled the full power of his gun batteries against the plunging aircraft, shooting down the first and damaging the second before it crashed his station in the conning tower and engulfed the immediate areas in a mass of flames. Although suffering from shrapnel wounds and painful burns, he rallied his concussion-shocked crew and initiated vigorous firefighting measures and then proceeded to the rescue of several trapped in a blazing compartment, subsequently carrying one man to safety despite the excruciating pain of additional severe burns. Unmindful of all personal danger, he continued his efforts without respite until aid arrived from other ships and he was evacuated. By his staunch leadership, capable direction and in indomitable determination throughout the crisis, Lieutenant McCool saved the lives of many who otherwise might have perished and contributed materially to the saving of his ship for further combat service. His valiant spirit of self-sacrifice in the face of extreme peril sustains and enhances the highest traditions of the United States Naval Service.

Harry S. Truman

LCS(L) 122 transferred her dead and wounded to the *U. S. S. Solace* (*AH 5*) and the *U.S.S. Rescue* (*AH 18*) and made her way back to Kerama Retto for repairs.

 From 12 to 13 June, *LCS(L) 66* was assigned patrol along the southern edge of Okinawa. At 1930 she noted a small enemy boat with several troops on board. Opening fire with her 40mm guns, she destroyed the craft and its occupants. The Japanese had been driven to the southern end of the island by American troops and many were within reach of American ships patrolling the coast. The *66* was ordered to proceed along the coast and attack targets of opportunity, which included troops that they might sight. On 13 June, the ship strafed the beaches and prepared to fire a salvo of rockets at the beach area. Her mission was aborted when two LSM(R)s with heavier firepower entered the area and did the job. The *66*, along with *LC(FF) 786*, *LCS(L)s 62* and *82* went back on patrol at Nakagusuku Wan.

Having spent two weeks on patrol in the bay, *LCS(L)(3) 61* was assigned a day on radar picket duty as she made her way back to Hagushi anchorage on the western side of the island. Unpleasant duty arrived on the 14 as the ship patrolled on station.

Anchored as before. 0525 Made all preparations for getting underway. Captain on the conn. 0530 Underway on port shaft proceeding to Radar Picket Station for support duty. Set course at 021(T) 025 *PGC) 025(psc) at standard speed of 8.5 knots. 0615 Patrolling on Radar Picket Station . . . in company with USS Twiggs (DD 591). Steaming on course . . . at standard speed of 8.5 knots . . . Steaming as before. 1020 Sighted body in water and interrupted patrol to investigate. 1030 Identified body as Japanese: nothing of intelligence value due to advanced decomposition. Resumed patrol. 1200 Orders from USS Twiggs departed patrol from station for Shimajiro-Ko on course 220(T) 224(pgc). (*Log LCS 61* 328).

Damage to the *LCS(L) 122* from *kamikaze* attack on 11 June, 1945. This view shows the damage to the base of the conning tower. In the foreground is the wheel of the Japanese aircraft. Official U.S. Navy Photograph, courtesy of Richard M. McCool.

On two occasions the ship had to leave formation to investigate floating bodies. Japanese pilots who had been shot down did not usually survive the crash. Their bodies, once afloat in the Pacific, soon became food for sharks. Usually their decomposed and half-eaten bodies were hauled aboard with the hope of finding some intelligence information. However, in both cases, nothing of value was found and the bodies were again returned to the sea. About the only gain from such events was an occasional souvenir as crew members removed a button or item of clothing from the body.

On that day, 14 June, as the *LCS(L)(3) 61* departed from the formation, her crew got their last glimpse of the *U.S.S. Twiggs (DD 591)*. The next day, the destroyer was ordered to head for the southern tip of Okinawa near Senaga Shima off the city of Naha. There she was to assist in attacking the last remnants of the Japanese army which had been driven to the coast. Caught between advancing infantry in front and naval bombardment to the rear, the Japanese army had little hope of survival. About 2030 hours on 16 June, the *U.S.S. Twiggs* was attacked by a *Jill* torpedo plane. It launched its torpedo into the port side of the destroyer, blowing up the *Twiggs'* Number 2 magazine. The plane then circled around and crashed into the ship. Captain George Philip rallied his men to fight the fires, but within a half hour, they reached the aft magazine and it exploded. When that blew up, the *Twiggs* was finished, taking with her 18 officers, 165 men and her Commanding Officer. *LCS(L) 14* was cruising only a few miles away and went immediately to her aid. The fires on the destroyer were so intense that the gunboat could not get close enough to come alongside. The best that she could do was search for survivors, she found none. A few days later, on 21 June, the Okinawa campaign was over. The *U.S.S. Twiggs* had become a casualty of the campaign. She was the twelfth destroyer sunk off Okinawa.

Fighting on the island continued, and with it the displacement of many civilians. Joe Staigar of the *61* recalls, "While at Buckner's Bay we saw many LCVPs going by with women and children. They seemed to be scared out of their minds" (Staigar letter). In many cases civilians got in the way of the firing and lost their lives. Whenever possible the American forces attempted to save the Okinawan civilians by placing them on small boats and taking them to parts of the island that had been pacified.

In June, Kume Shima was still held by the Japanese. In order to determine the size and strength of their forces, it was decided that a Marine Recon unit should land and evaluate the situation. *APDs 96* and *122* were assigned the task of landing troops on the island during the night of 15 June. *LCS(L) 13* was given the task of covering their withdrawal early the next morning at about 0300. Fortunately the Marine Recon men performed their task undiscovered and their withdrawal went without incident.

TEN-GO 10

The last of the *Ten-Go* operations took place from 21 to 22 June, 1945 and involved a total of 30 navy planes and 15 army planes. On 21 June, Radar Picket Station 5 was patrolled by the destroyers *U.S.S. Aulick* (*DD 569*) and U.S.S. *Knapp* (*DD 653*), as well as *LCS(L)s 31, 61, 64* and *81*. The next day, they were at general quarters frequently. *Corsairs* from the Combat Air Patrol shot down several planes but none came close enough to the ships to involve them in any action.

At RP 7 on 22 June, 1945 were the *LCS(L)s 34, 62, 81, 118* and the destroyers *U.S.S. Claxton* (*DD 571*), *U.S.S. Walke* (*DD 723*), and the *U.S.S. Van Valkenburgh* (*DD 656*). Two Japanese planes approached the station at 0048. Fortunately, the gunboats had the benefit of the destroyer's radar to keep them informed. A Betty passed to port, then circled around to the starboard side of the LCS(L)s. Under fire from the *62*, she was splashed 200 yards from the ship.

Good news came the following day when the battle for Okinawa was declared over. However, no one told the *kamikaze* pilots. Congratulatory messages were sent throughout the fleet and on the morning of 23 June, 1945 the ships received the following communique:

THIS MESSAGE RECEIVED QUOTE THE PRESIDENT OF THE UNITED STATES TODAY RECEIVED THE FOLLOWING MESSAGE FROM PRIME MINISTER CHURCHILL WHICH IS TO BE PASSED ON THE FORCES UNDER YOUR COMMAND X I WISH TO OFFER MY SINCERE CONGRATULATIONS UPON THE SPLENDID VICTORY GAINED BY THE UNITED STATES ARMY FLEET AIR FORCE IN OKINAWA X THIS STRENGTH OF WILL POWER DEVOTION AND TECHNICAL RESOURCES APPLIED BY THE UNITED STATES TO THIS TASK JOINED WITH THE DEATH STRUGGLE OF THE ENEMY OF WHOM 90,000 ARE REPORTED TO BE KILLED PLACED THIS BATTLE AMONG THE MOST INTENSE AND FAMOUS OF MILITARY HISTORY X IT IS IN PROFOUND ADMIRATION OF AMERICAN VALOR AND RESOLVE TO CONQUER AT WHATEVER COST MIGHT BE NECESSARY THAT I SEND YOU THIS TRIBUTE FROM YOUR FAITHFUL ALLY AND ALL YOUR BRITISH COMRADES IN ARMS WHO WATCH THESE MEMORABLE VICTORIES FROM THIS ISLAND AND ITS CAMPS ABROAD MAKE OUR SALUTE TO ALL YOUR TROOPS AND THEIR COMMANDERS ENGAGED UNQUOTE (*ALPOA*. 23 June 1945).

From 23 to 24 June, the *31, 61, 64* and *84* anchored in Nakagusuku Wan. On the morning of 24 June, the ships picked up staff gunnery instructors who were assigned to check out their gun crews. After proceeding to a target practice area, the LCS(L) gunners showed their stuff by quickly shooting down the drones sent by them. Katz recalls, "A radio controlled drone was launched from an LSM. We knocked it down in no time. They put up 2 more, and it didn't take but a few minutes to put them to bed. They got disgusted then and sent us back to the anchorage" (Katz 13).

On 26 June, the *LCS(L) 69* provided a smoke screen for the *LST 688* at Ie Shima. About 0013 her smoke generator failed and she was assigned anti-aircraft duty near the *Hastings Victory*. At 0110 a *Betty* passed over the anchorage and was taken under fire by other ships. Shortly thereafter, at 0124, a *Kate* headed in on a suicide run towards the LCS(L) and the *Hastings Victory*. Forty millimeter rounds from the gunboat hit the plane, which passed close over her, taking off sections of the mast and radio antenna. She splashed 75 yards off the gunboat's starboard bow. On the following day the island of Okinawa was declared secured and the infantry actions on the island were reduced to mopping-up operations. From that point on, the American military began to build up its air bases and supply depots for the coming invasion of the home islands. The strategic importance of the island as an air base for future *B-29* raids against Japan was recognized and at various locations supply depots and staging areas were to be constructed and the major airfields rebuilt for use against the main islands.

Nakagusuku Bay was to be the sight of major development as well and would figure heavily in the plans for the invasion of Japan (Operation Olympic, aimed at Kyushu, and Operation Coronet, aimed at Honshu). The area would gain new docks and port facilities. With the island finally lost, the Japanese strategy shifted. No longer would they send *kamikaze* planes to attack the invasion fleet around Okinawa but would hold them in reserve so that any fleet approaching Japan would be met by a greater number of planes.

LCS(L)s 61, 64, 101 and *120* took up position on Radar Picket Station 15, along with the *U.S.S. Converse* (DD 509), *U.S.S. Aulich* (DD 569), and *U.S.S. Foote* (*DD 511*). The ships went to general quarters twice during the day, with planes either not coming within range or identified as friendly. Remaining on duty at Radar Picket Station 15 and 15A for the next couple of days, they returned to Hagushi on 7 July, resumed patrol in the anchorage and provided antiaircraft cover for the anchored ships.

The pace of Japanese air attacks was slowing down, and from the end of June to the end of July, many ships from Flotillas Three and Four sailed for the Philippines to await the next major campaign, the invasion of Japan. As Flotilla Four ships departed from Okinawa, they received the following message:

ON DEPARTING THIS AREA I WISH TO THANK EACH AND EVERY OFFICER AND MAN IN FLOTILLA FOUR FOR THE MAGNIFICENT JOB DONE X YOU BROUGHT OUT A NEW AND UNTRIED WEAPON AND BY YOUR SKILL AND BRAVERY HAVE MADE YOURSELVES THE SCOURGE OF THE JAPS X YOU HAVE WELL EARNED THE ADMIRATION WITH WHICH THE ENTIRE FLEET NOW REGARDS THE LCS'S X YOUR PATIENCE AND GOOD HUMOR UNDER A PROLONGED PERIOD OF CROWDED AND UNCOMFORTABLE LIVING CONDITIONS WITH NO RECREATION OR REST PERIODS HAVE MY UNQUALIFIED ADMIRATION X I CONSIDER THE LCS OFFICERS TO BE THE HIGHEST TYPE OF AMERICANS X I CAN GIVE YOU NO GREATER COMPLIMENT THAN THAT X IT HAS BEEN A GREAT HONOR TO HAVE SERVED WITH YOU X WELL DONE X

> N. PHILLIPS COMMANDER, U.S.N.
> COMMANDER LCS(L)(3) FLOTILLA FOUR
> (*Commdr. Flot 4 Speedletter. 7 July 1945*).

During their tour at Okinawa, the LCS(L)s had attacked the Japanese ashore, shot down numerous Japanese planes, rescued countless sailors and destroyed a large number of suicide boats. What they needed the most at that point was some rest and recuperation as they prepared for the invasion of the home islands of Japan.

Although many ships headed south for a break, others continued on patrol duty. *LCS(L)s 125, 129* and *130*, along with *U.S.S. Callaghan (DD 792)*, the *U.S.S. Pritchett* (*DD 561*), and the *U.S.S. Cassin Young* (*DD 793*) patrolled RP 9A on 29 July. At 0034, the formation went to general quarters and at 0041 a low flying suicide plane crashed into the *Callaghan* near her Number 4 gun. A small explosion occurred at once, followed shortly by a large one, as the fires reached the gun's magazine. The LCS(L)s were ordered alongside to assist in rescue and firefighting. Exploding munitions made it difficult to close on the burning ship and the amount of water the ships could put on the fire was limited. More planes attacked the ships and the *Pritchett* also took a hit, causing slight damage. Overhead, the C.A.P. fought off other planes and the attack abated. After the raid, the LCS(L)s cruised the area, picking men from the water. At 0234, the *Callaghan* sank by the stern. Her depth charges went off shortly thereafter, giving rise to the speculation that any men in the water at that point were killed. No other survivors were picked up after that. *U.S.S. Callaghan (DD 792)* became the last destroyer sunk off Okinawa.

With the ending of the battle for Okinawa, the United States Navy recognized that it was one of the most costly in its history. Army and Marine losses ashore had been great, however the ships on the picket line and in the invasion force had suffered even more. Naval personnel lost in the fighting totaled 4,907. Twelve destroyers had been sent to the bottom, along with fifteen amphibians and nine other ships. In addition, 368 ships had suffered damage from shore batteries, *kamikazes* and friendly fire.

The hazards of radar picket duty were summed up by Captain F. Moosbrugger in his *Action Report on the Capture of Okinawa Gunto, 26 March to 21 June 1945* when he wrote:

> The radar picket station groups took every blow that the Japs could inflict and absorbed terrific punishment in personnel casualties and material damage but the mission was successfully and proudly completed. Never in the annals of our glorious naval history have naval forces done so much with so little against such odds for so long a period. Radar picket duty in this operation might well be a symbol of supreme achievement in our Naval traditions" (14).

A number of ships sent south to the Philippines for rest and relaxation had similar experiences. Although they were out of the danger zone around Okinawa, they were still at war. The trip to Leyte took five days. The voyage of Task Unit 99.1.28, which included *LC(FF)s 367, 1082, 1079* and *LCS(L)s 61, 62, 63, 64, 81*, and *82*, as well as a number of other LCS(L)s, was typical. On 11 July, 1945, as the convoy passed Formosa, it was approached by a Japanese reconnaissance plane, however the plane did not come within range of the ships' guns. Two submarines were reported in the area, and the crews could not relax because of the recurring calls to general quarters. Some additional hazardous duty was performed along the way as ships occasionally left the convoy to fire on and destroy mines. This was one of the jobs that the miniature destroyers were well suited for and they completed the task without injury to themselves.

At 1050 hours on the morning of 14 July, 1945, the ships entered Leyte Gulf and made anchorage at San Pedro Bay eight hours later. Much relieved, the crews looked forward to a break from the incessant calls to general quarters, the possibility of sudden death from the sky and as Powell Pierpoint so aptly put it, looked forward to "beer and liberty" (Pierpoint 8).

Life in San Pedro Bay was a decided improvement. Tied alongside a number of destroyers, the crews were able to go on board the larger ships to see movies. Pierpoint recalls, "The destroyers were very nice to us because theretofore they had always been the smallest ships in any joint operations and they were delighted to be fatherly to something smaller" (Pierpoint letter). Finally, on 20 July the ships anchored off San Antonio and the crews had a few hours of liberty ashore before departing for a new anchorage. Over the next several days the crews were able to go on liberty at San Pedro. A special treat was a USO show featuring Kay Kayser. As with most USO shows, the featured star was less interesting to the men than the pretty chorus girls who accompanied the show (Katz 14).

Certificate awarded to Flotilla Four sailors who participated in the battle for Okinawa. Courtesy of Robert F. Rielly

Many of the ships were in need of repair or routine maintenance. In the war zone this was frequently accomplished by loading the ship into a Landing Ship Dock. LSDs were innovative designs that could carry large numbers of smaller craft to the assault beaches. Once there, their holds were flooded and they discharged their cargos of landing craft and men. They could be used for repair work as well. Their 458' length allowed them to transport a great number of smaller vessels, however, for repair purposes, they could also take in an LCI(L) or an LCS(L). Normally operated by a crew of 17 officers and 309 men, the ships were a valuable asset to the amphibious forces.

Many of the crews had looked forward to liberty ashore and for a short period they were able to enjoy it. Unfortunately for the fleet, an outbreak of dysentery occurred and by 5 August, liberty was canceled in an attempt to halt its spread.

On 6 August, the LCS(L)(3) ships performed routine patrol and maintenance duties in San Pedro Bay. By the end of the day the anchored fleet was jubilant. News had come over the air that a huge bomb had been dropped on Japan (Hiroshima) and that the Japanese had surrendered. News of the surrender proved to be premature, and a few days later, the dropping of a second bomb on Nagasaki also led to speculation. However, since no surrender was forthcoming, the ships went out to sea frequently in August to engage in gunnery practice for the coming invasion of Japan. During this practice, they fired a number of their rockets, weapons that would be used a great deal in any invasion of the home islands of Japan. One must assume that had the invasion of Japan taken place, the LCS(L)(3) fleet would have been in the first wave of attack craft giving support to the Marines and Army infantry as they landed on the beaches of Japan.

American military leaders had developed an overall plan for the invasion of Japan's home islands. Code named Downfall, the plan called for two stages. The first stage, Operation Olympic, was scheduled for 1 November, 1945 and was aimed at Kyushu, the southernmost island of Japan. Fourteen divisions were to be landed in this operation. Once the island was secure, the harbors and airfields there would be used to complete the next stage of the plan, which was code named Operation Coronet. This second phase of the invasion was scheduled for 1 March, 1946 and was aimed at the Kanto Plains area around Tokyo and Yokohama. Twenty-five divisions would be landed there. After they had secured the area around the capitol, it was believed that the Japanese would be unable to continue the war.

Plans for Operation Olympic called for the use of over 3,000 ships in the invasion. After the larger ships pounded the beaches and fortifications with their heavy guns, the smaller support ships such as the LCS(L)s and the LCI(L)s that had been adapted to fire rockets and mortars would scour the beaches with rocket fire and clear the way for the waves of landing craft and ships that would set the troops ashore. It was this stage of the operation that was seen as most hazardous.

Shinyo **suicide boats at Sasebo, Japan, 18 October, 1945. If the invasion of Japan had been attempted, these craft would have assaulted the amphibious ships as they attempted to land their troops and supplies. Army Signal Corps Photo courtesy of the National Archives.**

The Japanese plan for the defense of their home islands was code named *Ketsu-Go (Decisive Operation)*. Japanese strategy at Okinawa had been to allow the American forces to disembark and move inland, so that they could not be supported by naval gunfire. Although this strategy made sense, the Japanese learned that the overwhelming material superiority of their enemy would make their onslaught unstoppable. As a result, they determined that the Americans should be stopped at the water's edge or their homeland would be lost.

Once defeat at Okinawa became a reality, the Japanese held their forces in reserve for the American invasion of Kyushu. They correctly predicted that the Americans would strike there first. In preparation for the defense of Kyushu, they had transferred many military units to the south so that they would be within striking distance of the American fleet. Coastal fortifications were strengthened, and as many ships and planes as possible were shifted within range of the target area. Japanese strategists felt that their reconnaissance aircraft would be able to spot the American invasion fleet while it was still 150 to 200 miles off shore, which would give them ample time to ready their forces.

Massive waves of *kamikaze* planes would be sent against the fleet. To that end, the Japanese estimated that they could have 10,000 planes ready on the day of the invasion. Their experiences with *kamikaze* raids at Okinawa had taught them that massed raids were the most successful and difficult to stop. Accordingly, they planned to use 5,000 of the planes within the first ten days of the invasion. Troop ships and other landing craft would be the primary targets. If the Americans could be prevented from gaining a toehold on the island, they might be convinced that the price for the invasion was too high. In addition to the suicide planes, the Japanese estimated that they could have at least 2,000 of the suicide boats ready to attack any ships that approached shore. American gunboats, such as the LCS(L)s, would have been heavily involved in fighting off these craft. In addition to the *kamikaze* planes and boats, the complete variety of suicide weapons would be placed in use, including manned torpedoes and midget subs. In order to increase the effectiveness of these diverse nautical weapons, they would be used mainly at night when they would be harder to see. By these methods, the Japanese planners believed that they could destroy about a quarter of the invasion force. Patrolling back and forth in the invasion anchorage would have been the LCS(L)s and other small ships which would have borne the brunt of these attacks. Fortunately, this was not to occur. On 15 August, word came to the assembled fleet at Leyte that the Japanese would surrender. "The announcement was the signal for a colorful celebration by the ships collected in the harbor. Searchlights played on the clouds, whistles and sirens sounded for hours, and all ships made earnest efforts to expend their supplies of pyrotechnique ammunition" (Pierpoint 10).

On 26 August, 1945 "Fleet Admiral Chester W. Nimitz's headquarters . . . announced the . . . composition of the Allied fleet assembled off Japan for operations in connection with the occupation of the home islands" (*List of Allied Warships* 42). Listed among the 354 ships slated for the occupation were 32 of the LCS(L)(3)s, all but *LCS(L)(3) 3* were from Flotilla 4. They were numbers *3, 57, 61, 62, 63, 64, 65, 66, 67, 68, 69, 81, 82, 83, 84, 85, 86, 87, 89, 90, 92, 93, 94, 95, 114, 115, 117, 118, 119, 121, 122, 123*, and *124*.

On 3 September, 1945, a number of the LCS(L)s left Leyte headed for Tokyo. During the nine day trip the convoy passed others en route to Japan and encountered some rough weather around 5 September. Their voyage ended when they tied up at the dock yards at deserted Yokosuka Naval Base.

Once situated in Tokyo Bay, the *Mighty Midgets* were assigned to assist the larger ships in providing liberty ashore for their sailors. This was an easy chore for the LCS(L) ships, since their shallow draft made it possible for them to get in close to any landing site in the port cities of Yokosuka, Yokohama and Tokyo. For the next week the LCS(L)s carried sailors ashore to investigate the conquered country. John Cardwell of the *61* recalls, "Because of our size, we were assigned liberty duty for the big boats, you couldn't put a battleship in there. We could go right into the docks. . . .We would load up with maybe 150 guys on top and take them into the docks for liberty, they would have to be back on the ship at 6 o'clock" (Cardwell interview). In all, the LCS(L)s served as liberty boats for approximately 7,000 sailors a day.

The crews of the LCS(L)s had an easier time than many of the sailors heading for liberty. Normally as the sailors were landed, the Military Police checked them for contraband that could be sold on the black market. Once the sailors had been checked and the Military Police had departed, the crews were able to wander about the port area of the city without going through that type of inspection. Normal liberty required the sailors to wear dress blues, however, many LCS(L) crewmen were able to wear their work clothes.

LCS(L)s 93, 95, 67, 89 and *81* **at Yokosuka, Fall, 1945. Photo courtesy of Allen R. Selfridge.**

LCS(L) 91 **at Yokosuka, January, 1946. Photo courtesy of Norman H. Wackenhut.**

The first official liberty granted to many of the crews was in Tokyo. Much of the area had been firebombed and, in many cases, the only identifiable structure in what had formerly been a business site was a metal safe, everything else had burned. As the crews wandered about the city, they were aware of the food shortages and the difficult conditions that the survivors of the war had to endure. In many instances small boats patrolled around the anchored ships, looking for garbage that might contain edible scraps. Many of the sailors saved leftovers for the hungry people, a number of whom were children.

From 16 to 18 November,1945, *LCS(L)s 61, 62, 66, 67*, went out on maneuvers and engaged in gunnery drills. In addition to firing at target sleeves pulled by aircraft, the ships fired off some of their rockets to complete their practice. After returning to Tokyo Bay, they resumed their duties as liberty boats. They were to perform a variety of tasks for the next few months before returning to the states.

Still other members of LCS(L) Flotilla Four, joined by ships from Flotillas Three and Five served in varied roles around the home islands of Japan. Units of Flotilla Three, Groups Eight and Nine, had been sent to Japan to support landings at Amori on Honshu Island. Following that, the ships were sent south to Sasebo where they were based for the next few months as they performed mine-sweeping duties in the Tsushima Straits. In all, over 40 ships were sent to assist in the occupation of Japan, while at least 20 were sent to Korea to support landings there and perform general minesweeping and patrol duties in the Yellow Sea between the West coast of Korea and the East Coast of China. Still another group of LCS(L)s numbering at least a dozen, principally from Flotilla Three, were sent to the southern areas and did patrol work and minesweeping in the area between Shanghai and Taiwan. A couple of the LCS(L)s even had assignments further south, where they were sent to the Gulf of Tonkin between China and Viet Nam and to sweep mines between Hong Kong, Haiphong and Hainan Island.

MINESWEEPING OPERATIONS

During the war an important tactic that the Japanese used to protect their ports and shipping lanes was the use of mines. Scattered throughout the approaches to each harbor were mine fields that allowed access to the protected waters by Japanese ships, but which would also prove to be a barrier to attacks by American submarines and surface craft. Numerous straits existed in the island chains of the Pacific and mines were sowed strategically in order to funnel Japanese ships through a secured area. American submarines attempting to attack Japanese convoys frequently encountered these fields and were thwarted in their attempts to get at the enemy ships. Still others had the misfortune to run into mines and were lost with all hands. One of the most successful American subs of the war, the *Barb*, under the command of the famous naval strategist Eugene B. Fluckey, frequently lost time and target opportunities when encountering such areas. Fluckey reported that a number of his fellow submariners were probably lost by striking mines (Fluckey 283).

Once Okinawa had been captured, the necessity for clearing mines from the planned invasion routes was urgent. Although minesweeping using the LCS(L)s had been going on for some time, the program was accelerated. The ending of the war did not diminish the need for minesweeping operations, however, the purpose of the program changed from invasion to occupation and the subsequent supply of allied occupation forces. Normal maritime traffic would resume throughout the western Pacific, and the mines needed to be cleared from as many shipping channels as possible. In addition to sweepers belonging to the Allied powers, Japanese minesweepers were also put to work on the more hazardous sites.

General minesweeping operations involving LCS(L)s usually involved a pair of them following in the wake of a YMS. Once the YMS had cut the mine's cable, it floated to the surface where it was visible to the crewmen on board the LCS(L). Usually the mines exploded when hit by rifle fire from the Springfield 03s that were on board the ship. If they proved stubborn, the heavier guns would be employed. In some cases, the mines did not explode, they just sank. Occasionally, if an LCS(L) came too close and was showered with debris from the explosion, a crewman might be injured or killed. One could never be certain what would happen when a mine was fired upon. In some cases they had simply corroded and become inactive or were defective from the start. In addition, the number of mines cleared was always less than the number that the Japanese claimed to have planted. This concerned mariners in the area for some time. Historian Peter Elliot described 20 post-war operations that cleared a total of 11,200 mines in the area around Japan (Elliot 177). In addition to Japanese waters, extensive minesweeping operations took place in the Yellow Sea, the Korean port of Inchon and the major ports in mainland China. Further minesweeping work involving LCS(L)s was undertaken around the island of Formosa, where LCS(L)s belonging to Flotilla Three worked out of the port of Keelung on the northern tip of the island.

A variety of other duties faced the LCS(L)s, including the escort of Japanese ships back to American held bases in Korea and other locations. This was necessary so that surrender of the ships might be made official and their crews sent back to Japan. On 29 September, 1945, *LCS(L)s 59* and *60*, accompanying the destroyers *Alfred A.Cunningham* (*DD 752*), *Herndon* (*DD 638*), and *YMS 97*, escorted six Japanese ships into Chinkai Bay, Korea, where they were taken into custody. These ships included the destroyers *Kure* and *Hatsu* along with *SCS Onuose* numbers *21, 23* and *28.* On their way into the harbor at Chinkai Bay, the American fleets passed two Japanese hospital ships heading for their homeland. As a courtesy, the Japanese ships saluted.

Patrolling operations lasted for the next several months in Korea. Occasional problems arose and mishaps occurred. On 21 November, 1945, the *LCS(L) 54* collided with the *LST 505*, which was anchored in the river at Jinsen. The *54* had been attempting to come alongside the LST to deliver mail, but the current proved to be more than the officers thought, and the *54* crashed into the lowered bow ramp of the LST. The result was that the starboard bow of the *54* was pierced just above the waterline from frame 15 to frame 33. Although the LST suffered no ill-effects, the LCS(L), seriously in need of repair, was temporarily sidelined. Her gash, one-and-one-half feet wide by 27-feet long, required repairs.

LCS(L)s 29, 46, 47 **and** *28* **at pier # 1, Tsingtao, China. These ships were instrumental in mine clearing and other activities in the immediate post-war period. Photo courtesy of Ken Krayer.**

The ending of the war caused a great psychological change in the sailors of the LCS(L) fleet. Their mission accomplished, they all wanted to be sent home. Unfortunately for most of them, the job was not completed since several major tasks lay ahead.

The first of these involved the remainder of the Japanese forces that had been bypassed in MacArthur's island hopping campaign. Pockets of soldiers, well supplied and willing to fight, existed on many of the islands of the south Pacific. Would they go along with their government's order to surrender, or would they decide to make the supreme sacrifice and fight in spite of their government's decree? A number of American forces had to be dispatched to each of the islands to accept surrender and transport the defeated Japanese back to their homeland. Large stores of Japanese supplies had to be confiscated as well. In addition, some of the bases that had been captured by the Americans were under development for their own use. These had to be closed down as their existence was no longer needed. All this would require that troops and supplies be transported by sea and numerous ships assigned to the task.

In addition to the Japanese garrisons in the bypassed islands, there existed the problem of Japanese army units in Korea and China. Korea alone held an estimated 270,000 regular army personnel along with additional civilian support personnel (Barbey 322). The numbers in China were considerably larger and matters were quite complicated. During the war Kuomintang forces under Chiang Kai Shek and the Communist forces under Mao Zedong had temporarily called off their civil war and focused their energies against the Japanese. With the demise of the Japanese threat, these two adversaries once again vied in a struggle that saw the Communists emerge victorious in 1949.

American troops had to be sent to China to accept the surrender of Japanese forces and keep order. But in areas where the Communists held control, they were opposed to any American intervention, since the Americans had backed the Kuomintang. Accordingly, American forces landing in China faced a mixed reception. In areas controlled by the Kuomintang, they were well received, however in Communist influenced areas, they were decidedly not welcome. This was made evident to Marines of the 1st Division when they landed at Tangku on the Hai Ho River. After being escorted upstream by LCS(L)s of Flotilla One, the Marines came under attack by Chinese Communist forces and suffered several casualties.

With various extra duties such as minesweeping and patrolling completed, the majority of the LCS(L) fleet headed for home at the end of 1945 and the beginning of 1946. Most steamed east from either Japan or Okinawa and made stops at Saipan and Hawaii before heading stateside. The trip from Tokyo to Saipan early in December, 1945, would prove to be memorable for a number of the ships, including the *61, 62, 63, 64, 82, 83, 84, 86, 87, 114, 115*, and *118* as they encountered the worst typhoon of their tour. Heading southeasterly towards Saipan, they were aware of the coming storm. As the wind began to pick up, Chief Bosun's Mates had the ships rigged for heavy weather. Extra life lines were added wherever needed, and the hatches were all battened down.

The storm came in from the starboard side and hit the convoy broadside. The flat-bottomed LCS(L)s heeled precariously throughout the 24 hours that the storm was at its peak. Waves during that time were estimated at 40 to 50 feet high and dwarfed the tiny fleet. Rated men were assigned to each life raft in case the need should arise. These life rafts could hold about 20 men and were stocked with provisions that would help them survive at sea. Whether or not they could survive on them in the storm was in question. All hands remained topside with their life jackets on.

LCS(L)s had significant fire fighting capabilities. Here, the *LCS(L) 71* fights a fire at the Marine Barracks in Sasebo, Japan after the war. Photo courtesy of Ray Baumler.

LCS(L) 44 at Jinsen Harbor, Korea late in 1945. The great tidal range in the
harbor made maintenance a bit easier. Ships could be grounded on the mud flats
to have their bottoms cleaned and painted. Photo courtesy of Nisi Dionis.

As the storm abated, the men prepared for their entrance into Saipan Harbor,
relieved at having weathered their worst storm and with renewed confidence in
the abilities of their ships. The convoy anchored in Saipan Harbor on 9 December,
1945 and remained there until 16 December, when they once again headed for the
states.

Between Saipan and Pearl Harbor the ships ran into another typhoon.
Christmas Day arrived and the weather had not abated. Longhurst of the *61*
recalls, "It was so rough that Cookie couldn't cook. The next morning on the
26 we crossed the date line and it was Christmas all over again, but he still
couldn't cook so he said that when we got to Honolulu he'd cook us a turkey
dinner, so we all agreed to that. Because it was too rough, all we got was
sandwiches" (Longhurst interview).

Homeward bound *LCS(L)s 28, 76* **and** *57* **at Saipan, 25 December, 1945. Photo courtesy of Ken Krayer.**

The voyage to Pearl Harbor lasted until 30 December, 1945, with the LCS(L)s running at their usual slow speed of eight to ten knots. At 1400 hours, the small fleet steamed into Pearl Harbor and the crew prepared to celebrate the New Year. Once there, the food situation improved greatly. Unencumbered by the constraints of war, the food supply depots basically opened their doors. Individual sailors simply walked in and asked for whatever they wanted with no paper work required. Men came back with cases of oranges, eggs, cans of ham and other items that had been in short supply. Of particular interest was fresh fruit and vegetables, since the canned varieties were the only kind available at sea. Each man in the crew became his own cook, and from that point on until the arrival in San Diego, much weight was gained by the crew members. After only a few days in the Hawaiian Islands, the ships were once again at sea, leaving Pearl Harbor on 4 January, 1946, and heading for San Diego.

THE FINALE

As the ships approached the United States, anticipation grew among their crews. The estimated time of arrival had been figured out in advance and they neared the coast about 7:00 AM on 14 January, 1946. Everyone crowded the forward part of the ships, straining their eyes to catch the first glimpse of land and they finally did. Not much detail could be seen of the California coast at that point, but everyone knew they had arrived home safely after a year at war.

The LCS(L)s remained in San Diego for varying lengths of time. In contrast to the beginning of the Pacific cruise, San Diego was almost deserted. Crews took liberty for a few days and many men were discharged from the service and sent home. Ships departed from San Diego and headed either north to the Portland area or to Florida for decommissioning.

LCS(L) 55 **returns home and passes under the Golden Gate Bridge. Photo courtesy of John Palco.**

LCS(L) 25 at pre-inactivation dry-dock in Portland, Oregon, April, 1946. Many of the LCS(L)s were mothballed in Portland, Oregon and Bremerton, Washington. Photo courtesy of Franklin Moulton.

As they steamed into their home ports to be mothballed, the ships had on board many of the original crew but also many new faces. Once they were berthed in Green Cove Springs, Florida, or Portland, Oregon, the men on board them got down to the arduous task of decommissioning. Cosmolene was used to coat the guns and other exposed fittings and cocoon-like covers were placed over machinery and equipment. When the job was finished the men transferred off to await discharge or new assignments. This was to be the procedure for many of the LCS(L) fleet as they were mothballed on both the east and west coasts. For most, this would be a temporary condition. Within a few years, the changing world situation would see them re-commissioned and sent to various places in the world for further service.

The Mothball Fleet at Green Cove Springs, Florida. Photo taken in October, 1950. The LCS(L)s are berthed in the upper right. Photo courtesy of the National Archives.

CHAPTER VII

THE FINAL CHAPTER

OTHER SERVICE

Although most had been mothballed, many LCS(L)s were soon back in commission. In fact the service performed by the ships for foreign navies was of much longer duration than that served for their own country. Within a few short years after the end of the second World War, it became obvious that the United States and its allies faced new threats, this time from the Communist bloc nations. Incursions into Vietnam and South Korea by the Communists put pressures on the NATO alliance in the west and forced the United States to re-commission the LCS(L)s. Re-designated as LSSLs (Landing Ship Support Large), they were transferred to friendly nations at a rapid rate.

One hundred and twenty-three LCS(L)s survived the war and 72 of them went on to serve again in foreign navies. During the war, five of them had been sunk in battle, one damaged beyond repair and sunk and a seventh grounded and declared a total loss. A number of others had been damaged. Within two years the sell-off had begun, with 17 sold to private individuals and companies. Reports on the official Navy List of 1948 indicated that 106 of the LCS(L) fleet were still in existence, some still actively used for training at various Reserve Commands. In addition, 25 of the Flotilla Flagships LC(FF) were shown to exist as well (Fahey *Victory Edition Addenda-Ships II*). Beginning in the early 1950s and lasting through the 1970s, many of the ships were transferred to friendly governments. This was done under various agreements such as the Mutual Defense Assistance Program and the Security Assistance Program. A number saw service in several countries before they were eventually decommissioned and sold as surplus.

The odyssey of *LCS(L)(3) 9* was not unlike that of many of her sister ships. Transferred to France under the MDAP in 1950, she was renamed the *Hallebarde* and given the NATO Pennant Number L 9023. After being used by the French in Indochina, she was transferred back to the United States in 1955, transferred to Japan as the *Asagao* in 1956, and then retransferred to the government of South Vietnam in 1965 and renamed *Doan Ngoc Tang* (*HQ 228*). As the communists took over in 1975, she escaped and made her way to the Philippines. She was then transferred to the Philippine government which renamed her *La Union* (*LLF 50*). In poor condition, the ship was used primarily for parts and eventually deleted from their official navy list in the mid-1980s.

LSSL 38 at dockside in Italy after her transfer. Ships in the Italian Navy had the first two letters of their name painted on the bow. Here, the letters BR, standing for *Bracco* are visible. Photo courtesy of the National Archives.

LCS(L)S IN ITALY

The specter of Communism on the rise throughout the world generated a number of agreements between the United States and its friends. Created in 1949, the Mutual Defense Assistance Program was designed to rearm the Europeans in the face of increasing pressure on the part of the U.S.S.R. The Security Assistance Program fulfilled a similar function. Two of the initial signatories of the NATO organization, founded in 1949, were Italy and France. Both countries received American naval vessels to bolster their fleets. Italy received six of the former LCS(L)s, which had been redesignated as LSSLs, through transfer under the Security Assistance Program on 25 July, 1951. Designated as the *Alano* class, they included the *34 (Alano), 38 (Bracco), 62 (Mastino), 63 (Molosso), 64 (Sugugio),* and *118 (Spinone).*

During their tour of duty in the Italian Navy, they served as support gun boats. GM diesels, which were their original source of power, were replaced by Gray Marine diesels and other equipment in order to keep them in service. The ships were on regular coastal patrol during the time that they served in the Italian fleet, and one even made it back to her native land. In conjunction with the American Bicentennial celebration, the Italians sent their sail training ship, the *Amerigo Vespucci,* to visit the United States. As she sailed into Hampton Roads in the summer of 1976, she was accompanied by the *Alano* (ex *34*).

FRANCE AND VIETNAM

Although the *Mighty Midgets* had been engaged in fierce fighting in the Pacific, the actual duration of their wartime activities was little more than half a year. In Vietnam, in the service of the French and later the Vietnamese, the ships were actively engaged in fighting for a period of nearly 24 years.

France, one of our NATO allies, was in a difficult position. With control of her colonies weakened by the war, she found herself under increasing pressure in Vietnam. The Mutual Defense Assistance Act, passed in 1949, authorized military aid to friendly nations. Western Europe was the major concern of the United States government at that time. Originally passed to authorize support for that area, it was amended to provide $75 million in aid for the Far East. This coincided with the victory of Mao Tse-tung's forces in China. At first it was not clear how this money was to be used, and the final determination was to be left to the discretion of the Commander in Chief. On 18 January, 1950, shortly after the passage of this legislation, the new government of Ho Chi Minh in North Vietnam received official recognition by the People's Republic of China. The alliance of these two countries, diametrically opposed to Western interests, changed the situation. Vietnam became a top priority and the American military determined that aid to the French in the struggle against the Communists was of great importance. Estimates of the French needs for the following year were placed at $100 million, of which only a portion was available. Equipment lists were submitted by both the French government and the Bao Dai government in Saigon. Recognizing the lack of military expertise of the Vietnamese and still smarting from the wasteful assistance program to Chiang Kai-chek's *Kuomintang,* the Americans decided to funnel all aid through the French government. In April of 1950, $15 million was allocated to support the French efforts in Indochina. Included in the allotment were funds to pay for the delivery of supplies, ships, and aircraft, among them six LSSLs. Within two months, the Korean War began and America's interest in the Far East increased. As a result, the efforts to send supplies to the French in Vietnam were accelerated. On 25 July, 1950, the French LST *Rance* left Puget Sound accompanied by six of the re-commissioned gunboats: *LSSLs 2, 4, 9, 10, 28* and *80.* After island-hopping across the Pacific, they arrived in Saigon on 17 November. At first the French designated the ships as numbers *1* through *6*, but they went through several hull number and name changes. This has caused some confusion, since early reports out of French Indochina used the first designation. By the end of 1951, the ships had been given new hull numbers, from *9021* through *9026.* Early in 1953, they were given official names, representing medieval weapons. In this chapter, the numbers and names appropriate to the year are used with the original LCS(L) hull numbers in parentheses to aid in identification.

It was not the first time that the LSSLs had sailed in Indochinese waters. In the aftermath of World War II, a number of LCS(L)s had been assigned to minesweeping and other miscellaneous duties in the Korea, China, Taiwan and South China areas. *LCS(L)s 30* and *50* and *102* patrolled in the waters off Vietnam from 20 October, 1945 through the beginning of November. From 5 November, 1945 to the beginning of January, 1946, the *96, 97 and 100* also swept mines in the area and the *LCS(L)s 43* and *97* were active there from the end of January to April, 1946.

After arriving in Vietnam, the ships were quickly pressed into service and were assigned a role in the newly formed *dinassaut* (River Assault Division). These units had been created by Captain Francois Jaubert of the Naval Brigade. Jaubert assembled a variety of small assault craft to patrol up and down the riverways in Vietnam to combat the *Viet Minh* forces under Vo Nguyen Giap. Although he died in battle early in 1946, his work paved the way for the further development of the *dinassaut* groups. These units usually consisted of from twelve to eighteen ships and boats comprised of a combination of LCTs, LCMs, and LCVPs. Many of these were greatly modified with the addition of armor, tank turrets, extra machine guns and mortars to increase their firepower. Until LSSLs appeared in 1950, an LSIL usually served as the command ship and supplied fire support. With their superior firepower, the LSSLs soon became the desired vessel for this task. Their tall conning towers gave them good visibility but made them an easy target. It also gave the officers on top of the conn the ability to see over river embankments and far off into the rice paddies, making it possible to direct fire more accurately. Although this procedure was useful for spotting the enemy, it frequently led to the wounding or death of the French spotter, as they were prime targets for snipers. It was not uncommon for the *dinassaut* unit to be spread over a lengthy stretch of river. Particularly troublesome were sections of rivers that wandered through lowlands and made visual communication between the boats difficult. The high conn on the LSSLs made them ideal for keeping track of the entire convoy.

LSSLs 2, 4, 9, 10, 28 and *80* at dry dock in Bremerton, Washington. This photo was taken on 13 June, 1950 shortly before they were sent to Indochina to serve in the French Navy. Photo courtesy of the National Archives.

Usually each *dinassaut* had one such fire support ship, but in important campaigns, two might be placed in the unit. As the war progressed and the Communist attacks strengthened it was not unusual to find a third LSSL assigned to a convoy. Although *Dinassaut 2* and *Dinassaut 6* both had LSSLs assigned to them, the assignments were not considered permanent. LSSLs were too valuable a weapon to limit their areas of use. In fact the *dinassaut* units frequently changed size and composition according to their activities.

LSSL HULL AND NAME CHANGES IN FRENCH SERVICE

LSSL No.	1st French Hull No.	2nd French Hull No.	French Name
2	1	9021	*Arbalete*
4	2	9022	*Arquebuse*
9	3	9023	*Hallebarde*
10	4	9024	*Javeline*
28	5	9025	*Pertuisane*
35	-	-	*Etendard*
65	-	-	*Oriflamme*
80	6	9026	*Rapiere*
105	-	-	*Framee*

French methods of conducting operations on the rivers varied according to the task. As they applied to the LSSLs there were two basic types. The *dinassaut*s might be used to transport supplies or be used in assaults against the enemy. A typical formation usually consisted of two groups, an opening group and a main group. Leading the entire convoy was an LCM Monitor. These 65 foot vessels were armed with machine guns and mortars. A half-dozen small minesweepers followed immediately behind them. Two to 300 meters to the rear was the first LSSL, leading the main body by about 50 meters. This main body had two components, one that supplied fire power and the other that carried either troops or cargo. Firepower was supplied by the LSSL or an LSIL and heavily armed LCM Monitors or LCTs. Next came the lead ships of the convoy, usually consisting of LCMs loaded with cargo. Bringing up the rear was a second LSSL which served as the command vessel for the division. If the convoy were vital to the French operations, it might also have the support of air cover. When an ambush occurred, the lead LCM Monitor opened fire on the enemy position, the convoy closed ranks and the LSSL opened up with her heavier firepower. This concentration created what the French referred to as a "ball of fire." The convoy increased speed and tried to pass through the enemy ambush as quickly as possible (*A Translation from* *the French* 178). This is where the LSSLs were at their best. With their twin 40mm guns and other weapons blazing, they insured that the enemy kept his head down. If he didn't, he ran the risk of being wiped out. Additional assistance might be needed, and frequently a convoy called in an air strike.

An LSSL operating in Indochina under the French flag in the early 1950s. Her forward 3"/50 deck gun was preferred over the single or twin 40mms. Photo courtesy of the U.S. Naval Historical Center.

The French were fortunate that the *Viet Minh* never developed an effective strategy for stopping river convoys. Although the most serious threat to the ships came from mines, other *Viet Minh* weapons were not as effective. It is not clear why the *Viet Minh* did so, but rather than concentrating their attack on a limited stretch of the river, they spread out their ambushes, allowing the French to overwhelm them with superior firepower. In one such ambush on the Day River in November, 1952, the *Viet Minh* used at least 20 weapons of 75mm and 57mm and some 150 automatic weapons spread out over a distance of seven kilometers (*A Translation from the French* 174). Recoilless rifles and mortars concentrated in an attack on an LSSL probably would have damaged it severely, and might have been able to put one out of action, but the *Viet Minh* did not group them effectively.

In order to thwart the enemy ambushes, the French planned their convoys carefully using overflights by *Moranes* to spot enemy emplacements. They also maintained contact with local artillery units and might call in gunfire on the enemy. While on convoy or patrol, all hands were at battle stations so that they could not be surprised by an ambush. In fact, if a section of the river bank seemed to be suspicious, it was simply raked with fire to pre-empt an enemy attack. Still another tactic involved the landing of commandos on the flank of the suspected enemy position. These troops could quickly put an end to the ambush. The problem with this tactic was that it required the beaching of some of the ships and left them open to mortar attack.

A second type of formation was designed to make river assaults as effective as possible. Ships engaging in the operation were divided into two groups, the opening group and the shock group. The opening group was led by an LCM Monitor and several minesweepers. One thousand to 1,500 meters behind them came the lead LSSL of the shock group, and sometimes a second LSSL 50 meters behind the first. Another LCM Monitor trailed these ships, followed by a number of armored LCMs containing assault troops. Lastly came another LCM Monitor and sometimes a third LSSL. When operating in this type of formation, the last LSSL was usually the command ship.

When the enemy was located along the river, the first Monitor turned to the opposite side to cover the river bank and the lead LSSL turned in to the shore facing the attackers. This maneuver was initiated with the full firepower of the LSSL engaging the enemy. Armored LCMs in the first group landed their troops as the second LSSL beached herself. A column of LCMs landed troops on the assault beach with an LSSL on each flank to provide firepower. The second group of LCMs accompanied by the third LSSL waited to the rear until the landing beach was established. Usually this was the larger of the two groups, but they were not landed until the beachhead was secured (*A Translation from the French* 180-182).

These assaults were successful when they worked according to plan. However, the *Viet Minh* usually attempted to take advantage of the difficult conditions under which the patrols and convoys had to operate. Reports from the United States Office of Naval Intelligence identified the problem:

Amphibious formations are highly vulnerable in the narrow and often winding waterways. Frequently they can be sighted from considerable distances by hidden enemy lookouts, while the amphibious formation itself can see little because of the walls of foliage or high banks along the waterways. Each new bend rounded may bring the formation face-to-face with an enemy ambush or blockade, and in the south the constant hazard of controlled river mines must be faced. Aerial reconnaissance may help the commander spot obvious river obstructions, large enemy formations, or fortifications, but the dense jungle growth usually provides ample cover for small enemy formations to fire at the advancing vessels with bazookas, machine guns, and small arms (United States Office of Naval Intelligence *Dinassasu* 31).

Heading out on convoy or assault, the ships and boats passed through familiar territory. Lining the banks were large and small villages and numerous deserted enemy observation posts. Once the ships had passed an area, the *Viet Minh* knew that it would only be a matter of time before they returned. When they did, they usually faced an ambush. Lining both sides of the river and firing from behind high riverbanks or from hidden bunkers, the *Viet Minh* poured a deadly fire on the vessels, assaulting them with mortar, bazooka, and machine gun fire. Such an ambush might be as much as seven kilometers long, and with the ships running at their usual slow speed, it was inevitable that casualties would occur.

The French use of the *dinassauts* and their supporting LSSLs was centered in two regions, one in the north and another in the south. In the north, the Red River Delta, which contained the major cities of Hanoi and Haiphong, was crucial to the *Viet Minh* forces. Within the Delta area the Vietnamese raised the bulk of their important rice crop, control of which could make continued resistance possible for the *Viet Minh*. Residing in this section of Vietnam were nearly 10,000,000 inhabitants, making French control of the area vital. As a result, the French concentrated at least a quarter of their troop strength in the area. Patrols up and down the Red River and its branches, most important of which was the Day, were necessary to insure French control of the area. The French had constructed over 900 outposts throughout the region, surrounding the critical approaches to the cities of Hanoi and Haiphong, as well as strategically located villages. These fortified outposts were manned by about 100,000 French troops. Attempts to keep them supplied by use of overland routes usually proved to be ineffective, with the *Viet Minh* easily able to ambush the convoys. With the large Vietnamese population in the area, the French were always in the position of being surrounded by the enemy. By 1953, it was estimated that 5,000 of the 7,000 villages in the region were controlled by the *Viet Minh* (Lancaster 265). It was almost impossible to keep the land routes between the French outposts open. The rivers were the only hope for resupply and reenforcement. Convoys on the river might also face ambush, but the accompanying firepower of the monitors and LSSLs made it possible for them to get through. Accordingly, the use of the river routes to supply these posts gained increasing importance. When ships did need repair from the ravages of use or damage caused by an ambush, they might go the Haiphong Naval Base. There, the ARL *Vulcain* was available for ship repairs. Facilities were limited, however, with Haiphong containing only one drydock large enough to handle the LSSLs or LSILs. Haiphong also had three marine railways which were capable of hauling an LCM out of the water. A civilian dry dock was used at times, but it was also limited to LCM size ships. Inland from Haiphong, small repair facilities were located at Nam Dinh and Hanoi.

As the newly rejuvenated LSSLs entered the Indochinese area of operations, it was midway in the war between the French and the *Viet Minh*. Numerous battles had been fought between the two sides, however, the highest priority for combat operations was in the north, where the *Viet Minh* forces were the strongest and supplied directly by the Chinese. As a result, much of the action for the newly arrived ships took place in the Red River Delta, where continual river patrols and convoys were effected in order to keep control of the region.

The first two ships to go into service were the *1* (ex *2*), which patrolled from Annam to Tonkin from mid-December, 1950 to 7 February, 1951 and the *2* (ex *4*) 4), which spent the last two weeks of December, 1950 on patrol in the Bassac River section of the Mekong Delta. Four of the six LSSLs spent only a couple of months in the southern areas before they were sent north to Haiphong. Only *LSSLs 2* (ex *4*) and *5* (ex *28*) spent any significant time in Saigon and in patrolling the Mekong. However, in February and March, 1952, they were sent north to Haiphong, where they remained on duty for the duration of the war.

LSSL ASSIGNMENTS FROM OCT., 1950 TO MAY, 1954

U.S LSSL	French Hull No	French Name	Assigned to Saigon Area	Assigned to Haiphong Area
2	1	*Arbalete*	Nov. 1950-Feb. 1951	Feb. 1951-1954
4	2	*Arquebuse*	Nov. 1950-Feb. 1952	Feb. 1952-1954
9	3	*Hallebarde*	Nov. 1950-Aug. 1951	Aug. 1951-1954
10	4	*Javeline*	Nov. 1950-Feb. 1951	Feb. 1951-1954
28	5	*Pertuisane*	Nov. 1950-Mar. 1952	Mar. 1952-1954
35	-	*Etendard*	No Data Available	
65	-	*Oriflamme*	No Data Available	
80	6	*Rapiere*	Nov. 1950-Mar. 1951	Mar. 1951-1954
105	-	*Framee*		Jan. 1954-

(Source: Michel, Vols. IV & V)

In Cochin China, the Mekong River delta south of Saigon was similarly important. Two of the LSSLs, the *2* (ex *4*) and the *5* (ex *28*) saw service there in the period
between the first quarter of 1951 and the beginning of 1952. Because their concentrated firepower was so valuable, the French were reluctant to assign them to a particular division. As a result, LSSLs were in a special category. With their shallow draft,
they were able to gain access to areas denied to the larger ships. This made it possible
to bring their guns to bear against the enemy in the smaller tributaries. To maintain
force flexibility, the LSSLs were assigned temporarily to duty where needed.

Saigon was a major port and contained repair facilities capable of handling the
largest naval vessels. LSSLs and their companion *dinassaut* ships might be repaired
there, however, it was more likely for them to be repaired at the base of the
Commander in Chief or at one of the smaller inland bases at Cau Doc, Vinh Long,
Can Tho, My Tho or even Phnom Penh, Cambodia.

Some modifications of the ships were needed to make them useful for river assignments. The rocket launchers that had helped them assault landing beaches in the
Pacific were of little use in the river areas since they had a fixed trajectory which would
cause them to overshoot their targets. Prior to transfer they were removed, and in
many cases, they were replaced with two or three 81mm mortars, which were more
useful in engagements against the *Viet Minh* since they had an adjustable range. Mortars could also be used to fire illumination flares for night identification of targets. The
first six ships transferred to the French all had 3"/50 forward deck guns. Of the last
three, the *Etendard* (ex *35*) and the *Oriflamme* (ex *65*) had a single 40mm gun forward
and the *Framee* (ex *105*) had a twin 40mm. It is not clear if this armament was requested or just happenstance, however, the 3"/50 gun gave the ships the added heavy
firepower that was sometimes necessary. The 3"/50 guns were mainly used against
supply dumps or fortifications. Smaller guns were useful as anti-personnel weapons.
The twin 40mm guns that had served so well as anti-aircraft weapons proved useful as
well. Although the guns had Mark 51 directors available, they were of little use in river
warfare and were frequently found to be in need of repair because of heat and humid-
ity. More useful were fire liaison parties, which could land and direct call-fire to selected targets. Since the ships might be subjected to intense small arms fire in the
course of an ambush, light armor plate was added to some areas, including the conning tower. Each of the LSSLs usually had an awning mounted on top of the conn in
order to protect the crew from the intense heat of the sun.

Shortages of manpower limited the number of personnel on board, and the French
LSSLs carried a compliment of three officers and 55 enlisted men. They were usually
commanded by a Lieutenant, and the *dinassaut* was under the command of a *capitaine
de corvette*, the French equivalent of a Lieutenant Commander in the American Navy
(United States Office of Naval Intelligence *Dinassau* 29).

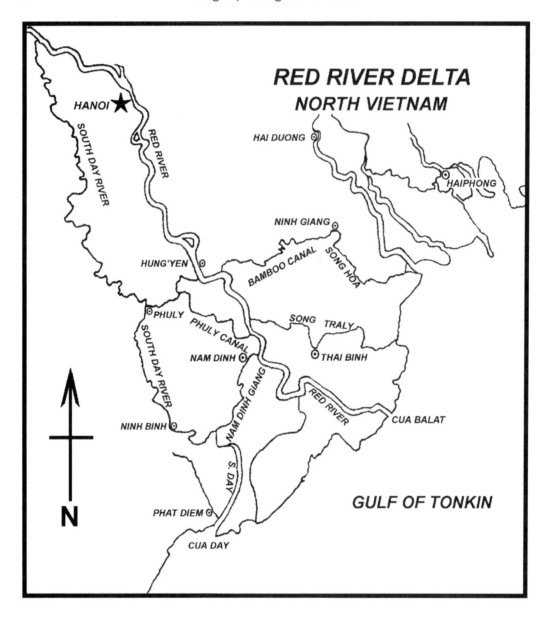

Within a short time the newly arrived *Mighty Midgets* saw action once again. The Red River Delta, near the port of Haiphong, was the scene of an attack by General Vo Nguyen Giap's forces which were attempting to capture the French outposts that surrounded the city. Fortunately the French were able to use the rivers to resupply their troops. On 23 March, 1951, the *Viet Minh* sent three divisions against the French at Mao Khe, near the Da Bach River. They were held at bay by support fire from six French ships, the light cruisers *Duguay-Trouin, La Grandier, Savorgnan de Brazza*, the corvette *Chevreuil* and the *LSSLs 1* (ex *2*) and *4* (ex *10*). Later, at nearby Bi-cho and Uong-bi, the *Savorgnan de Brazza, Chevreuil* and the *LSSL 4* (ex *10*) threw their combined firepower against other communist units. After 48 hours, the French ships were forced to withdraw in the face of overwhelming force. As this was taking place, *LSSLs 1* (ex *2*) and *6* (ex *80*), in company with French corvettes, were patrolling the coast and the entrance to the river, preventing the resupply of the enemy. Fighting continued in the area, and within the next couple of months, the French and *Viet Minh* forces both carried out bloody campaigns.

In *Operation Meduse,* which took place between 20 April and 4 May, 1951, the French assembled a massive force to combat the *Viet Minh*. Thirteen-thousand men and 30 ships were employed in the operation, among them the three *LSSLs, 1,* (ex *2*), *4* (ex *10*) and *6* (ex *80*). At that point, the LSSLs were the most modern design in the *dinassauts*. Based at Qui-cao, they were instrumental in supplying support fire for the troops as they were landed at various locations just to the south of Haiphong, in the quadrant formed by Song Thai Binh, the Bamboo Canal, Song Giem Ho and the sea. At the battle for Song Da Bach, both ships provided fire support for the landing of the Jaubert and Francois commando units and then patrolled the rivers assuring the marine blockade in the area of operation. After this was accomplished, the three LSSLs, along with the corvettes, cruised offshore, blocking enemy access to the estuaries.

The Red River Delta in the northern part of Vietnam was a crucial rice producing center. Located upstream on the river is the city of Hanoi, and at the northernmost edge of the delta, the port of Haiphong. Continued advances in the area by the *Viet Minh* were resisted fiercely by the French.

North Vietnamese General Vo Nguyen Giap had determined that an attack on the delta was necessary. Although he would have preferred to capture the major cities of Hanoi and Haiphong, the strength of the French forces made this impossible. Capture of the Catholic areas, primarily the provinces of Ninh Binh and Nam Dinh, would provide a significant propaganda coup and place the *Viet Minh* in a good position to threaten other areas of the delta. In order to divert French forces away from the target, Giap sent his 312th Division to the northwest corner of the delta to keep the French occupied. The attack was launched on 29 May, 1951 with the 308th Division attacking Ninh Binh and the 304th crossing the Day River to attack Phu Ly. Giap had committed a total of 70,000 men to the campaign. The *dinassauts* immediately went into action, and the Third River Patrol Division was ambushed while heading from Nam Dinh to Ninh Binh. This division included the *LCI 102*, four LCMs, three LCVPs and an LCT. As a standard procedure during an ambush, the LCI landed its troops and raked the shoreline with fire as the infantry put and end to the threat. Continuing on to Ninh Binh, the division reached its destination and beached itself to put troops ashore. The following morning, 30 May, 1951, the enemy launched an attack on the division using four battalions. *LCI 102* was hit and forced to withdraw to the opposite riverbank as the *Viet Minh* captured the station. Having been badly mauled by the enemy, the French unit was relieved to see the newly formed River Patrol Division A come to its aid. Included in the unit was the *LSSL 6* (ex *80*) under the command of Lt. Commander P. Schloesing. Accompanying the LSSL were six LCMs.

A few days later, on the morning of 4 June, the *6* (ex *80*) was beached at Ninh Binh. At 0500 the *Viet Minh* attacked the ship with 75mm guns, mortars and machine gun fire. Unfortunately for the enemy, the firepower of the LSSL was superior. Locating enemy positions by muzzle flash, the *6* (ex *80*), along with her accompanying LCMs, poured forth a withering fire, forcing the *Viet Minh* to withdraw. After the battle, the 6 (ex *80*) found that she had taken six hits from the enemy. However, none were serious and within a few hours she headed downstream on patrol (Brossard 157).

Yen Cu Ha was attacked the next day, 5 June. The town was saved by the intervention of *LSSL 6* (ex *80*). At 0700, Schloesing received an urgent message directing him to proceed to Yen Cu Ha to assist the garrison which was in danger of being overrun by the *Viet Minh*. Assembling a force as rapidly as possible, he loaded troops on two LCMs and set out for the beleaguered outpost. Along the way, one of the LCMs ran into trouble and had to be beached. Continuing on by itself, the *LSSL 6* (ex *80*) arrived about 0900 near the town station to find 15 French commandos surrounded and still engaged in combat. They had managed to fight off at least three enemy companies. Using her considerable firepower over a period of several hours, the LSSL managed to drive the *Viet Minh* troops away from the French defenders. The weather began to clear, and a *Morane* flew over the area and spotted the enemy emplacements. With that assistance, the fire from the *LSSL 6* (ex *80*) became increasingly accurate and the tide of battle began to turn. The LCMs arrived and landed additional troops, causing the *Viet Minh* to withdraw to the central tower of the station where they continued to resist. Gunner's Mate First Class Labele took careful aim and a round from the 76mm gun on the 6 (ex *80*) hit the *Viet Minh* command post, causing it to collapse on top of the enemy. Their leadership destroyed, the *Viet Minh* were driven from the city. When the fighting was ended, the French investigated the destroyed tower and found that 55 of the enemy were still alive. In and around the tower area were 87 dead enemy soldiers, most killed by fire from the gunboats. In addition to the bodies, a number of weapons were captured, including a 57mm recoilless rifle, eleven machine-guns and a large number of small arms (Schloesing 1331-1332). Two days later, on 7 June, the *Viet Minh* returned and repeated their attack on the station. *LSSL 6* (ex *80*) arrived at daybreak and added her firepower to the battle once again. Having experienced the severity of her guns before, the *Viet Minh* withdrew.

Throughout the region, the *Viet Minh* and French attacked and counter-attacked. Giap had committed a strategic error that compelled his forces to give up the campaign. In an attempt to capture one of the provinces, he had his 320th Division cross the Day River under cover of night. With the French river patrols tied up in other areas, this crossing was effected without incident. It proved to be a mistake. As the weeks wore on, the *Viet Minh* found themselves cut off from their supply routes. *Viet Minh* supply boats, attempting to carry food and munitions to the units, fell prey to the river patrol ships which took a devastating toll. By 18 June, Giap was forced to call off his offensive.

These engagements came to be known as the Battle of the Day River and were the first of any significance for the newly arrived LSSLs. Their superior firepower demonstrated to the French that they had a new and important weapon in the fight against the communists. In many cases, the concentrated firepower supplied by the LSSLs was instrumental in turning the tide of battle.

From 15 March to 8 April, 1952, the French forces conducted *Operation Mecure*. This venture was designed to harass the enemy and deny them the use of the rice harvest. Cruising up and down the coast between the Red River and the mouth of the Cua Diem Giang, *LSSLs 1* (ex *2*), *4* (ex *10*) and *6* (ex *80*), along with the *Savorgnan de Brazza*, blocked the coast and kept the enemy off balance. As a result of their actions, the *Viet Minh* suffered 1,580 regulars killed and 1,893 prisoners lost, including 43 officers. In addition, the force captured a large number of important weapons (Michel Vol. IV 335).

Later in the year, the LSSLs participated in *Operation Punaise,* between 5 and 9 November, 1952. By that time, they had been given official names and were no longer referred to by number. The purpose of this operation was to supply the outpost at Bui Chu and it was undertaken by one LSSL, one LCT and one LCM. The situation in the area was difficult. Up to that time it had been characterized by a massive infiltration of *Viet Minh* regulars who continually attacked outposts on the periphery. In an attempt to reinforce outposts in the area, the *Arquebuse* (ex *4*) escorted a landing by the Senee Commando unit. On the evening of 13 to 14 November, the sector was attacked by four *Viet Minh* battalions from the 314th and 320th Divisions. Within a short time, the enemy had encircled the French troops, but heavy fire from the LSSL drove them back and allowed the French to regain their positions.

LSSL 80 (early French hull number 6) patrolling on the Day River in 1951. Photo courtesy of the National Archives.

Later that day, the *Arquebuse* (ex *4*) and the *Hallebarde* (ex *9*), along with *LCTs 9064* and *9060*, attempted to land a battalion of the Foreign Legion at Phat Diem. As *LCT 9064* beached and began to unload its troops, they were ambushed by a battalion of the *Viet Minh* 320th Division. Under fire from 75mm recoilless rifles, bazookas, and heavy automatic arms, the ships fought back. French records indicate that the firepower of the two LSSLs was the primary reason for the defeat of the enemy (Michel Vol IV 380).

Throughout 1952, the LSSL ships continued on coastal patrol and river operations in the Tonkin area in the North, with two of the ships briefly assigned to the Mekong Delta region in the south. During 1951 and 1952, the heavy firepower of the ships enabled them to go on frequent patrols by themselves. This was possible since the *Viet Minh* did not have the best of equipment to combat them. In these undertakings, the ships frequently added an artillery forward observer who spotted enemy positions and directed call-fire. Under these conditions the actions of the ships were limited, as they had no infantry forces on board which could land and engage the enemy. However, by 1953 and 1954, the *Viet Minh* became increasingly well armed, and the ships were forced to operate with others to insure their safety.

Since the beginning of the *dinassaut* operations, the river forces had been plagued by continued ambushes. Usually these were launched against convoys, but lone LSSLs or assault groups might also fall victim to them. In the years when the French were operating the LSSLs on the rivers, the *Viet Minh* were not as well armed as they would be after the French left. Usually convoys came under attack from machine gun, mortar, and bazooka fire. On some occasions, larger weapons, such as 76mm guns, might be employed. However, the heavy weapons were more difficult to conceal and, in the case of a counter-attack, could be lost to the French. Consequently, the *Viet Minh* weapons were usually light. As the war continued into the mid-1950s, the use of ambushes escalated and ships and convoys had to increase their firepower in order to fight them off.

Over time, it became more difficult to protect convoys and anchorages. By the middle of 1953, the first river mines began to appear in the Red River Delta, giving the French ships still another hazard to confront (Michel Vol. V 181). These mines were visually controlled and set off as the ships passed over them. Buried in the river bottom, they resisted conventional minesweeping techniques. French minesweepers had to drag heavy wires through the mud in an attempt to pull them up. This was a slow and tedious method and very difficult, since the mines were controlled by wires running to hidden observation points on shore. If the dragger failed to eliminate the mine, it could still be set off as other members of the convoy passed over. Each convoy on the river was led by minesweepers in an effort to counter this problem, however, the menace was never eliminated. Frequently, the hidden *Viet Minh* positions were visible from the air and a *Grumman Goose* or *Morane* flying observation for the convoy spotted them. In such cases, the 81mm mortars proved to be effective remedies. Although losses from mines were kept to a minimum, they were considered to be a major problem. Still another threat came from *nageurs de combat* (combat swimmers). These frogmen swam to anchored or beached ships under cover of night and attached explosive charges to the hulls. A survey of damage to the LSSLs during this period shows them suffering from a variety of attacks.

In the first years of the decade it had been possible to send out a convoy with only one LSSL as a fire support vessel. By 1953, it was unthinkable not to send two or three LSSLs along for support. Anchorages that had once been safe from floating mines and frogmen became too hazardous. Nets had been tried in an attempt to keep out these attacks, but it made it too difficult for the ships to get underway in a hurry. This was particularly important since they might come under attack by mortar fire during the night. Sept Pagoda, an important river port, had to be abandoned in early 1954 for just this reason.

SELECTED ATTACKS ON LSSL SHIPS 1951-1954

Date	Location	Ship	Method of Attack	Damages/Ship Casualties
4May51	Ninh Binh	6 *(Rapiere)*	75mm gun	light damage
4Jun51	Ninh Binh	6 *(Rapiere)*	75mm gun & machine gun	light damage, some wounded
14Nov52	Phat Diem	*Hallebarde Arquebuse*	75mm gun, bazooka & machine guns	no damage
29Mar53	Phat Diem	*Hallebarde*	combat swimmer	light damage
9May53	Ninh Binh	*Hallebarde*	mine	damage to stern, 1 sailor killed
4Aug53	Song Ninh Co	*Arquebuse*	bazooka	light damage, 2 wounded
5Aug53	Song Ninh Co	*Pertuisane*	bazooka	light damage, 1 wounded
18Aug53	Ticu	*Arbalete*	automatic weapons	no damage
23Sept53	River North of Bamboo Canal	*Javeline*	automatic weapons & mortar	3 wounded
14Jan54	Bamboo Canal	*Javeline*	mine	light damage
2Feb54	Day River	*Pertuisane*	bazooka	light damage, 4 dead, 2 wounded
9Feb54	Nam Dinh Giang	*Arquebuse*	bazooka	light damage, unknown dead & wounded
17Mar54	River south of opening of Bamboo Canal	*Rapiere*	recoilless rifle	3 wounded
18Apr54	Hung Yen	*Rapiere*	57mm recoilless rifle & machine guns	no damage
7May54	Yours Lang	*Framee*	57mm recoilless rifle	no damage

Based on Michel, *La Marine Francaise en Indochine de 1939-1956 Vols. IV & V.*

By 1953, the French had determined that large scale amphibious assaults would be valuable in their fight against the Communists. Such assaults would be completed by division-sized forces. In order to effect such undertakings, an increase in amphibious assault craft and ships was needed. By the end of 1953, three more LSSLs, numbers *35 (Etendard)*, *65 (Oriflamme)* and *105 (Framee)* had been transferred to France. Additional MDAP transfers by the end of 1954 totaled over 150 ships and craft of various types.

In the early part of 1953, the *Pertuisane* (ex *28*) engaged in a series of operations. *Operation Dahomey* took place on 23 February in the area near Sam Son (Thanh

Hoa). Along with two other warships, the *Paul Goffeny* and the *Belladone* and one commando unit, the operation resulted in 34 enemy dead and 20 prisoners. *Operation Tarn,* two days later at Ho Trung (Thanh Hoa), included the *Pertuisane* (ex *28*), the *Paul Goffeny*, the *Cdt. Amyot d'Inville* and the *Senee* and Commando unit. A number of the enemy were killed and twelve taken prisoner. On 28 February, the same ships and commando units attacked Cua Trap. In a running gun battle, the ships destroyed 73 junks, killed three of the enemy, and took 26 prisoners. French losses for the operations were one dead and two wounded (Michel Vol. IV 395).

Also that month, the *Arquebuse* (ex *4*) was active in the region of Nam Dinh and Phat Diem in support of *Dina 3*. Several gun battles along the river were undertaken with the LSSL supplying fire support for the *Senee* commando unit. With this operation, an enemy camp and depot were destroyed and a number of weapons captured. The enemy lost six dead and had 80 taken as prisoners, whereas the French had no losses.

Etendard (ex *LSSL 35*) shortly after her transfer to France on 12 March, 1953. She flies a French flag off her transom but still has the original U.S. hull number. The rocket launchers, normally mounted in front of her Number 2 gun tub were removed prior to transfer. Official U.S. Navy Photo courtesy of Phillip E. Peterson.

At the end of March, the French launched *Operation Hautes Alpes*. This operation became necessary because of the increasing threats against the post at Thanh Hoa in the province of Phat Diem. *Dinassaut 3*, supported by *Hallebarde* (ex *9*) and several LCTs, participated in the campaign. During the fighting, the *Hallebarde* (ex *9*) was damaged by an explosive charge planted by an enemy frogman.

On 18 April, the *LCT Fataccioli* ran aground at the mouth of the Red River near Cua Balat due to a navigation error. Concerned with the possibility of an ambush by the *Viet Minh*, the French assigned the *Arquebuse* (ex *4*) another LCT, two LCMs, and two tugs to assist in freeing her. The LCT, protected by the firepower of the assembled vessels, was freed by May, but not before the enemy had launched several attacks on it. Fortunately, the enemy losses were serious and they withdrew from the area.

Between the 8 and 9 May, 1953, the *Hallebarde* (ex *9*), along with other ships of *Dinassaut 3*, landed a platoon of troops near Ninh Binh, surprising a company of *Viet Minh*. It was a successful raid, with 48 of the enemy killed and 50 taken prisoner. A number of weapons were captured. However, during the night, the *Hallebarde* (ex *9*) struck a mine, which damaged her stern and killed one of her crew. Two weeks later, on 22 May , the *Javeline* (ex *10*) rejoined *Dinassauat 3* near Ninh Binh. The following day, 23 May, the *Dina* cleared the village of Bach Cu five kilometers to the northwest of Ninh Binh. As this was being accomplished, other elements of the unit were participating in an operation on the Nam Din Giang near the entrance to the Red River. The *Rapiere* (ex *80*) patrolled on the lower part of the river and supported the post at Ngo Dong, which had been harassed by the *Viet Minh*. In this operation, the LSSL sank three junks that were trying to escape.

Pertuisane (ex *28*) was involved in fire support against various elements of the *Viet Minh* that were grouping near Nam Than on the lower Red River. This action took place on 10 July, 1953. On 20 July, the *Arquebuse* (ex *4*) was assigned to patrol the area where the Cua Lach Giang and the Song Ninh Co intersected the Red River. It became the first LSSL to patrol in that waterway. On 25 July, the *Arquebuse* (ex *4*) supported efforts against elements of a provincial battalion while escorting a convoy from Nam Dinh to Hanoi. Near the mouth of the Lach Giang the convoy encountered 27 junks and ferryboats, sinking or damaging many of them.

In August, of 1953 there were several engagements by the LSSLs. Grouped under the heading of *Operations Tarentaise* and *Operation Libourne,* they occupied the period from 1 to 19 August. *Arquebuse* (ex *4*) had just relieved the *Pertuisane* (ex *28*), which had been patrolling on the Lach Giang. In an ambush on 4 August, 1953, both ships were hit by bazooka fire in the Song Ninh Co and one man was wounded. The ships did not suffer any significant damage.

On 18 August, *Dina 4* evacuated the village of Tieu. As usual, the *Viet Minh* attempted an ambush as the operation was underway. *Arbalete* (ex *2*) put down the assault, which consisted of automatic arms fire. Still another evacuation, this time at Tra Ling on the Song Giem Ho, was undertaken that month, with the *Arbalete* (ex *2*) again supplying the firepower necessary to make the operation a success. Effective hydrographic work in the area, under the cover of the *Arbalete's* (ex *2*) guns the previous month, made the operation go smoothly.

Toward the end of the month, from 20 to 24 August, the amphibious forces undertook a major campaign against *Viet Minh* outposts along the coast. The force, consisting of the *Chevreuil, Rapiere* (ex *80*), *LCT 9067* and the *Tempete* and *Senee* commando units, made three strikes against the enemy at Cape Falaise, Sam Son, and the mouth of the Song Yen, near Cu Tham. This raid was quite successful, with the enemy losing 102 dead, two wounded and 155 taken prisoner. Also included in the haul were numerous documents, mines, grenades, and eleven junks, carrying a total of 70 tons of supplies.

Javeline (ex *10*) and several LCMs operated on the Day River in the area around Ninh Binh, Nam Dinh, and the Nam Dinh Giang between 19 and 20 September. In general clean-up operations, the ships netted 20 enemy dead and nine wounded. More importantly, about 100 members of the political-military framework of the *Viet Minh* were arrested along with about 300 suspects.

Operation Brochet took place from 23 September to 13 October, 1953. Two assault divisions, *Dina 4* and *12*, attacked the region between Hung Yen and the Bamboo Canal along the Red River. Elements of the *Viet Minh* 42nd Regiment had been a continual threat to communications between Hanoi and Haiphong. Three LSSLs, the *Javeline* (ex *10*), *Arquebuse* (ex *4*) and the *Hallebarde* (ex *9*), *LCI 947* and *LCTs 9063, 9064, 9066, 9069, 9070,* and *9071,* assisted *Dina 12* in operations west of the canal. This campaign was aimed at interdicting numerous sampans and other small craft that were attempting to resupply the enemy by use of the waterway. *Javeline* (ex *10*) was ambushed and hit by automatic arms and three bazooka rounds, killing one of her crew and wounding several others. By the end of the month, the campaign had resulted in the death of 514 enemy soldiers, 333 taken prisoner, 168 wounded, and 1,400 suspects taken into custody. These numbers seemed impressive, but in fact the 42nd Regiment had managed to split up and elude the trap. One part escaped to the north in the direction of Ninh Giang and the other two escaped to the south, in the direction of Nam Dinh. French losses were reported to be 128 dead and 589 wounded (*Chroniques* Nov. 1953 1409-1410).

Operation Gerfaut began on 12 December, 1953. Its purpose was to locate and destroy elements of the 46th and 50th Regiments that were active in the area of Thai Binh between the Song Traly and the Red Rivers. On the morning of 12

December, French troops landed on the south bank of the Song Traly, surprising the enemy. Supplying firepower for the soldiers ashore was the *Arquebuse* (ex *4*) and the *Hallebarde* (ex *9*), along with four LCMs. The operation successfully cleared the area of *Viet Minh* and the contributions of the LSSLs to the success of the operation was noted (Michel Vol. V 235).

On 27 December, 1953, the French were relieved to see the arrival of new ships that the United States had promised. *Framee* (ex *105*) had just been transferred from Japan to France and her arrival along with two LSILs was most welcome. The ships were immediately sent to the Tonkin area to assist in operations in the Red River Delta.

Patrols and convoys on the Red River continued throughout the end of 1953 and into the beginning months of 1954. Crucial to control of the area was the stretch of the Red River between Cua Balat at the mouth and Hung Yen, which lay part way up the river to Hanoi. About halfway up this stretch, the Nam Dinh Giang branched off to the south and the village of Nam Dinh was situated there. From the end of December through February, 1954, the *Viet Minh* staged a particularly intense offensive in the area designed to cut the connections between the French posts and bases. Along the Nam Dinh Giang and the Day River, they staged a repeated series of ambushes on 15 December and on 2, 9, and 16 February, successfully cutting the French connections to Ninh Binh and other villages. These severe attacks made the French reassess the capabilities of their ships. It was desirable to place heavier armor plate on the LSSLs and the LSILs to help defend against the increasing size and number of enemy guns, however, after careful surveys, it was deemed impractical.

On 2 February, 1954, the *Pertuisane* (ex *28*) was supporting a group of dredgers on the Day River, when the ships were ambushed around km 28. One of the ships had to be beached and it was subsequently destroyed. A number of French were wounded in the assault. A few days later, as the *Arquebuse* (ex *4*) supported operations on the Nam Dinh Giang, it came under attack. A number of bazooka rounds hit the LSSL and the other ships, killing the Commanding Officer and the Second Officer on the LSSL. *Arquebuse* (ex *4*) was later awarded the Cross of War pennant for her actions.

Dinassauat 12 arrived at Hung Yen on 14 February in an attempt to clear the route to the base at Hanoi. After evacuating their wounded, they regrouped at Nam Dinh on 16 February in order to open the river. The increasing violence against the river forces made reinforcements necessary. Commando Units 35 and 32 were sent to reinforce Commando Unit 63, which was usually attached to *Dinassaut 3* at Nam Dinh. Added to the reinforcements of the ships of *Dinassaut 3* were those of the Vietnamese *Dinassaut 2*, which were usually attached to *Dinassaut*

3. Joining them were LSSLs *Hallebarde* (ex *9*) and *Rapiere* (ex *80*), *LSIL HQ 31* (ex *9033*), twelve VVs (ex LCVPs), twelve LCMs and a major part of *Dinassaut 12*. Assigned to fly overhead on reconnaissance were a *Grumman Goose* and a *Morane*.

Casualties were light and during the month of February, the French lost 13 dead, including three officers and 56 men who were wounded in the four engagements from 2 to 16 February. Both *Pertuisane* (ex *28*) and *Arquebuse* (ex *4*) had been slightly damaged by bazookas in the attacks on 2 and 9 February respectively, and the *Rapiere* (ex *80*) was damaged by bazooka fire on the 16 of February and forced to go to Haiphong for repairs.

At the beginning of March, 1954, the *Viet Minh* launched a full scale offensive in the area designed to cut off a number of French outposts and seize control of the region. The area had always been difficult to protect, with the waterways under constant hazard from Communist ambushes and the countryside filled with hostile forces. French *dinassaut* ships were continually under attack, and the available pool of experienced officers was slowly being diminished. A number of ships were sidelined for repairs, leaving many of the convoys short of firepower. The *Rapiere* (ex *80*), which had been ambushed in the middle of February and forced to enter the drydock at Haiphong for repairs, rejoined the *Hallebarde* (ex *9*) at the end of February. *Hallebarde* (ex *9*) had been in continuous service on the Red River for over 70 days without relief. *LSIL HQ 31* (ex *9033*) was sent down to Haiphong for repairs at that point, leaving the LSSLs without her assistance.

Javeline (ex *10*) alternated with the *Chevreuil* in supporting the Haiphong Dina. They operated day and night along the Song Da Bach, up to the Quang Yen sector. Frequent ambushes were encountered, and on 17 March the accompanying troops captured eleven of the enemy. The entire area around Haiphong was continually on alert for enemy activity during that time.

By the middle of March, it was necessary to send an assault and supply convoy up the river to recapture some outposts and resupply others. Haiphong was the center of provisions for these outposts. Through her port flowed the constant supply of men, munitions and other war materials necessary to keep the region under French control. The center of operations ran between two poles, Cua Balat at the mouth of the Red River and Hung Yen, about halfway up the river to Hanoi. *Dinassaut* operations were centered at Hung Yen, which had been overrun.

Operations to recover control of Hung Yen began on 15 March, with a convoy heading up the river. It consisted of the LSSLs *Hallebarde* (ex *9*) and *Rapiere* (ex *80*), one LCI, three LCMs, and two minesweepers, accompanied by six LCMs which carried three commando units. Overhead, a *Grumman Goose* flew reconnaissance for the flotilla, attempting to spot ambushes in the area. The passage through Thanh Nga was difficult. However, Ngoai Thon proved to be even more problematic.

As the convoy passed near the village, they manned their posts, keeping their trigger fingers on the 20mm and 40mm guns and the 60, 81, and 120mm mortars. Strict fire and radio discipline was observed and all seemed to be quiet. As the convoy passed Ngoai Thon, they found themselves in a stretch of river where the banks were completely covered by groves of banana trees, making it impossible to see through the thick vegetation. Within minutes, the first mortar rounds had bracketed the lead ship, *Rapiere* (ex *80*). The thickness of the undergrowth on the river banks made it difficult to see where the mortar was located. Several hundred meters of banana groves extended inland, along with some cornfields. *Viet Minh* observers were well-situated, and the ships were sitting ducks. The intensity of the fire increased from three to five projectiles a minute, and the danger for the convoy increased. Fortunately the observer on the *Grumman Goose* was able to spot the location of the enemy emplacements. Fire from the *Rapiere* (ex *80*) was instantly forthcoming, and the earth 300 meters inland erupted from the impact of her 20mm and 40mm guns and her 81mm mortars. One of the LCMs was hit and another went to her aid along with the *Rapiere* (ex *80*). They maneuvered effectively, covering the ship with their supporting fire, but their position soon became untenable. Sitting on the river, they were exposed to deadly mortar fire and something had to be done. *Hallebarde* (ex *9*) closed to within 50 meters of *Rapiere* (ex *80*) and both ships unleashed a torrent of fire. A commando unit was landed and put and end to the ambush. When it was over, they counted 20 *Viet Minh* dead and captured a variety of weapons. Orders were given to regroup the convoy and proceed at flank speed past the banana groves. As they withdrew, another LCM took a hit from a bazooka. By 1630, the ships were back on course in the channel.

Upon arrival at Hung Yen, they surveyed the damage. *Rapiere* (ex *80*) had been hit by four shells and three of her men were wounded. Several of the ships had been hit by bazooka fire. None of the mortars had found their target. However, numerous hits from 12.7 and 7.5 rounds were counted. In the course of the next ten days of river activity, the ships would cover Cua Balat, Nimh Dinh, Jung Yen, and Nam Dinh without a more serious engagement (Julien-Binard 1592-94).

On 27 March the river forces were once again at Hung Yen. Their purpose on this mission was to transport much needed machinery and replacement parts to *Dinassaut 12* at Hanoi. Many of the ships there were in need of repair and some had been missing parts since February. The trip to Hanoi was accomplished in spite of the fact that during the night the *Viet Minh* managed to capture the post at Ninh Xuyen. The successful completion of the trip reestablished the river link between Hanoi and Nam Dinh.

At 0400 hours on the 28, the river force reformed for its return to the base at Nam Dinh. Included in the group were the Vietnamese *Dinassaut 2*, the *Rapiere* (ex *80*),

LSIL HQ 31, one monitor, two VVs (LCVPs), six LCMs with Commando Units 4, 32, 35, and 63 along with four LCM transports. Leading the convoy were minesweepers, and the *Rapiere* (ex *80*) maneuvered to stay within the area cleared by them. The morning had been clear, but as the ship descended the river, they were enveloped in a light mist sufficient enough to slow the convoy's progress. As the *Rapiere* (ex *80*) and *LSIL HQ 31* maneuvered along the left shoreline, light machine gun fire was directed at them from the port side of the river. Orders were given to hold automatic arms fire and launch mortar rounds at the suspected enemy positions, and the convoy was halted until the threat could be eliminated. In spite of their search, the ships could not discover the source of the enemy fire and since it had abated, they continued on their trip. Later that day, at about 1730, *HQ 31* opened fire on suspected enemy positions on the left bank, and shortly thereafter, a mortar round landed near the *Rapiere* (ex *80*). *Rapiere* opened fire, turned to the right river bank and passed a row of banana trees. *LSIL HQ 31* was about 120 meters behind her, followed by the LCMs with the commando units. Five-hundred meters to the rear were the other LCMs and transports. It was at this point that the *Viet Minh* unleashed their attack on the front and the rear of the formation. Numerous explosions from mortar rounds occurred, killing and wounding several men. *Rapiere* (ex *80*) took a hit on her stern post from a 57mm shell. Between the fog, smoke from the exploding shells and the smoke from the ship's guns, *Rapiere* (ex *80*) and *HQ 31* were totally hidden from sight. Both ships let loose with all of their automatic weapons. As they maneuvered to their assault positions the LCMs landed Commando Unit 31. *LCT 9067* and *HQ 31* also landed their troops which were able to encircle the Vietnamese in a cornfield near the village of Ngoai Thon. Concentrated fire from the ships and the commandos made short work of the enemy, and the little promontory soon resembled a graveyard with bodies strewn about. Their safety assured and the enemy driven off, the convoy regrouped and continued on to its destination.

As they landed, ambulances came to the docks and tended to the wounded. A survey of the convoy's action revealed the following tally:

French: 6 dead, 18 wounded
     9 hits from heavy weapons
     numerous hits from light weapons

Viet Minh: 43 dead — killed by commandos. Number of losses from ship fire — uncertain
     Arms captured:
     1 - 57mm RR and 10 shells
     2 bazookas (90mm)

2 machine guns of 12.7 cal. and 20 cases of ammunition
2 light machine-guns
3 rifles
1 enemy outpost destroyed

(Julien-Binard 1595-1607).

Enemy activity in the region continued to expand. During the month of April, 1954, there was intense activity in the Red River Delta near the region of Song Tay, northwest of Hanoi. *Rapiere* (ex *80*), in support of the Vietnamese *dinassaut* ships in the area near Hung Yen, suffered an ambush near km 85 on the Red River. The ships launched a strong counter-attack and killed 43 of the enemy, who lost three recoilless rifles and four machine guns in the encounter (*Chroniques* June, 1954 805).

May of 1954 proved to be extremely busy for the LSSLs of the French river forces. On 3 May, in the region around Ning Giang, the *Arbalete* (ex *2*) patrolled on the Song Van Uc. In this area only a few days before, the gunboat and an LSU it was escorting were ambushed by the *Viet Minh*. No injuries were reported. However, the village of Tat Cau had to be evacuated. *Arbalete* (ex *2*) destroyed three sampans used by the rebels and continually fought off ambushes at night on the Song Da as the evacuees traveled to the sea.

On l7 May, the *Rapiere* (ex *80*) was escorting a convoy down the Red River from Nam Dinh and the sea. At km 155 they came under attack and landed two commando units at Cua Balat in order to clean out the resistance. Twenty of the enemy were killed and three French wounded. Also that day, in the area around Yours Lang, the *Framee* (ex *105*), and an accompanying LCT were ambushed. The LCT took five hits from a 57mm recoilless rifle and had several men injured. *Framee* (ex *105*) drove off the attackers with her mortars.

During the second half of the month the French launched four operations, *Galere, Gondola II, Fregate* and *Rocambeau. Pertuisane* (ex *28*) participated in *Operation Galere* on 16 May. Along with an LCT, they disembarked a commando unit near Ha Tray. Enemy losses were one dead, ten suspects arrested, arms and documents seized and ten large junks destroyed.

Operation Gondola II took place on 17 May. *Pertuisane* (ex *28*) was escorting a convoy to resupply the garrison at Phat Diem. Their landing was unopposed, with the LSSL standing by for fire support, and the return was relatively uneventful. The *Pertuisane* (ex *28*) frequently raked the shoreline where suspected enemy ambushes were likely. By the time the convoy had returned, two *Viet Minh* had been killed and ten suspects arrested.

On 19 May the French launched *Operation Fregate. Pertuisane* (ex *28*) and *Intrepide* escorted commando units to the mouth of the Lach Yapp, south of the estuary of the river at Thanh Hoa. Both ships supplied heavy firepower and the commando units landed. Thirty-four enemy soldiers were killed and ten taken prisoner. Seventy mines and other armaments were captured and the French suffered only three wounded. *Javeline* (ex *10*) was escorting an important river group on 21 May near Hung Yen when the convoy came under fire. A *Grumman Goose* flew over and identified the enemy position and the ships opened fire, killing some of the enemy. After landing and investigating, the troops found a tunnel complex in which the *Viet Minh* had hidden.

In *Operation Rocambeau* on 22 May, the *Pertuisane* (ex *28*) escorted the commando units *Marinade*, *Tempete* and *Senee* in an attack on a company of *Viet Minh* at Thanh Hoa and Cape Rond. A secondary objective was the evacuation of the village of Do Xuyen and the destruction of enemy depots. Troops were landed at 1300 and within three hours had accomplished their mission. The *Viet Minh* had given away their positions by a mortar attack on one of the LCTs and drawn heavy return fire. Sixty-six of the enemy were killed and 17 taken prisoner. Ten junks of 20 tons each were captured, and a blockhouse destroyed along with 30 mines. French losses were light (*Chroniques* July 1954 940-942).

The area near Hai Yen had come under strong attack in the early part of June, and the French decided to evacuate their outpost near the west entrance of the Bamboo Canal. Two *dinassauts* were engaged in the operation on 8 and 9 June, with the *Hallebarde* (ex *9*) providing fire support. Overhead, *Corsairs* attacked the two battalions of *Viet Minh* engaged in the fighting. Exiting the canal was difficult, with continued ambushes along the way. One of the French river craft was set afire and had to be towed out. Fortunately, the combined firepower of the LSSL and air support by the *Corsairs* enabled the convoy to escape with light injuries. *Viet Minh* losses were estimated at over 500 (*Chroniques* June 1954 1072-1073).

In spite of many successful missions, French control of the region was slowly being diminished by the successes of the *Viet Minh*. Development of a Vietnamese Army and Navy to assist the French efforts was deemed necessary, and the first plans had been agreed upon in 1952. On 10 April, 1953, the first Vietnamese naval unit was placed on active duty. It was assigned to patrol the rivers and harbors and was considered to be part of the *dinassaut*. By 1954 the plans had been modified to include three river assault groups. Among these units were four LSSLs. Ultimately, by 1958, there would be four *dinassauts*, including two additional LSSLs, and by 1960, six *dinassauts*.

French plans for the new Vietnamese Navy, however, would not reach fruition under her direction. Her defeat at Dien Bien Phu on 7 May, 1954 foretold the end of the French Empire in Southeast Asia. From that point on, the *Viet Minh* increased their attacks on the Red River Delta area. Roads between the outposts were mined daily, with the French obliged to spend much of their time digging up the mines only to have them replaced the next night. Increasing use of the river forces was necessary, but with the growing *Viet Minh* strength, only the most heavily armed convoys stood a chance of getting through unscathed. Recognizing the imminent assault on the delta area, the French drew up plans for the contraction of their area of control. The last bastion was to be at Haiphong, where naval gunfire might assist in holding on to the city. Vietnamese Army forces continued to fight on in the other areas of the Red River Delta.

With the signing of the Geneva Accords, the French began to evacuate the north. Along with the French, hundreds of thousands of Vietnamese decided to leave the area and relocate to South Vietnam. French ships, formerly used for convoy and river patrols, stopped at various villages throughout the delta, picking up refugees and transferring them to larger ships for the journey south. *Pertuisane* (ex *28*), along with *LSIL 9035* and *LSM 9015*, spent the second half of October, 1954 collecting and escorting refugees. In a public statement on 2 December, 1954, French Minister Guy la Chambre indicated that by 20 October the total number of refugees escorted south was 373,304, with 122,459 transported by air and 250,845 transported by sea (*Chroniques* Jan. 1955 108).

As her role in Vietnam ended, France began the transfer of LSSLs and other ships to the Vietnamese Navy. The first transfer took place in Saigon on 12 October, 1954. *Arbalete* (ex *2*) was officially transferred to the Vietnamese Navy and renamed *No Than HQ 225* (*Magical Arbalete*). Since LSSLs were new to the Vietnamese, the officers and 25 of the crew were French and acted in the role of instructors. Thirty Vietnamese sailors formed the remaining part of the crew and the ship served as a training vessel for them. Although it was nominally assigned to the Vietnamese Navy, actual control of the *No Than HQ 225* (ex *2*) remained in French hands. By the end of 1955, the ship was deemed unseaworthy and taken out of service. It was transferred to Taiwan for parts in 1957.

Arquebuse (ex *4*) was transferred in 1955 and renamed the *Linh Kiem HQ 226* (*Sacred Sword*). It was the practice at that time to name navy ships after ancient battles or weapons. The names assigned to the two LSSLs were the names of weapons used by ancient kings and thus reflective of Vietnamese history. LSSLs transferred after that were named after Vietnamese naval officers who had died in battle. In 1970, both the *No Than* and *Linh Kiem* received name changes to make them consistent with other ships in the class. Thus the *No Than* became the *Nguyen Van Tru* and the *Lien Kiem* became the *Le Trong Dam*.

The last LSSL to carry the French flag was the *Framee* (ex *105*), which had arrived in 1953. It was officially transferred to Vietnam in March, 1956, and given the name and number previously assigned to the *Arbalete* (ex *2*), which was *No Than HQ 225*. Two others, the *Etendard* (ex *35*) and the *Oriflamme* (ex *65*) were transferred to Greece in 1957 and 1958. *Rapiere* (ex *80*) was returned to the United States in 1955 and then transferred to Japan. In 1956 *Hallebarde* (ex *9*) and *Javeline* (ex *10*) were returned to the United States. *Pertuisane* (ex *28*) was transferred to Taiwan in 1957. Its condition did not warrant re-commissioning, and it was used for parts by the Taiwanese who already had three of the vessels in commission, the *Lien Yung* (ex *56*), *Lien Chin* (ex *81*) and *Lien Jen* (ex *95*).

From their arrival in late 1950 until the transfer of *Framee* (ex *105*) in 1957, the LSSLs engaged in numerous assaults against the Communists under the French flag. Their role in the struggle firmly established, the LSSLs continued their service under the Vietnamese flag.

As they reviewed their practices and efforts in the war against the *Viet Minh*, the French surveyed their ships. They noted the advantages and disadvantages of the LSSLs for use in Indochina. As assets they noted the excellent effect of the twin 40s and the 76mm guns. The high conning tower received applause and condemnation. It gave the watch on the ships the ability to see over the river banks and spot the enemy. However, it was too high to pass under many of the low bridges. The ships were vulnerable to massed mortar attack. In addition, their extreme draft of six-and-one-half feet made it impossible for them to get into some of the smaller streams. Machine gun stations were not adequately protected, causing the wounding and death of many of the gunners (Michel Vol. V 363). It was, however, considered superior to the LSIL (LCI) in that it had heavier firepower and was of more recent construction. Although it could not carry as many troops as the LSIL, it was still considered more useful, particularly since it had the dual role of river and sea patrol. The single proposal for change on the LSSL was that it should be equipped with protective shielding around the 76mm gun so that the gunners working there would not be such easy targets. In all, both LSSLs and the LCIs were considered to be well-adapted to the type of warfare that the French had conducted (Michel Vol V 393).

With the consolidation of power in the north by the *Viet Minh*, activities for the newly formed Vietnamese Navy centered on the Mekong River Delta area. Units that had been supporting the French in the Red River Delta were transferred south to the Mekong where they were joined to the existing River Assault Groups (RAGs).

The new Vietnamese Navy had a great deal of pride, particularly in their LSSL ships. Captain Kiem Do, former Deputy Chief of Staff for Operations, recalls, "LSSLs were the first real combat ships transferred to our navy. They were our pride. Their firepower was formidable in close combat. A terror for the VC in the 50s . . . Their firepower and their mobility were very much appreciated at a time where the VN Air Force's capability was still limited and divisional artillery rarely available to provide support to small scale clearing operations at remote areas" (Do letter 19 June, 1998).

TRANSFERS OF SHIPS FROM FRANCE AND U.S. TO VIETNAM

U.S. LSSL Number	French Name	Vietnamese Name
2	*Arbalete*	*No Than HQ 225* — taken out of service in 1956 and sold to Taiwan for scrap in 1957 — the name and number was then assigned to the newly transferred *Framee* (ex *105*)
4	*Arquebuse*	*Linh Kiem HQ 226* — renamed *Le Trong Dam* in 1970
9	*Hallebarde*	*Doan Ngoc Tang HQ228*
10	*Javeline*	*Le Van Binh HQ 227*
96	-	*Nguyen Ngoc Long HQ 230*
101	-	*Luu Phu Tho HQ 229*
105	*Framee*	Transferred to VN in March, 1956 and named *No Than HQ 225* — renamed *Nguyen Van Tru* in 1970
129	-	*Nguyen Duc Bong HQ 231*

Vietnam's Navy had three basic components. The first was a shore-based division for overall control of the ships and their assignments, as well as general headquarters duties, training and command duties and administration of the bases. A second division was the Sea Force, which was primarily concerned with coastal patrol, interdiction of enemy supplies and troop movements and minesweeping. A third division focused on the river patrols and included the *dinassauts* and their LSSL command ships.

By the summer of 1955, the Vietnamese Navy was heavily engaged in operations in the Mekong Delta. From 5 June to 19 June, 1955, *Dinassauts 22, 23* and *25* were in action against units of the Hoa Hao near Can Tho. Within the first day of action, the enemy's headquarters and two of their battalions had been captured. On 7 June, the three *dinassauts* staged an action on the Bassac River near Tra On, 20 miles south of Can Tho. There they landed a force of 2,000 troops, capturing six enemy patrol boats and two LCMs. During these operations, the *No Than HQ 225* (ex *2*) served as the command ship for the Vietnamese forces. Intense action followed for the next twelve days as the Vietnamese Navy *dinassauts* continued to pound at the forces of the Hoa Hao leader, Ba Cut. By the end of the operation the 3,500 men under him had been driven from the area.

The Mekong Delta continued to be problematical for the Vietnamese and in

December, 1955 regular patrols were set up on the Mekong River from its mouth to the Cambodian border. Additional coastal patrols covered the area from Ha Tien to Cape Vung Tau. Assigned to patrol the coast from Saigon to Cape Bai Bung, was the *No Than HQ 225* (ex *2*).

Operating out of Danang and later in the south, LSSLs participated in the interdiction of Communist shipping. On 6 November, 1956, an LSSL, accompanied by six other patrol and amphibious ships, sailed from Cape Vung Tau in exercises designed to demonstrate their presence. Relations between Cambodia and Vietnam deteriorated in the mid-1950s, and from 29 May to 5 June, 1957, the Vietnamese conducted maneuvers in the Gulf of Siam. These operations were designed to protect the fishing fleets which were being harassed by the Cambodians and involved the use of LSSLs.

Nguyen Ngoc Long HQ 230 (ex 96) on the Go Cong River, November, 1967. Changes to the ship are in evidence here, including the newly mounted 76mm forward gun and the armor around the gun mounts. Photo courtesy of the National Archives.

The Vietnamese Navy continued to grow in size and strength, from 1,900 in 1955 to 3,500 by 1960, with six River Assault Groups (RAGs) including about 1,900 officers and men. Primarily under the command of the Army, they did not have their own assault troops but relied on Army units. The Sea Force operated without such interference but frequently fell victim to political maneuvering, which placed it in a subordinate position to the Army. American aid and support continued, and the Vietnamese Navy grew to 6,200 officers and men by 1963. Under its control, at that time, were 258 vessels, including patrol ships, river craft, and an assortment of amphibious craft. By 1972, the total manpower of the South Vietnamese Navy was over 47,000. The Fleet Command was organized into five divisions and had nearly 1,600 ships and craft in its force.

Division	Types of Ships
Sea Patrol	PC, PCE
Inshore Patrol	PGM
River Patrol	LSSL, LSIL
Logistics Lift	LST, LSM, LCM, AKL, YOG
Minecraft	MSC, MLMS, UDT

Nguyen Duc Bong HQ 231 (ex *LSSL 129*) **on the Bassac River south of Saigon, circa late 1960s. In evidence here is the protective screening arond the conning tower, designed to protect the ship from B-40 rockets. Photo courtesy of the U.S. Navy Historical Center.**

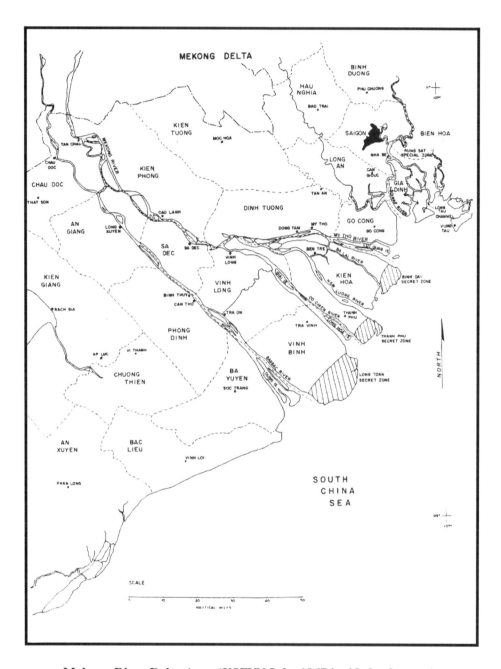

Mekong River Delta Area (*USFVN* July, 1967 inside back cover).

Increasing American involvement in the Vietnamese war led to additional transfers of LSSLs to the Saigon government. A number of the ships had originally been loaned to Japan but were no longer needed there and had been returned to the United States. In 1965 and 1966, the Americans transferred five LSSLs to the Vietnamese. Newly named for Vietnamese officers who had given their lives in the fight against the Communists, they were the *Doan Ngoc Tang* (ex *9*) and *Le Van Binh* (ex *10*) which were transferred on 15 September, 1965, the *Luu Phu Tho* (ex *101*) transferred on 2 October, 1965, and the *Nguyen Ngoc Long* (ex *96*) which was transferred on 8 December, 1965. The following year, the *Nguyen Duc Bong* (ex *129*) was transferred on 19 February, 1966. French influence had waned by this time, and units formerly referred to by the old French designation *dinassaut*, were renamed RAGs or River Assault Groups.

Linh Kiem HQ 226 (ex *4*) was assigned to the Vietnamese Navy Sea Force. One of the missions of this division was patrol of the river system and support of RAG operations. From 4 to 5 October, 1965, the *Linh Kiem* (ex *4*) came into some heavy action and demonstrated her value in river warfare. RAG 23 was preparing to land the 41st Vietnamese Ranger Battalion near Ben Tre on the Ham Luong River in Kien Hoa Province. Their mission was to seek out and destroy a Viet Cong unit that had been operating in the area. *Linh Kiem* (ex *4*), along with another LSSL, was escorting the convoy toward its destination and was in the rear guard position. The lead LSSL noticed movement on shore and fired into what it suspected was an enemy position. Unfortunately, the convoy had steamed into an ambush. Enemy forces held both banks, and with automatic weapons and recoilless rifles, managed to heavily damage two of the LCMs in the convoy. Both had to be beached to save them and the LSSLs turned their full firepower on the enemy to keep them at bay. *Linh Kiem* (ex *4*) and her sister ship were instrumental in driving off the enemy (Croizat 101).

The city of Saigon is located inland on the Saigon River. Ships heading up the river from the sea had to pass through a region known as the Rung Sat. Heavily wooded with mangrove trees and difficult to traverse, the region became a stronghold for the Viet Cong who made every attempt to interfere with shipping. In 1964 this area was so dangerous that it became a special assignment for the Vietnamese Navy.

Constant patrols by the RAGs were necessary to keep the shipping lanes open, and LSSLs were frequently at work there and in the Fourth Riverine Area. Since Viet Cong infiltration was significant, the duty was extremely hazardous. Although fire from the river banks was always a peril, the greatest danger to the LSSLs came from enemy swimmers and the mines that they planted. At 0231, on the morning of 2 October, 1966, the *Le Van Binh HQ 227* (ex *10*) was anchored about 800 yards west of the VNN RAG base at My Tho, when she became the victim of sabotage. Two large explosions were heard, and the ship began to settle to the bottom. Fortunately the water was not deep and she came to rest on the bottom with her decks barely clear of the water. Her crew quickly began to pump her out and were able to patch her up and refloat her.

Lt. Commander Tran Van Triet, Commanding Officer of the Vietnamese Navy's 27th River Assault Group, took charge of the rescue. With Tran as the convoy commander, *HQ 227* was towed back to Saigon by *LCM 8*, where she was surveyed. Damage to her was so severe that she was not salvageable and was decommissioned. The Viet Cong saboteur had disguised himself as a member of the Vietnamese Popular Forces and was a passenger on board. At the appropriate time, he apparently slipped over the side and assisted in the planting of the mines.

Viet Cong swimmers were a constant hazard in the Mekong Delta rivers. Under cover of darkness one would swim downstream to an anchored ship towing a mine with a timing device. He would attached the mine to the ship's anchor cable and both the swimmer and the mine were then carried downstream by the current. After a few minutes the mine exploded. Presumably, the swimmer had cleared the area and would live to fight again. Since LSSL ships anchored by the stern, the damage to them from mines was in their aft sections.

On occasion the LSSL ships were put to work at unusual tasks. In December of 1966, the Commanding Officer of *Luu Phu Tho HQ 229* (ex *101*) received an unusual request. The District Chief, a friend of his, was desperate to get supplies to an outpost which was under Viet Cong pressure. This was not an approved use for the ship, but he gave in to the request in order to help alleviate the situation. Since the outpost was cut off, re-supply by the river was the only possibility. The outpost was in need of animals to build their stock, and so it was decided to transport one ox and four cows on board the LSSL. Unfortunately, the ship hit some rough weather and two of the animals suffered broken legs, but the livestock did get delivered, albeit somewhat the worse for the voyage. When news of the event leaked out, the Commanding Officer was given a court martial for illegal transportation of livestock. The court martial was subsequently dismissed and the CO received a light punishment.

In combat, errors in communications are not uncommon, and sometimes they are costly. During February of 1967, the *Nguyen Duc Bong HQ 231* (ex *129*) was assigned to the 4th River Force Command at Can Tho. The following month she was ordered to support an assault by the 7th Army Division on the Ham Luong river. Arriving at the site of the operation about 0530, her Commanding Officer discovered that the assault had been canceled, but he had not been notified. Within minutes the ship was under attack in a Viet Cong ambush, which extended for a half mile along the river bank. The Commanding Officer, Lt. Sinh The Nguyen, found himself in a difficult position. A combination of low tide, swift currents, and high riverbanks gave a decided advantage to the enemy, who attacked the *HQ 231* (ex *129*)with mortars and recoilless rifles. The tried and true strategy of beaching the vessel and fighting it out was not workable, due to the terrain. Using her full firepower, the ship withdrew from the area, but it was costly. Nguyen was wounded and his Executive Officer, the American advisor, and 27 crewmen were killed. The ship made it back to Saigon under its own power, was repaired and put back into action (S. Nguyen letter 2 June, 1998).

LSSL ships saw a great deal of action in 1967. Much of this had to do with protecting nearly 1,000 isolated Popular Force outposts that were scattered throughout the delta region. Manned by local forces, they were designed to give the impression that the Saigon government had more control than it actually did. LSSLs frequently acted as escorts for supply convoys. One such operation occurred on 4 June, 1967, 18 miles south of Vinh Long. A Popular Force outpost at Duc My was under attack by a platoon of Viet Cong and the *Doan Ngoc Tang HQ* 228 (ex *9*) came to its aid. The fire support of the ship was considered the major factor in repelling the enemy. A couple of weeks later, on 17 June, the gunboat, assisted by two PBRs, helped fight off two platoons of Viet Cong which were attacking the outpost at nearby Lo Xe. Ten days later, on 27 June, the same LSSL, along with eight PBRs, intercepted 102 junks and found one that belonged to the enemy. It was promptly sunk and one Viet Cong was killed in the operation (USNFVN Supplement June, 1967 28). The remainder of the year was filled with similar operations involving the LSSL ships.

The first half of 1968 was an extremely busy time for the *Linh Kiem HQ 226* (ex *4*). Under the command of Lt. Le Van Rang, the ship continually supported allied actions against the Viet Cong in the Mekong Delta. Among them was the defense of Saigon on 31 January, after the New Year's truce was canceled. A few days later, from 3 to 5 February, the ship saw a great deal of night action on the Co Chien River, east of Vinh Long. Enemy units were attempting to surround the city and the ship maneuvered continually under difficult conditions, firing on the Viet Cong and thwarting their attempts to gain a foothold. Much of the *Linh Kiem's* activities were related to the defense of isolated government outposts on the branches of the Mekong. On 2 March, 1967, the ship was ambushed while providing support for an outpost in the Binh Minh District. Rang's Executive Officer and one crewman were wounded, but the ship continued firing on the enemy and drove them off. From the end of January to the beginning of March, the ship participated in over 36 gunfire support missions with Rang in command. For his efforts under fire, he was awarded the Bronze Star with Combat V by the President of the United States (Rang letter 8 July, 1998).

On 6 May, 1968, the *Linh Kiem HQ 226* (ex *4*) was steaming on the Co Chien River six miles east of Vinh Long when she was ambushed by the Viet Cong, who fired on her from both banks of the river. The ship sustained only minor damage, but five of her crew were wounded. Still another attack occurred a few days later on 10 May, when the *Luu Phu Tho HQ 229* (ex *101*), under the command of Lt. Trong Luu Vo, was ambushed five miles north of Vinh Long on the My Tho River. Her pilot house was damaged and she was forced to use her emergency steering to get back to her base. Seven of her crew were wounded in the attack (*USNFVN Supplement* May, 1968 116).

Such ambushes were frequent and usually caused casualties for the LSSL ships. Part of the problem was that many ships simply returned fire and then cruised out of range. As a result, the Viet Cong were encouraged to attack them, since there was usually little loss on their side. Some of the commanding officers realized that this was a poor strategy.

In May of 1968, Lt. Ngoc Nguyen took command of the *No Than HQ 225* (ex *105*). Realizing that the old strategy was not working, he instituted new procedures on his ship. In many cases, the crews were not in combat readiness at all times, so he made sure that they were each time they departed their anchorage. While other ships shot and ran, he followed the French tactic of beaching the ship and firing back. He had picked up this idea from older veterans of the service who had served with the French. With its superior firepower, the LSSL was easily able to drive off the enemy without incurring serious losses. Within a short time, the *No Than* was not subject to ambush as were the other LSSLs and LSILs.

On 16 February, 1969, the *No Than HQ 225* (ex *105*), under the command of Lt. Ngoc Nguyen, was returning to Vinh Long after a night patrol on the Co Chien River. About 0330, as they approached the district headquarters, the Captain was informed that it was under attack by the Viet Cong. The ship dropped anchor in mid-river and supported the shore base with fire from its 76mm gun. Within one hour, the Viet Cong had withdrawn. The headquarters command informed Lt. Nguyen that his efforts had resulted in the deaths of 25 of the enemy (N. Nguyen letter 26 May, 1998).

On 28 November, 1969, the *No Than*, now under the command of Lt. Ba The Duong, responded to a Viet Cong ambush at Tam Giang, Dam Doi while on patrol. Under attack by 57mm recoilless rifles and machine guns, the ship beached and concentrated her firepower on the enemy. Within a half hour, the Viet Cong had been driven off (N. Nguyen E-mail 26 May, 1998).

Improvements in tactics in the late 1960s made the work of the LSSLs more effective. On 25 February, 1970, the *Doan Ngoc Tang HQ 228* (ex *9*) was transiting toward the mouth of the Do De River (WQ 16367) when the ship came under B-40 and automatic weapons fire. The enemy fire was immediately returned and within two minutes, two Black Pony aircraft were overhead, followed shortly thereafter by USN Seawolves. After the OV-10s had placed strikes into the area and the LSSL had ceased her direct fire a Kit Carson Scout reaction team was inserted by USN PCFs 17 and 36 (*USNFVN* February, 1970 119-120).

These new tactics gradually caused the decline of the LSSLs in attack operations as their role increasingly was taken over by helicopter gun ships and other aircraft.

Throughout the 1960s, the LSSLs were frequently used in river assaults, for convoy patrol and the interdiction of Viet Cong sampans. However, as time wore on, the situation began to change and with it the role of the ships. Increases in the heavy weaponry of the Viet Cong made the river patrols more hazardous, and with frequent attacks by recoilless rifles, rockets and mines, the LSSLs and their companion craft had their hands full. Where once they were the most important element in the assault landings, they now found that many such troop movements involved the use of helicopters and that the role of the LSSLs had changed. Increasingly, they became used as fire support for convoys going up and down the rivers carrying supplies.

As the war in Vietnam progressed, it spread across the borders into Laos and Cambodia. Prince Norodom Sihanouk, unable to drive the Viet Cong from their sanctuaries in his country, gave up his leadership of Cambodia in July of 1969. He was replaced by Lon Nol. In an attempt to assist the new and friendly Cambodian government, the United States and Vietnam launched attacks on the Viet Cong enclaves in Cambodia. Part of this effort involved convoys of munitions and other supplies from Saigon to Phnom Penh.

One of the tragic side effects of the war on the Vietnam-Cambodian border was the displacement of many Vietnamese, who fled from the fighting and took up residence in the southern part of Cambodia. Ethnically different from the Khmers, they subsequently became the victims of persecution. With this newly developed situation, the river runs to Phnom Penh, Cambodia became increasingly urgent. In June of 1970, the *No Than HQ 225* (ex *105*), was assigned to support operations between Phnom Penh and Neak Luong, Cambodia. Cambodian communists had begun killing Vietnamese civilians living in their country. Lt. Quyen Ngoc Nguyen, Commanding Officer of the *No Than* at that time, recalls "seeing many dead bodies floating on the surface of the river, with their backs up and their hands and feet tied" (E-mail 17 June, 1998).

The Vietnamese Navy docks at Phnom Penh, Cambodia in June of 1970. *Linh Kiem HQ 226* **(ex** *4***) is at dockside while** *No Than HQ 225* **(ex** *105***) stands by. Both ships were sunk by enemy mines within a few months. Army Signal Corps Photo courtesy of the National Archives.**

Shortly after that assignment ended, the *No Than HQ 225* (ex *105*) was assigned to the Seafloat base at Nam Can. This was a joint effort of the U.S. and Vietnamese forces. A large island consisting of pontoons was constructed in the middle of the river and anchored to the river bottom. Moored to this island were numerous small gunboats and supply vessels. Their purpose was to interdict and disrupt Viet Cong water traffic deep within its territory. It was a hazardous undertaking, since the entire area was under enemy control. Regular canine patrols and sensors were used to indicate enemy presence on the river banks and pre-empt attacks.

Viet Cong frogmen continued to be a hazard. In order to keep them at bay, MK 3 grenades were thrown into the water around the ships every few minutes. Unfortunately for the *No Than*, the supply was limited, which may have led to her sinking. Early in the morning of 30 July, 1970, the *No Than* was tied up at the Nam Can naval base on the Bo De River. Around 0200, a large explosion blew a hole aft in her starboard side. The ship began taking on water rapidly. Lt. Quyen Ngoc

Nguyen, Commanding Officer, recalls, "I sent the order to abandon the ship after seeing the water flood 1/3 of the ship in only a few minutes. I was very sad about the number of crewmen who died because they went down into the ship to save some personal property" (Q. N. Nguyen letter 17 June, 1998). Within minutes she had gone to the bottom with only ten feet of her bow above water. Rescue teams from the Seafloat worked feverishly, pulling many crewmen to safety. Efforts to raise the ship were not considered, as the area was too dangerous and the current too swift. Seventeen of her crew were reported missing and presumed killed in the attack. Subsequent investigations revealed a length of nylon line attached to her mooring cable, an indication that she was the victim of a mine planted by a Viet Cong swimmer (USNFVN July, 1970 7).

Linh Kiem HQ 226 (ex *4*) was also sunk by a mine at 0520 on 3 October, 1970. She was anchored in the Co Chien River when a Viet Cong frogman from Con Giai Island swam downstream to her and attached a mine to her mooring cable. The ensuing explosion blew a hole in her aft port side, wounding two of her crew and sending the ship to the bottom in eight meters of water. No attempts were made to salvage her (USNFVN October, 1970 35).

From the early 1970s through 1975, the ships were primarily used to escort convoys up the Mekong to Tan Chau, a Vietnamese city on the border with Cambodia. As noted above, it soon became necessary for the LSSLs to go further upriver, as far as Neak Luong and Phnom Penh, Cambodia. It was on these runs that the ships suffered their heaviest casualties, as they were usually cruising through enemy-held territory. LSSLs, designed during World War II, had begun to outlive their usefulness. With their 14 knot top speed, they had difficulty making much headway upstream during the dry seasons, when the rivers were narrower and the current swifter. In areas where the communists controlled the riverbanks, they were too slow to escape attack. Smaller, faster craft, that had been developed for the American brown-water navy, began to replace them. One factor that spared them was the communists' practice of focusing their firepower on the freighters, tugs, and cargo barges. If a tug were put out of commission, the barge and its supplies would be lost (Do E-mail 19 June, 1998).

In January of 1971, the first war-related supply convoy reached the capital at Phnom Penh. These convoys carried food and munitions up the Mekong River as part of the program of the Cambodian Relief Tripartite Commission and required the use of escort vessels like the LSSLs. The ships were frequently under attack and in 1974, two LSILs were sunk (Do 196). River supply of the Cambodian government continued until its fall in April of 1975.

By the beginning of that year, continued Khmer Rouge advances had left the capitol isolated and placed them in control of the countryside. From the Vietnamese border up to Neak Luong, the communists held the riverbanks and were able to block-ade the convoys. This was a crucial blow for the Khmer government. With their over-land highways cut off by the communists, fully ninety percent of their supplies had to come in by river convoy. On 30 January, 1975, the last supply ship made it to Phnom Penh. The cities of Neak Luong and Phnom Penh, cut off from their river supplies and totally isolated, fell in April, placing the Khmer Rouge in power.

As the spring of 1975 approached, the situation in South Vietnam became grim; the collapse of the government was only a matter of time. Captain Kiem Do, Deputy Chief of Staff for Operations, was contacted by his American counterpart, Richard Armitage on 25 April, 1975. Fearful that the Vietnamese Navy would fall into the hands of the communists, they had devised a plan for the evacuation of the Navy and its personnel, the E-Plan. Concerns were voiced that too much activity on the part of the ships might lead to panic and disorder, so the preparations had to be carried out in secret. Plans for the evacuation involved keeping the seaworthy ships as close to the base as possible and repairing those that might be used in the escape (Do 194-195).

At 1800 hours on 29 April, 1975, as the South Vietnamese government was in its last hours, E-Plan was activated (Do 199). Although there were numerous ships and craft in the South Vietnamese Navy, many were not capable of making the voyage across the sea to the Philippines, Guam or other friendly ports. A number of them were river or coastal craft with limited ranges and still others were not seaworthy and in need of repair. At total of 37 ships, carrying 30,000 Vietnamese, made it out of the country and arrived in the Philippines.

The ensuing debacle attendant with the demise of the Vietnamese government made a strict accounting of naval vessels difficult, if not impossible. Ships left behind fell into the hands of the North Vietnamese. At first it was thought that some of the LSSLs had been captured by the enemy, however, they had managed to escape. Heavily laden with refugees, the former *LSSLs 9, 96, 101* and *129* made their way to the Philippines. Shortly after their arrival, they were transferred to the government of the Philippines and remained on the official navy lists there until they were deleted in the 1980s. Only the *9, 96* and the *129* were operational, the *101* was suitable only for parts.

The Vietnamese Navy operated its LSSLs for 20 years in battle against a difficult enemy. Although the Saigon government eventually fell, their navy men had upheld a long-standing tradition. At the end, they had not surrendered their ships, but had taken them *en masse* out of the country. Their heroic exploits were many and in the end they brought honor and credit to the ranks of the LSSL sailors. LSSLs had gone down in combat in WWII and Vietnam, but none had ever been taken by the enemy.

Doan Ngoc Tang (ex *LSSL 9*), under the command of Lt. Hong Vo Duong, arrives at Subic Bay, Philippine Islands with refugees, 5 May, 1975. A small boat with Vietnamese refugees is tied up in the foreground. Photo courtesy of the National Archives.

PHILIPPINES

LSSL ships had seen their first action in the Philippines, the waters were familiar to them. During the 1970s, the Philippine government acquired seven of the vessels from the United States. Included in their number were the four ships which had escaped from Vietnam in 1975 and had been transferred to the Philippine government. That same year, *LSSLs 68, 87* and *88* were transferred from Japan to be used for parts. Although they had a total of seven ships, only three of them were operational. *LSSL 9* was recommissioned as the *La Union*, the *96* became the *Sulu* and the *129* was christened the *Camarines Sur*. They were used in the campaign against piracy, smuggling, and the secessionist movement in southern Philippines (Tunacao letter 4 August, 1993). Gradually the ships were stricken from the Philippine naval register and sold as scrap. The last of them was decommissioned on 22 July, 1986.

RYUKYUS

Immediately after the war, the United States government found itself in the position of administering a number of overseas areas that had been captured during the war. Although the main effort in the Far East was aimed at control of Japan proper, the island of Okinawa was also under American domination. In order to bring some order to the area, the United States placed five of the LSSLs in the service of the Ryukyuan Coast Guard. *LSSLs 54, 56, 81, 95* and *105* began their service in February, 1952 and most served until 1954 before they were transferred to other countries. Number *54* was transferred to Korea in October, 1952 and the *105* was transferred to France for use in Indochina in December, 1953

JAPAN

It seem ironic that a ship destined to fight the Japanese should eventually see service in their Navy. Over the years, a number of United States Navy veterans have voiced their disapproval of the transfer to and use by Japan of the ships that had been theirs. That was the case with the LCS(L)s. Japan was the recipient of more of the vessels than any other nation, with a total of 53 eventually serving in her Maritime Self-Defense Force. Designated as the *Yuri* class, which translates as *Lily*, the ships were named after various flowers.

At the end of the war, several problems had to be solved. First and foremost was the danger posed by thousands of mines surrounding the home islands of Japan and a number of other areas in the western Pacific. LCS(L)s and other ships spent the last part of their time in that area engaged in the process of clearing mines from the sea lanes. This was a hazardous duty, and during the war, many American ships had been damaged in the attempt to clear them. In order to save American lives, a few elements of the former Imperial Japanese Navy were allowed to remain on active duty in order to fulfill this mission. The task was difficult and required a great deal of caution and time. Between the end of the war and 1952, the Japanese minesweeping details cleared "937 influence mines . . . at a cost of 19 ships sunk and 77 lives lost"(Auer 52). With this type of duty, the precedent was set for allowing the Japanese a certain amount of naval activity.

Within a short time, the Korean War broke out, and with it came increasing demands on the United States Navy ships in the western Pacific. Many of these vessels had been engaged in patrolling in the Far East and were needed in the war effort. In order to maintain coastal security around the Japanese islands, the

Congress of the United States determined that it would be more feasible to have the Japanese bear some of the responsibility. This would allow the United States Navy to focus its activities on the Korean peninsula.

The Mutual Security Act had been passed by the United States. However, Japan did not qualify for assistance under that legislation. Both the United States and Japanese governments passed the Charter Party Agreement which went into effect on 27 December, 1952. It authorized the loan of Patrol Frigates and LCS(L)s to Japan for a five-year period and could be renewed for an additional five years. Accordingly, the first ships were transferred to Japan at Yokosuka on 14 January, 1953. Others quickly followed, and by the end of the year, a number of LCS(L)s had been sent to Japan. By the middle of the decade there were 53 listed in service.

Although the ships had been moth-balled at the end of the war, many were not in good shape. Typical of the problems were those identified by J.H. Sims, Commanding Officer of the *LSSL 67*. Sims was ordered to take command of the newly re-commissioned *67* early in 1952. The first stop was at Charleston Naval Shipyard in South Carolina where a number of problems with the ship were addressed. On 6 March, 1952 the ship sailed for its eventual destination at Yokosuka, Japan. It arrived there on 9 July, 1952 after stops at a number of ports. Repairs to the ship and its equipment were undertaken at Mt. Hope Shipyard in Coco Solo, Canal Zone, Long Beach Naval Shipyard in California and Pearl Harbor Naval Shipyard in Hawaii. In his report dated 16 July, 1952, Sims listed six pages of deficiencies, including leaking rudder posts, dirty fuel tanks, defective engine gears, and jammed and inoperable guns (OIC *LSSL 67* 16Jul52). The expense attendant in refurbishing the LSSL ships appears to have been significant.

As the decade progressed, their need for the ships had ended and Japan began to return some of them. Between 1958 and 1959, a total of 27 were returned. The ships, which had originally been assigned under the Charter Party Agreement in 1952, had all been reassigned under the U.S -Japan Mutual Defense Assistance Agreement of 1954. Between 1965 and 1970 an additional nine ships were returned, and from 1971 to 1977, the rest were remanded to U.S. custody (*Kaijo Jietai* 186). Many of them were in poor condition and the U.S. used them for target practice. A number were sunk in an area about 80 miles south-southeast of Tokyo. Among the ships sunk were the *12, 13, 18, 20, 25, 52, 57, 67, 98, 100, 109, 119* and *130*. In 1958, one ship, the *Hamagiku* (ex *87*), was refitted as a drone target carrier. She was the last LCS(L) used by Japan and remained a part of the Japanese Maritime Self-Defense Forces until she was returned to the U.S. in 1975.

Transfer of LSSLs and PFs in Yokosuka on 14 January, 1953. At the top (not in order) are *LSSLs 57* (*Kiku*), *104* (*Ran*), *107* (*Yuri*) and *130* (*Hagi*). Within the next few years Japan would receive an additional 49 of the ships. Photo courtesy of the National Archives.

LSSL fleet at Yokosuka late in 1953. The ships had not fared well during their period of storage and most of their gear had to be replaced. Photo courtesy of Jack Jewell.

KOREA

Prior to the outbreak of the Korean War, the United States had already begun to bolster its allies throughout the Far East. Korea had been the recipient of some 30 ships, and among them were several of the LSSLs: *54* (*Po Song Man*), *77* (*Yung Huang Man*), *86* (*Yong Il Man*) and *91* (*Kang Hwa Man*). The *77* and the *91* were transferred to her on 24 January, 1952 and the *54* and *86* towards the end of the year. Primarily used as gunboats, they were carried on the lists of the South Korean Navy until they were no longer of use. Both the *77* and the *91* were decommissioned on 15 November, 1960 and the *54* and the *86* on 31 October, 1962.

Transfer of LSSL ships to the Republic of Korea at Astoria, Oregon on 24 January, 1952. *LSSLs 77* **and** *91* **are in front and** *PCs 485* **and** *600* **are in back. Photo courtesy of the National Archives.**

GREECE

Greece joined NATO in 1952 and was also assisted by the transfer of two of the former LCS(L)s, number *35* (*Plotarkhis Ulachavas*) and *65* (*Plotarkhis Maridakis*). Received by transfer under the Foreign Military Sales arrangement, the *35* was delivered on 12 August, 1957 and the *65* in June of 1958. They were used as gunboats and for patrol duty until they were scrapped in 1976.

TAIWAN

Communist expansion throughout Asia posed an imminent threat to the United States and her allies. With the defeat of Chiang Kai-chek's Kuomintang forces in 1949 and their subsequent withdrawal to the island of Taiwan, new problems arose. In order to assist the Nationalist Chinese, the United States arranged to have a number of vessels transferred to the island nation. The former *LSSLs 56, 81*, and *95*, on loan to Japan since the early 1950s, were formally transferred to Taiwan at the Yokosuka Naval Yard in Japan on 19 February, 1954 and renamed the *Lien Yung* (ex *56*), *Lien Chih* (ex *81*) and *Lien Jen* (ex *95*). Two other LSSLs in the French service in Vietnam, the *2* (*Arbalete*) and the *28* (*Pertuisane*) were later turned over to the Taiwanese for cannibalization. The *Lien Yung* (ex *56*), *Lien Chih* (ex *81*) and the *Lien Jen* (ex *95*) were carried on the lists as active ships until they were stricken in 1971.

THAILAND

Only one ship of the 130 LCS(L) fleet still remains on active duty at this time (1999), the former *LCS(L) 102*. She began life at the Commercial Iron Works in Portland, Oregon and was commissioned on 17 February, 1945. After serving at Okinawa, she was moth-balled at the end of the war and then re-commissioned as the *LSSL 102*. Transferred to Japan in 1953, she was renamed the *Himawari*. She was returned to the United States in the mid-1960s, and then transferred to Thailand in 1966. There she was renamed the *Nakha*, the name she carries to the present day. Updated with newer engines and equipment she still carries the same armament with one exception, the rocket launchers have been removed. Mounted in their place are six 81mm mortars. She carries more modern navigation equipment, specifically a Raytheon 1500B I-band radar setup. The eight GM diesels that gave her an estimated 1,600 horsepower have been replaced. She now has two

GM diesels that together put out a total of 1,320 horsepower. Since she is the last remaining LSSL afloat, the National Association of LCS(L) 1-130 members have campaigned to have her returned to the United States and placed in a museum. At this writing, there is a tentative agreement between the United States and Thailand for this to occur, and the United States Naval and Marine Corps Amphibious Forces Museum in Boston, Massachusetts has set aside a berth for her.

TERMINUS

The 51 ships not discussed above were deemed to be surplus items. They were sold off to private companies. In many cases they were scrapped. However, some were put into commercial use. Investigations by historian Ray Baumler led to the conclusion that several of the original LCS(L) fleet was still in existence in the Pacific northwest area, where they had been converted to fishing boats. One of the ships, formerly the *LCS(L) 50*, had been renamed the *Seabird* and was rusting away at a dock in Seattle. She had originally been sold to the Copper River Packing Company of Seattle, Washington in October of 1947. Photographs by researcher Ron MacKay, Jr. demonstrated the sorry state of repair of this vessel (Baumler Search 1-2). Standard sell-off prices for the ships varied from around $8,000 to $10,000, however, the final journey of the *61* was representative. On 20 March, 1951, she was sold to the Condenser Service and Engineering Company, Inc. of Hoboken, New Jersey for $9,864. After delivery to that company on 10 May, 1951, she was scrapped. Major purchasers of the surplus ships included The Learner Company which purchased 14, Dulien Steel Products which bought nine and the Southwest Steel Corporation which bought five. It is not possible to determine the final disposition of each and every ship, but it is likely that after their use as commercial vessels ended most were scrapped.

The LCS(L)s existed as United States warships from their commissioning in 1944 to their decommissioning in the late 1940s and early 1950s. Although their active life in the United States Navy was brief, they went on to serve the allies of the United States for varying lengths of time and in various capacities.

Nakha (ex *LSSL 102*) is the last of the *Mighty Midgets* still in service. This photo of her was taken at the entrance to Songkhla Navy Base in Thailand on 31 January, 1997. Photo courtesy of NAVPIC-Holland.

APPENDICES

AH — Hospital Ship

AK — Cargo Ship

AKA — Cargo Ship — Attack

AM — Fleet Minesweeper

AO — Oiler

AP — Transport

APA — Transport — Attack

APD — High Speed Transport

ARD — Floating Dry Dock

ARG — Repair Ship — Internal Combustion Engine

ARL — Repair Ship — Landing Craft

ARS — Salvage Vessel

ATB — Amphibious Training Base

ATR — Ocean Tug — Rescue

BB — Battleship

CA — Heavy Cruiser

CAP — Combat Air Patrol

CL — Light Cruiser

CTF — Commander Task Force

CTG — Commander Task Group

CV — Aircraft Carrier

CVB — Aircraft Carrier — Large

CVL — Aircraft Carrier — Light

CVE — Aircraft Carrier — Escort

DD — Destroyer

DE — Destroyer Escort

DM — Light Minelayer

DMS — High Speed Minesweeper

DUKW — Heavy Amphibious Truck

Higgins Boat — see LCP(L)

LC(FF) — Landing Craft — Flotilla Flagship

LCI(D) — Landing Craft Infantry — Demolition

LCI(G) — Landing Craft Infantry — Guns

LCI(L) — Landing Craft Infantry — Large

LCI(M) — Landing Craft Infantry — Mortars

LCI(R) — Landing Craft Infantry — Rockets

LCM — Landing Craft Mechanized (Mark) also (G) and (R) versions Guns and Rockets

LCP(L) — Landing Craft Personnel — Large

LCS(L) — Landing Craft Support — Large

LCT — Landing Craft — Tank

LCVP — Landing Craft Vehicle Personnel

LSIL — Landing Ship Infantry Large — redesignation for LCI(L)s

LSM — Landing Ship Medium

LSM(R) — Landing Ship Medium — Rockets

LSSL — Landing Ship Support Large — re—designation for LCS(L)s

LST — Landing Ship Tank

LV — Landing Vehicle

LVT — Landing Vehicle Tracked

PBR — Patrol Boat River

PC — Submarine Chaser

PCE — Submarine Chaser Escort

PGM — Motor Gunboat

PT — Motor Torpedo Boat RP — Radar Picket Station

TF — Task Force

TG — Task Group

UDT — Underwater Demolition Team

YMS — Motor Minesweeper

YOG — Gasoline Barge

APPENDIX II

LCS(L)(3) SPECIFICATIONS

Dimensions: Length, 158' ½" o.a. - Beam, 23' 3"

Displacement:

	Draft
Loaded, 387 tons	4' 9" fwd., 6'6" aft
Light Service, 312 tons	3' 9½" fwd., 5' 8" aft
Light, 250 Tons	4' ¼" mean

Tons-per-inch immersion, 7 (full load), 6.9 (light service)

Armament: Bow Gun: one 40mm single or one 3"/50 or one twin 40mm. Other guns — two 40mm twins, four 20mm, four .50 caliber machine guns and ten Mk. 7 rocket launchers

Armor: 10-lb STS splinter shield to gun mounts, pilot house and conning tower

Endurance: 5,500 miles @ 12 knots, @ 45" pitch (350 tons displ.)

Speed: 15.5 knts. (max.) @ 650 shaft rpm: 14.5 knts. (cont.) @ 585 shaft rpm.

Propulsion: 8 GM diesels, 4 per shaft - max. BHP: 1,600 twin variable pitch propellers

Fuel, Store: 76 tons fuel oil, 10 tons Fresh Water, 6 tons Lubrication Oil, 8 tons provisions and stores at full load

Fresh Water: Distillery with the capacity to make 1,000 gallons per day

Crew: 6 officers, 65 crew

Above based on: Baker, A.D. *Allied Landing Craft of World War II* , 47.
Lawley, George & Son Corporation. *Instructions for LCS(L)(3) Class.*
Original Plans of LCS(L)(3) by George Lawley & Sons Corp.

SHIP CONSTRUCTION AND LAUNCHING DATA

LCS(L) Official Number	Builder	Keel Laid	Ship Launched	Date of First Commission
1	Lawley*	28 Apr 44	15 May 44	20 June 44
2	"	10 May 44	10 Jun 44	19 July 44
3	"	14 Jun 44	5 Jul 44	31 Jul 44
4	"	5 Jul 44	15 Jul 44	11 Aug 44
5	"	17 Jul 44	27 Jul 44	21 Aug 44
6	"	17 Jul 44	3 Aug 44	27 Aug 44
7	"	31 Jul 44	9 Aug 44	29 Aug 44
8	"	28 Jul 44	11 Aug 44	31 Aug 44
9	"	7 Jul 44	17 Aug 44	6 Sept 44
10	"	10 Aug 44	19 Aug 44	10 Sept 44
11	"	12 Aug 44	22 Aug 44	13 Sept 44
12	"	14 Aug 44	24 Aug 44	17 Sept 44
13	"	17 Aug 44	26 Aug 44	21 Sept 44
14	"	19 Aug 44	28 Aug 44	23 Sept 44
15	"	23 Aug 44	3 Sept 44	26 Sept 44
16	"	25 Aug 44	4 Sept 44	28 Sept 44
17	"	28 Aug 44	4 Sept 44	30 Sept 44
18	"	29 Aug 44	6 Sept 44	30 Sept 44
19	"	4 Sept 44	11 Sept 44	7 Oct 44
20	"	4 Sept 44	13 Sept 44	10 Oct 44
21	"	12 Sept 44	20 Sept 44	14 Oct 44
22	"	13 Sept 44	22 Sept 44	16 Oct 44
23	"	20 Sept 44	29 Sept 44	18 Oct 44
24	"	23 Sept 44	1 Oct 44	20 Oct 44
25	"	29 Sept 44	8 Oct 44	24 Oct 44
26	Commercial**	10 Jul 44	13 Aug 44	26 Aug 44
27	"	10 Jul 44	13 Aug 44	31 Aug 44
28	"	17 Jul 44	19 Aug 44	8 Sept 44
29	"	24 Jul 44	27 Aug 44	12 Sept 44

LCS(L) Official Number	Builder	Keel Laid	Ship Launched	Date of First Commission
30	"	24 Jul 44	27 Aug 44	16 Sept 44
31	"	7 Aug 44	2 Sept 44	20 Sept 44
32	"	14 Aug 44	10 Sept 44	23 Sept 44
33	"	14 Aug 44	10 Sep 44	27 Sept 44
34	"	19 Aug 44	16 Sept 44	30 Sept 44
35	"	28 Aug 44	17 Sept 44	3 Oct 44
36	"	28 Aug 44	17 Sept 44	4 Oct 44
37	"	2 Sept 44	23 Sept 44	10 Oct 44
38	"	11 Sept 44	1 Oct 44	13 Oct 44
39	"	11 Sept 44	1 Oct 44	16 Oct 44
40	"	16 Sept 44	7 Oct 44	20 Oct 44
41	"	18 Sept 44	8 Oct 44	24 Oct 44
42	"	18 Sept 44	8 Oct 44	26 Oct 44
43	"	23 Sept 44	14 Oct 44	30 Oct 44
44	"	2 Oct 44	22 Oct 44	2 Nov 44
45	"	2 Oct 44	22 Oct 45	6 Nov 45
46	"	7 Oct 44	27 Oct 44	9 Nov 44
47	"	9 Oct 44	29 Oct 44	13 Nov 44
48	Albina***	25 May 44	7 July 44	26 Aug 44
49	"	2 Jun 44	20 Jul 44	31 Aug 44
50	"	8 Jun 44	29 Jul 44	11 Sept 44
51	"	15 Jun 44	5 Aug 44	16 Sept 44
52	"	21 Jun 44	14 Aug 44	23 Sept 44
53	"	27 Jun 44	22 Aug 44	30 Sept 44
54	"	19 Jul 44	5 Sept 44	9 Oct 44
55	"	31 Jul 44	2 Sept 44	16 Oct 44
56	"	5 Aug 44	7 Sept 44	23 Oct 44
57	"	15 Aug 44	14 Sept 44	30 Oct 44
58	"	22 Aug 44	22 Sept 44	6 Nov 44
59	"	2 Sept 44	2 Oct 44	14 Nov 44
60	"	7 Sept 44	7 Oct 44	22 Nov 44
61	"	15 Sept 44	14 Oct 44	29 Nov 44
62	"	22 Sept 44	23 Oct 44	4 Dec 44
63	"	2 Oct 44	2 Nov 44	11 Dec 44
64	"	9 Oct 44	7 Nov 44	18 Dec 44
65	"	16 Oct 44	14 Nov 44	26 Dec 44
66	"	24 Oct 44	23 Nov 44	2 Jan 45
67	"	2 Nov 44	2 Dec 44	8 Jan 45
68	"	9 Nov 44	7 Dec 44	15 Jan 45
69	"	15 Nov 44	14 Dec 44	22 Jan 45
70	"	24 Nov 44	22 Dec 44	29 Jan 45

LCS(L) Official Number	Builder	Keel Laid	Ship Launched	Date of First Commission
71	"	2 Dec 44	2 Jan 45	5 Feb 45
72	"	8 Dec 44	8 Jan 45	14 Feb 45
73	"	15 Dec 44	16 Jan 45	19 Feb 45
74	"	23 Dec 44	30 Jan 45	26 Feb 45
75	"	3 Jan 45	9 Feb 45	6 Mar 45
76	"	9 Jan 45	15 Feb 45	12 Mar 45
77	"	17 Jan 45	26 Feb 45	19 Mar 45
78	"	31 Jan 45	28 Feb 45	26 Mar 45
79	Commercial	9 Oct 44	29 Oct 44	20 Nov 44
80	"	14 Oct 44	7 Nov 44	21 Nov 44
81	"	23 Oct 44	12 Nov 44	24 Nov 44
82	"	23 Oct 44	12 Nov 44	27 Nov 44
83	"	27 Oct 44	17 Nov 44	30 Nov 44
84	"	30 Oct 44	19 Nov 44	4 Dec 44
85	"	30 Oct 44	19 Nov 44	9 Dec 44
86	"	7 Nov 44	30 Nov 44	14 Dec 44
87	"	13 Nov 44	3 Dec 44	18 Dec 44
88	"	13 Nov 44	3 Dec 44	22 Dec 44
89	"	17 Nov 44	7 Dec 44	27 Dec 44
90	"	20 Nov 44	17 Dec 44	30 Dec 44
91	"	20 Nov 44	17 Dec 44	4 Jan 45
92	"	30 Nov 44	22 Dec 44	8 Jan 45
93	"	4 Dec 44	23 Dec 44	13 Jan 45
94	"	4 Dec 44	23 Dec 44	16 Jan 45
95	"	7 Dec 44	3 Jan 45	20 Jan 45
96	"	18 Dec 44	6 Jan 45	24 Jan 45
97	"	18 Dec 44	6 Jan 45	29 Jan 45
98	"	23 Dec 44	13 Jan 45	2 Feb 45
99	"	23 Dec 44	13 Jan 45	5 Feb 45
100	"	6 Jan 45	27 Jan 45	9 Feb 45
101	"	6 Jan 45	27 Jan 45	13 Feb 45
102	"	13 Jan 45	3 Feb 45	17 Feb 45
103	"	13 Jan 45	3 Feb 45	24 Feb 45
104	"	27 Jan 45	17 Feb 45	28 Feb 45
105	"	27 Jan 45	17 Feb 45	5 Mar 45
106	"	3 Feb 45	24 Feb 45	9 Mar 45
107	"	3 Feb 45	24 Feb 45	13 Mar 45
108	"	17 Feb 45	10 Mar 45	22 Mar 45
109	Lawley	1 Oct 44	10 Oct 44	26 Oct 44
110	"	3 Oct 44	12 Oct 44	29 Oct 44
111	"	9 Oct 44	17 Oct 44	3 Nov 44

LCS(L) Official Number	Builder	Keel Laid	Ship Launched	Date of First Commission
112	"	11 Oct 44	19 Oct 44	6 Nov 44
113	"	12 Oct 44	22 Oct 44	9 Nov 44
114	"	17 Oct 44	26 Oct 44	12 Nov 44
115	"	19 Oct 44	28 Oct 44	14 Nov 44
116	"	22 Oct 44	30 Oct 44	17 Nov 44
117	"	26 Oct 44	4 Nov 44	19 Nov 44
118	"	28 Oct 44	6 Nov 44	23 Nov 44
119	"	31 Oct 44	8 Nov 44	27 Nov 44
120	"	4 Nov 44	14 Nov 44	29 Nov 44
121	"	7 Nov 44	16 Nov 44	1 Dec 44
122	"	9 Nov 44	18 Nov 44	8 Dec 44
123	"	14 Nov 44	24 Nov 44	11 Dec 44
124	"	10 Nov 44	27 Nov 44	14 Dec 44
125	"	19 Nov 44	1 Dec 44	17 Dec 44
126	"	25 Nov 44	5 Dec 44	20 Dec 44
127	"	27 Nov 44	6 Dec 44	26 Dec 44
128	"	1 Dec 44	9 Dec 44	29 Dec 44
129	"	5 Dec 44	13 Dec 44	31 Dec 44
130	"	7 Dec 44	15 Dec 44	3 Jan 45

*George Lawley & Sons Corp., Neponset, Massachusetts
** Commercial Iron Works, Portland, Oregon
***Albina Engine & Machine Works, Inc., Portland, Oregon
(Above based on *Ships' Data* 219-222 and *WW II Hist*. D-7-9, D-21-24)

APPENDIX IV

FLOTILLA ORGANIZATION AS OF 4 MAY, 1945

FLOTILLA ONE
Capt. R. E. Arison USNR
LCI(R) 778

Group 1
Lt. W. I. Hunt USNR
LCS(L) 30*

Division 1		Division 2	
LCS(L) 7	Lt. Franklin L. Elder	*LCS(L) 26*	Lt. Herbert Chernin USNR
LCS(L) 8	Lt. R. T. Daniel USN	*LCS(L) 27*	Lt (jg) J. M. Bledsoe Jr. USN
LCS(L) 9	Lt. D. R. Ellis USNR	*LCS(L) 28*	Lt. R. H. Bost USNR
LCS(L) 10	Lt. A. C. Eldridge USNR	*LCS(L) 29*	Lt. J. Pierrepont USNR
LCS(L) 48	Lt. D. E. Widel USNR	*LCS(L) 30*	Lt. C. H. Sanders USN
		LCS(L) 49	Lt. H. W. Smith USNR
		LCS(L) 50	Lt. B.T. Clark USNR

Group 2
Lt. M. C. Fitzgerald USNR
LCS(L) 42

Division 3		Division 4	
LCS(L) 41	Lt.(jg) A.P. Marincovich USNR	*LCS(L) 46*	Lt. W. P. McCarthy USNR
LCS(L) 42	Lt. R.S. Sondree 00140	*LCS(L) 47*	Lt. F.R. Butler USNR
LCS(L) 43	Lt. W.A. Moore USNR	*LCS(L) 59*	Lt. N.L. Claxton USNR
LCS(L) 44	Lt. J. M. Leggat USNR	*LCS(L) 60*	Lt. W. H. White 21209
LCS(L) 45	Lt. E. M. Lang USNR	*LCS(L) 79*	Lt. J. D. Fleming 21160
LCS(L) 58	Lt. D. Gregory USNR	*LCS(L) 80*	Lt. T. C. Lynch USN

FLOTILLA THREE
Capt. T. C. Aylward USN
LC(FF) 988

Group 7
Lt. Cmdr. E. P. Stone USNR
LC(FF) 484

Division 13		Division 14	
LCS(L) 32	Lt. J. M. Evans 16659	*LCS(L) 53*	Lt. M. F. Steldt USNR
LCS(L) 33	Lt. C. J. Boone USNR	*LCS(L) 54*	Lt. J. Synan USNR
LCS(L) 34	Lt. J. B. Seely USNR		Lt. J. P. Murphy USNR**
LCS(L) 35	Lt. K. C. Huff USNR	*LCS(L) 55*	Lt. A. B. Cooper USNR
LCS(L) 36	Lt. Joseph Sansone	*LCS(L) 56*	Lt.(jg) H. M. Scherling USNR
LCS(L) 51	Lt. H. D. Chickering	*LCS(L) 57*	Lt. H. L. Smith
LCS(L) 52	Lt. J. O. Harper USNR	*LCS(L) 31*	Lt. K. F. Mahacek USNR

Group 8
Lt. Cmdr. E. C. Thomas USNR
LCS(L) 12

Division 15		Division 16	
LCS(L) 11	Lt. M. E. White USNR	*LCS(L)18*	*Lt.* J. F. Lehman USNR
LCS(L) 12	Lt. G. J. O'Hare USNR		Ens. A. O. Hungerford USNR
LCS(L) 13	Lt.(jg) B. R. Hart USNR	*LCS(L) 19*	Lt. F. Woods III USNR
LCS(L) 14	Lt.(jg) J. R. Todd USNR	*LCS(L) 20*	Lt. L. R. Hof USNR
LCS(L) 15	Lt. N. H. Brower USNR	*LCS(L) 21*	Lt. J. C. Geib USNR
LCS(L) 16	Lt. H. O. White Jr. USNR	*LCS(L) 22*	Lt. B. G. Brewster USNR
LCS(L) 17	Lt.(jg) J. M. Sharpe USNR		

Group 9
Lt. B. A. Thirkield USNR
LCS(L) 24

Division 17		Division 18	
LCS(L) 23	Lt. W. D. Wilson USNR	*LCS(L) 40*	Lt. (jg) T. T. Hollen USNR
LCS(L) 24	Lt. W. A. Russell USNR	*LCS(L) 109*	Lt. (jg) M. L. Smith USNR
LCS(L) 25	Lt. J. M. Willette USNR	*LCS(L) 110*	Lt. (jg) H. W. Blose USNR
LCS(L) 37	Lt. S. M. Brickhouse USNR	*LCS(L) 111*	Lt. L. E. Culp USNR
LCS(L) 38	Lt. J. C. Smith USNR	*LCS(L) 112*	Lt. A. H. LaMotte USNR
LCS(L) 39	Lt. R. A. Anderson USNR	*LCS(L) 113*	Lt. T. H. Smith USNR

FLOTILLA FOUR
Cmdr. N. Phillips USN
LC(FF)1082

Group 10
Lt. Cmdr. J. A. Dodson USN
LC(FF) 1079

Division 19		Division 20	
LCS(L) 114	Lt. G. W. Mefferd USNR	*LCS(L) 120*	Lt. F. H. Lamartin Jr. 24656
LCS(L) 115	Lt. A. P. Gliemke USNR	*LCS(L) 121*	Lt. W. C. Lewis 00969
LCS(L) 116	Lt. A. J. Wierzbicki USNR	*LCS(L) 122*	Lt. R. M. McCool USN
LCS(L) 117	Lt. E. R. Stanford Jr. USNR	*LCS(L) 123*	Lt. D. A. Oliver Jr. 20895
LCS(L) 118	Lt. P. F. Gilmore Jr. USNR	*LCS(L) 124*	Lt. D. Ward
LCS(L) 119	Lt. E. Saroch Jr. USNR		

Group 11
Lt. Cmdr. C. E. Montgomery USNR
LC(FF) 367

Division 21		Division 22	
LCS(L) 61	Lt. J. M. Kelley USN	*LCS(L) 83*	Lt. J. M. Faddis 20968
LCS(L) 62	Lt. E. F. Greenleaf USNR	*LCS(L) 84*	Lt. J. A. Noye USNR
LCS(L) 63	Lt. W. E. Pfau USNR	*LCS(L) 85*	Lt. C. E. Randall 21215
LCS(L) 64	Lt. C. W. Fogg USNR	*LCS(L) 86*	Lt. (jg) H. N. Houston USNR
LCS(L) 81	Lt. C. C. Lockwood 21366	*LCS(L) 87*	Lt. H. N. Martin USNR
LCS(L) 82	Lt. P. G. Beierl USN	*LCS(L) 88*	Lt. C. L. Bigos USNR
			Lt. (jg) Mark V. Sellis USNR

Group 12
Lt. Cmdr. B. D. Vogelin USNR
LC(FF) 789

Division 23		Division 24	
LCS(L) 65	Lt. T. B., Bannister USNR	*LCS(L) 90*	Lt. W. N. Birt USNR
LCS(L) 66	Lt. (jg) E. M. Eakin 13476	*LCS(L) 91*	Lt. S. A. McCray USNR
LCS(L) 67	Lt. J. R. Bullock USNR	*LCS(L) 92*	Lt. J. J. Cardamone USNR
LCS(L) 68	Lt. M. G. Loessig 13497	*LCS(L) 93*	Lt. C. F. Botright USNR
LCS(L) 69	Lt. F. W. Harlow USNR	*LCS(L) 94*	Lt. J. L. Cronk USNR
LCS(L) 89	Lt. J. A. Kidston USNR	*LCS(L) 95*	Lt. D. Bowerman USNR

FLOTILLA FIVE
Capt. J. M. McIssac USN
LCS(L) 126

Group 13
Lt. Cmdr. R. L. Jackson USN
LCS(L) 96

Division 25		Division 26	
LCS(L) 96	Lt. O. K. Franklin USNR	*LCS(L) 125*	Lt. H. C. Cobb USNR
LCS(L) 97	Lt. R. H. Woodside USNR	*LCS(L) 126*	Lt. R. S. Gunn USNR
LCS(L) 98	Lt. J. C. Price USNR	*LCS(L) 127*	Lt. J. N. Kelly USNR
LCS(L) 99	Lt. O. L. Miles	*LCS(L) 128*	Lt. J. B. Myers USNR
LCS(L) 100	Lt. F. J. Dimenna USNR	*LCS(L) 129*	Lt. L. A. Brennan USNR
LCS(L) 101	Lt. G. C. Ferris USNR	*LCS(L) 130*	Lt. W. H. File Jr. USNR

Group 14
Lt. Cmdr. K. E. Curley USN
LCS(L) 72

Division 27		Division 28	
LCS(L) 70	Lt. R. J. Liechti USNR	*LCS(L) 102*	Lt. R. L. Jones USNR
	Lt. G. E. Hart Jr.	*LCS(L) 103*	Lt. R. K. Crawford USNR
LCS(L) 71	Lt. R. B. Brokaw USNR	*LCS(L) 104*	Lt. F. M. Adams USNR
LCS(L) 72	Lt. F. R. Jaeger USNR	*LCS(L) 105*	Lt. G. W. Smith USNR
	Lt. (jg) H. R. Schwartz USNR	*LCS(L) 106*	Lt. H. W. Griswold USNR
LCS(L) 73	Lt. P. S. Carlton USNR	*LCS(L) 107*	Lt. (jg) G. S. Brown USNR
LCS(L) 74	Lt. H. J. Wittman USNR		Lt. (jg) D. A. Glover USNR
LCS(L) 75	Lt. R. B. Rivel USNR		

Group 15
Lt. Cmdr. H. Heine USNR
LCS(L) 108

Division 29		Division 30	
LCS(L) 2	Lt. J. B. Whitmore USNR	*LCS(L) 108*	Lt. R. E. Hone USNR
LCS(L) 3	Lt. T. J. Ryan USNR		Lt. H. W. Chanidas USNR
LCS(L) 4	Lt. E. W. Welch Jr. USNR		
LCS(L) 76	Lt. B. H. Eklund USNR		
LCS(L) 77	Lt. R. C. Shannon 10614		
LCS(L) 78	Lt. T. N. Fortson USNR		

PERMANENTLY ASSIGNED TO TRAINING IN THE UNITED STATES

LCS(L) 1   Lt. William K. Townsend
             Lt. (jg) Leo H. Bishkin
             Lt. (jg) L.T. Kermon
LCS(L) 5   Lt. Joe Kendall
             Lt. (jg) R. H. Kistler
LCS(L) 6   Lt. (jg) Edward S. Wright

Based primarily on: Commander Amphibious Forces, U.S. Pacific Fleet. LCS(L)(3) FLOTILLAS, *AMPHIBIOUS FORCES, PACIFIC FLEET: - Organization of* 4 May, 1945.

*Flotilla and Group Commanders were supposed to direct their units from ships designed for that purpose and designated as Landing Craft - Flotilla Flagship or LC(FF). In some cases, these specialized ships were not available and the Flotilla or Group Commander was aboard one of the LCS(L)s.

** Some ships had more than one Commanding Officer. As they became eligible for transfer their ship was turned over to a new Commanding Officer for the duration of its service life. The list above is based primarily on the source shown which lists the Commanding Officers as of 4 May, 1945. Where multiple names are listed, as in the case of the training ships, alternate sources were used.

APPENDIX V

SHIP DISPOSITION DURING AND AFTER WORLD WAR II

LSSL No., Transferred or Sold To, New Name, Date of Final Disposition

1　Sold to Northern Metal Company, Philadelphia, PA 21Nov50 for $8,353

2　Transferred to France 15Aug50 *Arbalete L 9021*, to S. Vietnam 12Oct54 *No Than HQ225,* to Taiwan 1957 for parts, scrapped 1958*

3　Sold to Dulien Steel Products of Seattle, WA 28Dec50

4　Transferred to France 15Aug50 *Arquebuse L 9022,* to S. Vietnam 1955 *Linh Kiem,* then renamed *Le Trong Deim HQ 226,* sunk in S. Vietnam 3Oct70

5　Sold to S. Paul Dooley, Fort Lauderdale, FL 6Jun47

6　Sold to Northern Metal Company, Philadelphia, PA 28Feb51

7　Sunk at Mariveles Harbor, Philippines 16Feb45

8　Sold to Dulien Steel Products of Seattle, WA 14Nov46

9　Transferred to France 15Aug50 *Hallebarde L 9023*, ret. to US 1955, to Japan 7May56 *Asagao*, to S. Vietnam 15Sept65 *Doan Ngoc Tang HQ 228*, escaped Vietnam 1975, to Philippines *La Union LF 50* for parts, deleted *circa* 1980s

10　Transferred to France 15Aug50 *Javeline L 9024*, ret. to US 1955, to Japan 7May56 *Hinageshi* , to Vietnam 15Sep65 *Le Van Binh HQ 227*, sunk in S. Vietnam 2Oct66

11　Sold to Dulien Steel Products of Seattle, WA 26Dec50

12　Transferred to Japan 30Jun53 *Sekichiku*, ret. to US 30Jun58, recommended for disposal and use as target to destruction, sunk by gunfire 12Mar59

13　Transferred to Japan 30Jun53 *Oniyur*i, ret. to US 30Jun58, recommended for disposal and use as target to destruction, sunk by gunfire 9Feb59

14　Transferred to Japan 16Feb53 *Sumir*e, ret. to US 30Sep75**

15　Sunk at Okinawa 22Apr45

16　Sold to Dulien Steel Products of Seattle, WA 9Feb51 for $8,211

17　Sold to the Learner Company of Alameda, CA 8Jan51

18　Transferred to Japan 30Jun53 *Yamayuri*, ret. to US 30Jun58, recommended for use as target to destruction, sunk by gunfire Dec58

19　Sold to Dulien Steel Products of Seattle, WA 29Dec50

20　Transferred to Japan 29Jul53 *Himeyuri*, ret. to US 29Aug58, recommended for use as target to destruction, sunk by gunfire Dec58

21 Sold to The Learner Company of Alameda, CA 16Mar51 for $10,870
22 Transferred to Japan 30Mar53 *Nogiku*, ret. to US 6Aug71
23 Sold to The Learner Company of Alameda, CA 16Mar51 for $10,870
24 Transferred to Japan 30May53 *Ezogiku*, ret. to US 31Mar59
25 Transferred to Japan 30Jun53 *Suzuran*, ret. to US 30Jun58, recommended use as target to destruction, sunk by gunfire 12Mar59
26 Sunk at Mariveles Harbor, Philippines 16Feb45
27 Transferred to Japan 30Apr53 *Azami,* ret. to US 19Oct76
28 Transferred to France 15Aug50 *Pertuisane*, to Taiwan 1957 for parts, scrapped 1958
29 Sold to The Learner Company of Alameda, CA 8Jan51
30 Sold to Dulien Steel Products of Seattle, WA 29Dec50 for $8,211
31 Sold to H.H. Buncher Co., Pittsburgh, PA 27Jan47
32 Sold to Southwest Steel Corp. Of Memphis, TN. 13Dec50 for $7,313.12
33 Sunk at Okinawa 12Apr45
34 Transferred to Italy 25Jul51 *Alano L 9851*, scrapped 1983
35 Transferred to France *Etendard* 12Mar53, ret. to US at Subic Bay, Philippines 1957, to Greece 12Aug57 *Plotarkhis Ulachavas*, discarded 1976
36 Sold to Northern Metal Co., Philadelphia, PA 13Feb51 for $9,009
37 Severely damaged at Okinawa, declared unfit for service, stripped and destroyed 7Mar46 at Naval Repair Base, Manicani Island
38 Transferred to Italy 25Jul51 *Bracco L 9852*, scrapped 1983
39 Sold to Martin B. Dahl, Seattle, WA 7Oct47
40 Sold to A.B. Anderson, Seattle, WA 9Oct47
41 Sold to Martin B. Dahl, Seattle, WA 7Oct47
42 Sold to Martin B. Dahl, Seattle, WA 7Oct47
43 Sold to Nick Bez, Seattle, WA 7Oct47
44 Sold to Western Fisheries Co., Seattle, WA 23Oct47
45 Sold to Fred Markley, Seattle, WA 7Oct47
46 Sold to Carl E. Anderson, Seattle, WA 7Oct47
47 Sold to Nick Bez, Seattle, WA 7Oct47
48 Sold to Fred Markley, Seattle, WA 7Oct47
49 Sunk at Mariveles Harbor, Philippines 16Feb45
50 Sold to Copper River Packing, Seattle, WA 8Oct47
51 Sold to Copper River Packing, Seattle, WA 22Sept47
52 Transferred to Japan 29Jul53 *Sasayuri*, ret. to US 29Aug58, recommended use as target to destruction, sunk by gunfire Dec58
53 Sold to The Learner Company, Alameda, CA 8Jan51
54 Transferred to Ryukyuan Coast Guard 1Feb52, to Korea 20Oct52 *Po Song Man*, decommissioned 31Oct62***
55 Sold to Dulien Steel Products of Seattle, WA 29Dec50
56 Transferred to Ryukyuan Coast Guard 1Feb52, to Taiwan 19Feb54, *Lien Yung*, stricken *circa* early 1970s
57 Transferred to Japan 14Jan53 *Kiku*, ret. to US 27Mar58, recommended use as target to destruction, sunk by gunfire *circa* Oct58

58   To Japan 29Jul53 *Susuki*, ret. to US 31Mar59
59   Sold to Southwest Steel Corp., Memphis, Tenn. 14Dec50 for $6918.51
60   Transferred to Japan 30Sep53 *Keido*, ret. to US 30Sep58
61   Sold to Condenser Service & Engineering Co., Hoboken, NJ 1May51 for $9,864
62   Transferred to Italy 1953 *Mastino L 9853*, scrapped 1983
63   Transferred to Italy *Molosso L 9854*, scrapped 1983
64   Transferred to Italy *Segugio L 9855*, scrapped 1983
65   Transferred to France 1951 *Oriflamme*, to Greece Jun58 *Plotarkhis Maridakis*, sold 1976
66   Sold to Alfred Ghezzi, Jr. & E. W. Hundley, Seattle, WA 12Jan48
67   Transferred to Japan 29Jul53 *Karukaya*, ret. to US 29Aug58, recommended use as target to destruction, sunk by rockets and bombs May59
68   Transferred to Japan *Hamayu* 30Jun53, to Philippines 17Nov75, not commissioned
69   Sold to Joseph Rosenthal's Sons, Inc., NY 20Mar51 for $9,550.55
70   Sold to The Learner Company, Alameda, CA 8Jan51
71   Sold to Dulien Steel Products of Seattle, WA 28Dec50 for $8,311
72   Transferred to Japan 30Apr53 *Shiragiku*, ret. to US 15Feb72
73   Sold to The Learner Company, Alameda, CA 8Jan51 for $8,156
74   Transferred to Japan 30Sep53 *Suisen*, ret. to US 30Sep58
75   Transferred to Japan 16Feb53 *Fuji*, ret. to US 6Aug71, sold to Honda Metal Traders, of Kyoto, Japan 10Jul72
76   Transferred to Japan 30Apr53 *Kaido*, ret. to US 20Oct69
77   Transferred to Korea 1952 *Yung Huang Man*, decommissioned 15Nov60
78   Transferred to Japan 16Feb63 *Bara*, ret. to US 8Mar76
79   Transferred to Japan 30Apr53 *Rindo*, ret. to US 23Apr76
80   Transferred to France 15Aug50 *Rapiere*, ret. to US 1955, to Japan 7May56, *Nadeshiko*, ret. to US 1963
81   Transferred to Ryukyuan Coast Guard 1Feb52, to Taiwan 19Feb54 *Lien Chih*, stricken 1971
82   Transferred to Japan 30Mar53 *Yamagiku*, ret. to US 6Aug71
83   Transferred to Japan 30May53 *Hinagiku*, ret. to US 31Mar59
84   Transferred to Japan 30May53 *Sawagiku*, ret. to US 31Mar59
85   Transferred to Japan 30May53 *Tsuta*, ret. to US 31Mar59
86   Transferred to Korea *Yong Il Man*, decommissioned 31Oct62
87   Transferred to Japan 30Mar53 *Hamagiku*, refitted as a drone carrier in 1958, stricken in 1967, to Philippines for parts 17Nov75
88   Transferred to Japan 30Apr53 *Ajisai*, ret. to US 1964, to Philippines 17Nov75, not commissioned
89   Transferred to Japan 30May53 *Hasu*, ret. to US 31Mar59
90   Transferred to Japan 30May53 *Shida*, ret. to US 31Mar59
91   Transferred to Korea 1952 *Kang Hwa Man*, decommissioned 15Nov60
92   Sold to The Learner Company, Alameda, CA 16Mar51 for $10,870
93   Sold to The Learner Company, Alameda, CA 16Mar51 for $10,870

94   Transferred to Japan 30May53 *Suiren*, ret. to US 24Oct69

95   Transferred to Ryukyuan Coast Guard 12Mar52, to Taiwan 19Feb54 *Lien Jen*, scrapped 1971

96   Transferred to Japan 30Jun53 *Shobu*, ret. to US 28Apr65, to S. Vietnam as *Nguyen Ngoc Long HQ 230* on 8Dec65, escaped to Philippines 1975, to Philippines as *Sulu,* non-operational 1983

97   Sold to The Learner Company of Alameda, CA 18Mar51 for $10,870

98   Transferred to Japan 30Mar53 *Aoi*, ret. to US 27Mar58, recommended use as target to destruction, sunk by gunfire 20Nov58

99   Sold to Dulien Steel Products of Seattle, WA 26Dec50 for $8,511

100 Transferred to Japan 30Mar53 *Akane*, ret. to US 27Mar58, recommended use as target to destruction, sunk by gunfire 20Nov58

101 Transferred to Japan 30Apr53 *Tsutsuji*, ret. to US 28Apr65, to S. Vietnam 2Oct65 *Luu Phu Tho HQ 229*, escaped Vietnam 1975, to Philippines for parts 1975

102 Transferred to Japan 30Apr53 *Himawari*, ret. to US 18Apr66, to Thailand 1966 *Nakha* (extant)

103 Transferred to Japan 30Sep53 *Yaguruma*, ret. to US 30Sep58

104 Transferred to Japan 14Jan53 *Ran*, ret. to US 31Mar59

105 Transferred to Ryukyuan Coast Guard 12Mar52, to France 28Dec53 *Framee*, to Vietnam 1957 *No Than HQ225,* renamed *Nguyen Van Tru* in 1970, sunk in S. Vietnam 30Jul70

106 Transferred to Japan 30Mar53 *Isogiku*, ret. to US 27Jun75

107 Transferred to Japan 14Jan53 *Yuri*, ret. to US 27Mar58

108 Sold to The Learner Company, Alameda, CA 16Mar51 for $10,870

109 Transferred to Japan, 30Jun53 *Kanna*, ret. to US 30Jun58

110 Transferred to Japan 30Mar53 *Fuyo*, ret. to US 6Aug71

111 Transferred to Japan 16Feb53 *Keshi*, ret. to US 21Jul70

112 Sold to The Learner Company, Alameda, CA 18Mar51 for $10,870

113 Sold to The Learner Company, Alameda, CA 17Mar51 for $10,870

114 Transferred to Japan 30Apr53 *Hiiragi*, ret. to US 14Feb66

115 Transferred to Japan 16Feb53 *Ayame*, ret. to US 11Feb66

116 Transferred to Japan 30May53 *Yamabuki*, ret. to US 31Mar59

117 Sold to The Learner Company, Alameda, CA 17Mar51 for $10,870

118 Transferred to Italy 25Jul51 *Spinoni L 9856*, scrapped 1983

119 Transferred to Japan 29Jul53 *Kikyo*, ret. to US 29Aug58, recommended use as target to destruction, sunk by rockets and bombs May59

120 Transferred to Japan 30Apr53 *Iwagiku*, ret. to US 12Jul71

121 Sold to Southwest Steel Corp., Memphis, TN. 14Dec50 for $6,941.16

122 Sold to J.C. Berkwit & Co., NY, NY 23Feb51 for $8,444.44

123 Sold to James L. Teagle, Hampton VA 14Aug47

124 Sold to Southwest Steel Corp., Memphis, TN. 14Dec50

125 Sold to Condenser Service & Engineering Company, Hoboken, NJ 1May51 for $10,307

126 Transferred to Japan 30May53 *Renge*, ret. to US 30May58

127 Grounded at San Clemente Island, CA 5Mar45, salvage impossible, Board of Investigation declared the ship a total loss to the govt. on 28Mar45, with the exception of the equipment salvaged (*Log LCS(L) 127* 189)

128 Sold to Southwest Steel Corp., Memphis, TN 14Dec50

129 Transferred to Japan 30Jun53 *Botan*, ret. to US 28Apr65, to S. Vietnam 19Feb66 *Nguyen Duc Bong HQ 231*, escaped 1975 to Philippines, to Philippines 1975 *Camarines Sur LF 48*, deleted 1989

130 Transferred to Japan 14Jan53 *Hagi*, ret. to US 27Mar58, recommended use as target to destruction, sunk by gunfire 14Nov58

*Some confusion exists over the identification of the first six LSSLs transferred to France in 1950. At first the French simply designated them as hull numbers *1* through *6*. Literature from 1950 to early 1952 frequently refers to *LSSL 1* or *LSSL 6*, etc. The numbers designated by the French at first correspond to the following: *1* = *LSSL 2*, *2* = *LSSL 4*, *3* = *LSSL 9*, *4* = *LSSL 10*, *5* = *LSSL 28* and *6* = *LSSL 80*. Within a short time, the French had assigned new hull numbers *9021* through *9026* and shortly thereafter gave names to the vessels. For a complete list of names and numbers see page 208.

**Many ships returned to the U.S. in the 1950s were used for target practice. Complete data is unavailable for these ships. Others were remanded to U.S. custody in Japan and sold there to Japanese scrap dealers.

***Ships in the service of the Ryukyuan Coast Guard were not renumbered, they carried their original U.S. Navy numbers.

Most dates are administrative transfer dates, actual delivery usually took place within a few months.

BOOKS-PERIODICALS-NEWSPAPERS

Appleman, Roy E., James E. Burns, Russell A. Lugeler, *et al. Okinawa: The Last Battle.* Washington, D.C.: Department of the Army, Historical Division, 1948.

Auer, James E. *The Postwar Rearmament of Japanese Maritime Forces, 1945-71.* New York: Praeger Publishers, Inc., 1973.

Baker, A.D. III. *Allied Landing Craft of World War Two.* Annapolis: Naval Institute Press, 1985.

Barbey, Vice Admiral Daniel E. *MacArthur's Amphibious Navy Seventh Amphibious Force Operations 1943-1945.* Annapolis: United States Naval Institute Press, 1969.

Baumler, Raymond A. "How Many LCS(L)s, What Types of Bow Guns?" *LCS(L)(3) 1-130 Association Newsletter* Vol 5 No. 1: Winter, 1993. 9.

————. "Search for the Seabird" Typescript, 1996.

The Beachmaster Final Edition. U.S.N.A.T.B. Solomons, Maryland. February, 1945.

Brossard, Maurice Raymond de. *Dinassaut.* Paris: Editions France-Empire, 1952.

Building the Navy's Bases in World War II History of the Bureau of Yards and Docks and the Civil Engineer Corps 1940-1946 Volume I. Washington: United States Government Printing Office, 1947.

"Chronique Des Forces Maritimes D'Extreme-Orient." in *La Revue Maritime.* Editions of November, 1953, 1407-1411, June, 1954, 803-806, July, 1954, 1071-1078, January, 1955 105-109.

Costello, John. *The Pacific War 1941-1945.* New York: Atlantic Communications Inc., 1981.

Croizat, Victor H. *Vietnam River Warfare 1945-1975.* New York: Blandford Press, 1986.

Do, Kiem and Julie Kane. *Counterpart A South Vietnamese Naval Officer's War.* Annapolis: Naval Institute Press, 1998.

Dyer, George C. *The Amphibians Came to Conquer: The Story of Admiral Richmond Kelly Turner Vol. I & II .* Washington, D.C.: Department of the Navy, 1969.

————. "Naval Amphibious Landmarks." *United States Naval Institute Proceedings.* Annapolis: Naval Institute Press, August, 1966. 50-60.

Fahey, James C. *The Ships and Aircraft of the United States Fleet - Victory Edition.* Annapolis: Naval Institute Press, 1977.

Fluckey, Rear Admiral Eugene B. *Thunder Below! The USS Barb Revolutionizes Submarine Warfare in World War II.* Chicago: Unversity of Illinois Press, 1992.

Footner, Hulbert. "Simple Life at Solomons Becomes Thing of Past as Result of War," Baltimore: *The Sun,* 17 January, 1943: 20+.

Frank, Benis M. *Okinawa: The Great Island Battle.* New York: Talisman-Parrish Books, Inc., 1978.

Friedman, Norman. *U.S. Small Combatants, including PT boats, sub-chasers, and the brown water navy: an illustrated design history.* Annapolis: Naval Institute Press, 1987.

Hill, Lt. Perry C. Jr. "Love Charlie Item." *United States Naval Institute Proceedings.* Annapolis: Naval Institute Press. June, 1945. 675-679.

The History of the United States Naval Research and Development in World War II. University of Pittsburgh Historical Staff at US Office of Naval Research. (Cited as Pittsburgh Papers).

Hoyt, Edwin P. *The Last Kamikaze The Story of Admiral Matome Ugaki* . Westport, Ct.: Praeger, 1993.

"Japanese Rocket Bombs With Human Pilots Used at Okinawa but Stir Only Derision." *The New York Times.* 28 April, 1945: 8.

Julien-Binard, Louis. "Souvenirs de Nam-Dinh mars 1954," *La Revue Maritime,* Special Edition Noel, 1956. 1583-1607.

Kaijo Jietai 25 Nenshi/Henshu Kaijo Jietai 25 - Nenshi Hensan Iinkai. (Maritime Self-Defense Forces: 25 Year History) Tokyo: Boeicho Kaijo Bakuryao Kanbu, 1981.

Karig, Walter, Earl Burton and Stephen L. Freeland. *Battle Report Victory in the Pacific.* New York: Rinehart & Company, Inc. 1949.

Katz, Larry. *Diary of a Radioman.*

Kemp, Paul. *Underwater Warriors.* Annapolis: Naval Institute Press, 1996.

"Kerama Isles Won by 77th Division." *The New York Times.* 12 April, 1945: 4.

Krayer, Kenneth R. *On a Ship with No Name The USS LCS(L)(3) 28 in World War Two.* Erie, PA: Kenneth R. Krayer, 1995.

Lancaster, Donald. *The Emancipation of French Indochina.* New York: Octagon Books, 1974.

Lawley, George & Son Corporation. *INSTRUCTIONS FOR LCS(L) (3) I CLASS 1711 - 111 - 30.* Boston (Neponset): MA: George Lawley & Son Corporation, 1944.

"List of Allied Warships Closing In on Jap Isles," *New York Daily News.* 27 August, 1945:42.

Michel, Jacques, Capitaine. *La Marine Francaise En Indochine de 1939 a 1955. Vol. IV Jan. 1950 to April 1953.* Paris: Marine Nationale, Etat-major de la Marine, Service Historique, 1972-1977.

———. *La Marine Francaise En Indochine de 1939 a 1955. Vol. V April 1953 to May 1956.* Paris: Marine Nationale, Etat-major de la Marine, Service Historique, 1972-1977.

Morison, Samuel Eliot. *History of the United States Naval Operations in World War II Vol. XIV Victory in the Pacific 1945.* Boston: Little, Brown and Company, 1960.

Murphy, J.P. Lieut. USNR. *"Well Done Mighty Midgets."* Unpublished essay. 21 July, 1945.

Nagatsuka, Ryuji. *I Was a Kamikaze.* New York: MacMillan, 1974.

O'Neill, Richard. *Suicide Squads, W.W. II: Axis and Allied Special Attack Weapons of World War II.* New York: St. Martin's Press, 1982.

Pierpoint, Powell *The History of the War Cruise of the LCS(L)(3) 61.* Typescript: 1945.

Roberts, Stephen S. "U.S. Navy Building Programs During World War II" *Warship International.* No. 3, 1981: 257.

Sakai, Saburo with Martin Caidin and Fred Saito. *Samurai!* New York: E.P. Dutton and Company, Inc., 1957.

Schloesing, P. "Un Exemple de Collaboration Interarmes Yen-Cu-Ha." in *La Revue Maritime* (October 1951) 1326-1332.

Ship's Data U.S. Naval Vessels Vol. II Mine Vessels (Less CM & DM) Patrol Vessels, Landing Ships and Craft. Washington, D.C.: United States Government Printing Office, 1946.

A Translation from the French: Lessons of the War in Indochina Volume 2. trans. By V.H. Croizat. Santa Monica, CA: The Rand Corporation, 1967.

U.S. Office of Naval Intelligence, " The Dinassau Units of Indochina," *The ONI Review, Secret Supplement*, Autumn 1952. 26-34.

Weller, Colonel Donald M. "Slavo-Splash! The Development of Naval Gunfire Support in World War II." *United Statets Naval Institute Proceeedings*. Annapolis:United States Naval Institute, August, 1954. 839-849.

Woodburn, Alberta. "Is This 'Solomons' Anymore?" *Calvert Independent*. Barstow, Md. 10 June 1943.

World War II History of the Supervisor of Shipbuilding, USN Portland Oregon. circa 1945.

OFFICIAL REPORTS

Commander Amphibious Forces. U.S. Pacific Fleet. *LCS(L)(3) FLOTILLAS, AMPHIBIOUS FORCES, PACIFIC FLEET - Organization of.* 4 May 1945.

Commander in Chief U.S. Pacific Fleet and Pacific Ocean Areas. *Operations in the Pacific Ocean Area During the Month of April 1945.*

Commander Task Flotilla Five (CTG 51.5/31.5). *Action Report Capture of Okinawa Gunto 26 March-21 June 1945.*

Commander Task Force 52 (Amphibious Support Force). *Operations of Task Force 52 in the Iwo Jima Campaign from 10 February to 19 February 1945.*

Commanding Officer *USS LCS(L)(3) 94.* Radar Picket Patrol, Tactical Plans for 20 June, 1945.

Secret Information Bulletin No. 24 *Battle Experience Radar Pickets and Methods of Combating Suicide Attacks off Okinawa March-May 1945.* United States Fleet Headquarters of the Commander in Chief.

United States Naval Forces Vietnam Monthly Historical Summary for October, 1966, December, 1966, March, 1967, July, 1967, June, 1967 (Supplement), May, 1968 (Supplement), February, 1970, July, 1970, October, 1970.

U.S. Naval Technical Mission to Japan. "Report No. S-02 Ships and Related Targets Japanese Suicide Craft." in *Reports of the U.S. Naval Technical Mission to Japan 1945-1946*. 15 January, 1946.

U.S.S. LCS(L)(3) SHIP LOGS

U.S.S. LCS(L)(3)		
	10	10Sep44 to 30Jun45
	21	14Nov44 to 30Jun45
	24	20Oct44 to 30Jun45
	37	10Oct44 to 30Jun45
	51	16Sep44 to 30Jun45
	53	30Sept44 to 30June45
		1Jul45 to 28Feb46
	61	29Nov44 to 30Jun45
	62	4Dec44 to 30Jun45
	64	18Dec44 to 30Jun45
	82	27Nov44 to 30Jun45
	83	30Nov44 to 30Jun45
	84	4Dec44 to 30Jun45
	86	14Dec44 to 30Jun45
	118	23Nov44 to 30June45
	122	8Dec44 to 30Jun45
	127	7Jan45 to 30Jun45

DESTROYER SHIP LOGS

USS Wickes DD 578

INDIVIDUAL SHIP ACTION REPORTS

Action Report - *LCS(L) 18*, 14 April, 1945.

Action Report - *LCS(L) 19*, 18 May, 1945.

Action Report - *LCS(L) 21*, 6 May, 1945.

Action Report - *LCS(L) 27*, 7 March, 1945.

Action Report - *LCS(L) 29*, Manggar-Balikpapan, 2 July, 1945.

Action Report - *LCS(L) 31*, Capture and Occupation of Iwo Jima, 19 February - 8 March, 1945 - 10 March, 1945.

Action Report - *LCS(L) 32*, Capture and Occupation of Iwo Jima, 19 February, 8 March, 1945 - 10 March, 1945.

Action Report - *LCS(L) 33,* Capture and Occupation of Iwo Jima, 19 February - 8 March, 1945 - 10 March, 1945.

Action Report - *LCS(L)(3) 33,* 4 April, 1945.

Action Report - *LCS(L)(3) 35,* 24 April, 1945.

Action Report - *LCS(L) 36,* Capture and Occupation of Iwo Jima, 19 February - 8 March, 1945 - 10 March, 1945.

Action Report - *LCS(L)(3) 40,* 8 August, 1945.

Action Report - *LCS(L) 48,* Mariveles Harbor-Corregidor Operation, 17 February, 1945.

Action Report - *LCS(L) 48,* Philippine Mine Sweeping Operations, 26 February, 1945.

Action Report - *LCS(L) 48,* Sadau and Tarakan Island, Borneo, 1 May, 1945.

Action Report - *LCS(L) 51,* Iwo Jima Island, 10 March, 1945.

Action Report - *LCS(L) 52,* Iwo Jima Island, 11 March, 1945.

Action Report - *LCS(L)(3) 52,* 1 May, 1945.

Action Report - *LCS(L) 54,* Assault and Capture of Iwo Jima, 19 February - 8 March, 1945 - 14 March, 1945.

Action Report - *LCS(L) 55,* Capture and Occupation of Iwo Jima, 19 February - 8 March, 1945, - 10 March, 1945.

Action Report - *LCS(L)(3) 57,* Battle of Okinawa at RP Station # 1, 12 April, 1945 - 15 April, 1945.

Action Report - *LCS(L) 60,* Brunei Bay Operation, 12 June, 1945.

Action Report - *LCS(L) 60,* Miri-Lutong Operation, 21 June, 1945.

Action Report - *LCS(L)(3) 62,* 6 June, 1945.

Action Report - *LCS(L) 80,* Macajalar Bay Operation, 14 May, 1945.

Action Report - *LCS(L)(3) 82,* 12 May, 1945.

Action Report - *LCS(L)(3) 85,* 18 April, 1945.

Action Report - *LCS(L)(3) 86,* 10 June, 1945.

Action Report - *LCS(L) 91,* 3 June, 1945.

Action Report - *LCS(L)(3) 113,* 16 May, 1945.

Action Report - *LCS(L)(3) 114,* 16 April, 1945.

Action Report - *LCS(L)(3) 114,* 12 August, 1945.

Action Report - *LCS(L)(3) 115,* 16 April, 1945.

Action Report - *USS LSM(R) 190*, 18 August, 1945.

LSM(R) 189 Report of Anti-Aircraft Action by Surface Vessels. 1 May, 1945.

OFFICIAL DISPATCHES, LETTERS, COMMUNIQUES

ALPOA Dispatch 23 June, 1945.

CINCPAC-CINCPOA, Monthly Operations Report, May, 1945.

Commander in Chief Amphibious Training Command (Undated, *circa*. 1946).

Commander LCS(L)(3) Flotilla Four. Speedletter. 7 July, 1945.

Commander Task Force 51, Okinawa. U.S. Naval Communications Service. Official Dispatch. 28 April, 1945.

Commander Task Force 51. 24 May, 1945.

Commander Task Force 51. 28 May, 1945.

Commander Task Force 51. 29 May, 1945.

Commander Task Group 51 to TF 51. 24 April, 1945.

Commander Task Group 51.5. Dispatch 1230. 29 April, 1945.

Commanding Officer *DD 774*. 15 May, 1945.

Commanding Officer *LCS(L)(3) 61*. Letter to Commander LCS(L)(3) Group 11. 1 April, 1945.

Commanding Officer *LCS(L)(3) 61*. Letter 11 July, 1945.

Commanding Officer *LCS(L)(3) 61*. "Monthly War Diary of LCS(L)(3) 61, 81, 82 and 83." 1 April, 1945.

ComPhibGroup Six Attack Plan.

COMSERVPAC to CNO 30 June, 1945.

DD 475 Dispatch 0155 5 June, 1945.

Memo for Capt. C.D. Wheelock, Head, Design Br. Shipbuilding Division BuShips, 23 May 1944, no file, subj: LCI(L) Origin of Design.

Officer in Charge *LSSL 67* to Commander, Florida Group, Atlantic Reserve Fleet. 16 July, 1953.

SHIP AND FLOTILLA HISTORIES

Arison, R.R. *War History Commander LCS(L) Flotilla One* 20 November, 1945.

Division of Naval History, Ship's History Section, Navy Department. "History of USS LCS(L) or *LSSL 10, 31, 33, 38, 53, 84*" Most compiled in 1945 or 1955. Individual 2-3 page reports.

Phillips, N. Commander *LCS(L) Flotilla Four. War History*: 8 January, 1946.

PERSONAL INTERVIEWS

Blakley, Earl A. Commanding Officer *LCS(L) 43.* Telephone interview 2 February, 1997.

Cardwell, John H. *LCS(L) 61.* Personal interview. 25 August, 1995.

DeCoursey, Edgar. *LCS(L) 61.* Personal interview. 25 August, 1995.

Jensen, Albert P. *LCS(L) 61.* Personal interview. 25 August, 1995.

Longhurst, Walter. *LCS(L) 61.* Personal interview. 28 July, 1995.

Rielly, Robert F. *LCS(L) 61.* Personal interview. 10 June, 1995.

Scrom, William J. *LCS(L) 61.* Personal interview. 25 August, 1995.

CORRESPONDENCE

Baumler, Raymond. *LCS(L) 14.* Letters of 12 August, 1996 and 4 November, 1997.

Columbus, Joe. *LCS(L) 61.* Letter to the author. 25 August, 1995.

Do, Kiem. Deputy Chief of Staff for Operations, Vietnamese Navy. Letter to the author. 19 June, 1998.

McCool, Richard M. Commanding Officer *LCS(L) 122.* Letter to the author. 22 May, 1997.

Nguyen, Ngoc. Commanding Officer *No Than HQ225* (ex *105*). Letter to the author. 26 May, 1998. E-mail to the author. 26 May, 1998.

Nguyen, Quyen Ngoc. Commanding Officer *No Than HQ 225* (ex *105*). Letter to the author. 17 June, 1998. E-mail to the author. 17 June, 1998.

Nguyen, Sinh The. Commanding Officer *Nguyen Duc Bong HQ 231* (ex *129*). Letter to the author. 5 June, 1998.

Pierpoint, Powell. *LCS(L) 61.* Letter to the author. 18 September, 1995.

Rang, Le Van. Commanding Officer. *Linh Kiem HQ 226* (ex *4*). Letter to the author. 8 July, 1998.

Scrom, William J. *LCS(L) 61.* Letter to the author. 16 May, 1995.

Sellis, Mark V. Executive Officer *LCS(L) 61.* Letter to the author. 8 July, 1995.

Staigar, Joseph. *LCS(L) 61.* Letter to the author. 17 July, 1995.

Tunacao. Diofonce F. Naval Adjutant, Philippines Navy. Letter to L. Richard Rhame. 4 August, 1993.

WORKS CONSULTED

BOOKS - PERIODICALS - NEWSPAPERS

Angelucci, Enzo and Paolo Matricardi. *World War II Airplanes Volume 2*. New York: Rand McNally & Company, 1977.

The AMPHIBS Amphibious Training Command United States Atlantic Fleet. Atlanta: Albert Love Enterprises.

Aoki, Michiko Y. and Margaret B. Dardess. "The Popularization of Samurai Values A Sermon by Hosoi Heishu." *Monumenta Nipponica* XXXI, 4 (1976) 393-413.

"'Baby Flat Top' Hit By A Suicide Plane." *New York Times*. 19 August 1945: 3.

Bagnasco, Erminio. *Submarines of World War Two*. Annapolis: Naval Institute Press, 1977.

"A 'Baka Bomb' Tries to Hit a Destroyer." *New York Times*. 20 May 1945: 2.

Ball, Donald L. *Fighting Amphibs The LCS(L) in World War II*. Williamsburg, VA: Millneck Publications, 1997.

Bartley, Lt. Col. Whitman S. *Iwo Jima: Amphibious Epic*. Washington, D.C.: U.S. Government Printing Office, 1954.

"Battle of the Seas." *Time Magazine*, 9 July 1945.

Baumler, Raymond A. *Ten Thousand Men and One Hundred Thirty "Mighty Midget" Ships The U.S.S. LCS(L)s in World War II*. Rockeville, MD: PIP Printing, 1992.

Belote, James and William. *Typhoon of Steel, The Battle for Okinawa*. New York: Harper & Row, 1970.

Benedict, Ruth. *The Chrysanthemum and the Sword*. Cleveland: Meridan Books, 1967.

Bertoch, Marvin J. *The Little Ships*. Salt Lake City: J.B. Bertoch, 1989.

Blackman, Raymond V.B. ed. *Jane's Fighting Ships 1950-73* 23 Vols. New York: Arco Publishing Co., 1950-1972.

Borton, Hugh. *Japan's Modern Century*. New York: The Ronald Press Company, 1955.

Brooks, Lester. *Behind Japan's Surrender*. New York: McGraw-Hill Book Company, 1968.

Bradley, John H. and Jack W. Dice. *The Second World War: Asia and the Pacific*. Wayne, NJ: Avery Publishing Group, Inc. 1989.

Breuer, William B. *Retaking the Philippines America's Return to Corregidor and Bataan: October 1944-March 1945*. New York: St. Martin's Press, 1986.

Brown, Delmer M. *Nationalism in Japan*. Berkeley: University of California Press, 1955.

Bureau of Ships Number LCS(L)(3) - 1 - SO107 - 527661 Designed by George Lawley & Son, Corporation Boston (Neponset), Mass. USA. (directions for running the ship and its equipment).

Caiger, John. "The Aims and Content of School Courses in Japanese History, 1872-1945" in *Japan's Modern Century* ed. by Edmund Skrzypczak. Tokyo: Sophia University, 1968. 51-81.

"Chronique Des Forces Maritimes D'Extreme-Orient." in *La Revue Maritime*. Editions of March, April, May, July, August, Sept., Oct., 1953, March, April, May, Aug., Christmas, 1954, Jan. 1955.

"Chronique de la Marine Militaire Francaise," *La Revue Maritime*.(Oct. 1952) 1315-1324.

Chumbley, Stephen., ed. *Conway's All The World's Fighting Ships 1947-1995*. Annapolis: Naval Institute Press, 1983.

Cole, Merle T. *Cradle of Invasion: A History of the U.S. Naval Amphibious Training Base, Solomons, Maryland, 1942-1945*. Solomons , MD: Calvert Marine Museum, 1984.

Coletta, Paolo E. "Daniel E. Barbey Amphibious Warfare Expert." in Leary, William M. ed. *We Shall Return! MacArthur's Commanders and the Defeat of Japan 1942-1945*. Lexington, KY: University Press of Kentucky, 1988. 208-243.

———. Ed. *United States Navy and Marine Corps Bases, Domestic*. Westport, Connecticut: Greenwood Press, 1985.

Colton, F. Barrows. "Winning the War of Supply." *The National Geographic Magazine*. December, 1945, 705-736.

Commander First Naval District. *United States Naval Administration in World War II*. Vols. VIII & IX. 1946.

Commander in Chief Pacific Fleet. *United States Naval Administration in World War II Amphibious Forces*. Volumes 1,2,3,4.

Connery, Robert H. and Paul T. David. "The Mutual Defense Assistance Program," *The American Political Science Review*. June, 1951. 321-347.

Conway's All The World's Fighting Ships 1947-1982. Part II: The Warsaw Pact and Non-Aligned Nations. Annapolis: Naval Institute Press, 1983.

Cooney, David M. *A Chronology of the U.S. Navy 1775-1965*. New York: Franklin Watts, Inc., 1965.

Craig, William. *The Fall of Japan*. New York: Dial Press, 1967.

Craven, Wesley F. and James L. Cate, eds. *The Pacific: Matterhorn to Nagasaki, June 1944 to August 1945*. Chicago: University of Chicago Press, 1948-58.

Davis, Jim. *The USS LCS(L)(3) 112: a history*. Typescript, February, 1997.

"Destroyer Set To Go Home is Sunk, 152 Lost." *New York Times*. 7 July, 1945: 3.

Devillers, Philippe and Jean Lacouture. *End of a War Indochina, 1954*. New York: Frederick A. Praeger, Publishers, 1969.

Dictionary of American Naval Fighting Ships Vols. I - IV 1950-1969. Washington: United States Government Printing Office, 1959, 1963, 1968, 1969.

Dolloz, Jacques. *The War in Indo-China 1945-54*. trans. By Josephine Bacon. Savage, MD: Barnes and Noble Ltd., 1990.

Downes, James W. Y2c USNR. *The Mighty Midgets*. Typescript. 1945.

Eller, Rear Admiral Ernest McNeill, *et. al.* eds. *Dictionary of American Naval Fighting Ships Volume V 1970*. Washington: United States Government Printing Office, 1970.

Elliot, Peter. *Allied Minesweeping in World War 2*. Annapolis: Naval Institute Press, 1979.

Fahey, James C. *The Ships and Aircraft of the United States Fleet — 1939 First Edition*. Annapolis: Naval Institute Press, 1977.

————. *The Ships and Aircraft of the United States Fleet — Two-Ocean Fleet Edition*. Annapolis: Naval Institute Press, 1977.

————. *The Ships and Aircraft of the United States Fleet — War Edition*. Annapolis: Naval Institute Press, 1977.

Fairbank, John K., Edwin O. Reischauer and Albert M. Craig. *East Asia The Modern Transformation*. Boston: Houghton Mifflin Company, 1965.

Feifer, George. *Tennozan The Battle of Okinawa and the Atomic Bomb*. New York: Ticknor & Fields, 1992.

Feis, Herbert. *Japan Subdued The Atomic Bomb and the End of the War in the Pacific*. Princeton: Princeton University Press, 1961.

Friedman, Norman. "Amphibious Fire Support," *Warship Vol. IV*. London: Conway Maritime Press, 1980. 199-205.

————. "Amphibious Fire Support: Post War Development," *Warship Vol. IV*. London: Conway Maritime Press, 1980. 234-243.

Fukuya, Hajime and Martin E. Holbrook. "Three Japanese Submarine Developments," *United States Naval Institutes Proceedings*. Annapolis: Naval Institute Press, August, 1952. 863-867.

Fulton, William B. Major General. *Riverine Operations 1966-1969*. Washington, D.C.: Department of the Army, 1973.

"General MacArthur Establishes Authority in Tokyo." *New York Times*. 8 September 1945: 2.

Gow, Ian. *Okinawa 1945 Gateway to Japan*. New York: Doubleday & Company, Inc. 1985.

"Greatest Sea Air Battle." The Milwaukee Journal. April 4, 1950.

Gregory, Barry. *Vietnam Coastal and Riverine Forces Handbook*. Wellingborough, Northamptonshire, England: Patrick Stephens Limited, 1988.

Grosvenor, Melville Bell. "Landing Craft for Invasion." *The National Geographic Magazine* July, 1944: 1-30.

Harbold, Commander Robert P. Jr. "Letter Response to Kaiten Article by Yokota." *United States Naval Institute Proceedings*. Annapolis: Naval Institute Press. July, 1962. 118-119.

Harrison, E.J. *The Fighting Spirit of Japan.* London: W. Foulsham & Co., Ltd. (no date given)

Historical Section Amphibious Training Command. *Commander in Chief Atlantic Fleet Amphibious Training Command. Vol. II.*

Hooper, Edwin Bickford, Dean C. Allard and Oscar P. Fitzgerald. *The United States Navy and the Vietnam Conflict Volume I The Setting of the Stage to 1959.* Washington, D.C. Naval History Division, Department of the Navy, 1976.

Hoshino, Kota. *The Mission of Japan and the Russo-Japanese War.* Yokohama: Fukuin Printing Company, 1904.

Hoyt, Edwin P. *MacArthur's Navy.* New York: Orion Books, 1989.

Hoyt, Edwin P. *Closing the Circle: War in the Pacific, 1945.* New York: Van Nostrand Reinhold Company, 1982.

"The Human Buzz Bomb." *The New York Times.* 3 June 1945: 8E.

Inoguchi, Rikihei and Tadashi Nakajima, with Roger Pineau. *The Divine Wind: Japan's Kamikaze Force in World War II.* Annapolis: U.S. Naval Institute, 1958.

Isley, Jeter A. and Philip A. Crowl. *The U.S. Marines and Amphibious War.* Princeton: Princeton University Press, 1951.

Kaijo Jietai Zen Kan Tei to Ko Kuki (Maritime Self-Defense Forces: All Warships, Small Boats and Naval Aircraft). Tokyo: Kaijo Jieitai, 1960.

Karig, Walter, Earl Burton and Stephen L. Freeland. *Battle Report The Atlantic War.* New York: Rinehart & Company, 1946.

Kawamura, Yoya. "Letter Response to Kaiten Article by Yokota." *United States Naval Institute Proceedings*. Annapolis: Naval Institute Press. July, 1962. 119.

King, Fleet Admiral Ernest J. *U.S. Navy At War 1941-1945 Official Reports to the Secretary of the Navy.* Washington: United States Navy Department, 1946.

Kirsch, Robert W. ed. *The Story of a New Ship of War L.C.I. (L). . .Landing Craft Infantry (Large).* USS LCI National Association, 1997.

Koburger, Charles W. *The French Navy in Indochina: Riverine and Coastal forces, 1945-54.* New York, Praeger, 1991.

Ladd, J.D. *Assault from the Sea 1939-45.* New York: Hippocrene Books, Inc. 1976.

Lawrence, W.H. "Plane Losses Top Japanese Output." *The New York Times,* 25 April, 1945: 9.

———. "Ryukyu Glory Won by Little Ships". New York: *The New York Times,* 29 June 1945: 3.

LCS(L) Landing Craft Support (Large). Paducah, Kentucky: Turner Publishing Company, 1995.

"The Little Ships". *Time Magazine* 9 July 1945: 37.

Lorelli, John A. *To Foreign Shores U.S. Amphibious Operations in World War II.* Annapolis: Naval Institute Press, 1995.

Lott, Arnold S. *Brave Ship Brave Men.* Annapolis, Md. United States Naval Institute, 1986.

Love, Robert W. Jr, *History of the U.S. Navy 1942-1991.* Harrisburg, Pa.: Stackpole Books, 1992.

Luvas, Jay and John F. Shortal "Robert L. Eichelberger MacArthur's Fireman." in Leary, William *We Shall Return! MacArthur's Commanders and the Defeat of Japan 1942-1945.* Lexington, KY: University Press of Kentucky, 1988. 155-177.

Marolda, Edward J. *By Sea, Air, and Land: an Illustrated History of the U.S. Navy and the War in Southeast Asia.* Washington: Navy Historical Center, Dept. of the Navy, 1994.

Martin, Arthur. *LCS (L) (3) 88 - Brief History of the Ship -* Typescript. *circa* 1995.

Martin, Paul W. "Kamikaze!" *United States Naval Institute Proceedings.* Annapolis: United States Naval Institute, August, 1946. 1055-1057.

Mason, William J. *U.S.S. LCS(L) (3) 86 "The Mighty Midget."* San Francisco: William J. Mason, 1993.

McCandless, Rear Admiral Bruce. "Letter Response to Kaiten Article by Yokota." *United States Naval Institute Proceedings.* Annapolis: Naval Institute Press. July, 1962. 119-120.

McClintock, Robert. "The River War in Indochina," *United States Naval Institute Proceedings,* December, 1954. 1303-1311.

Medal of Honor 1861-1949 The Navy.

Meyer, Richard M. "The Ground-Sea Team in River Warfare." in *Riverine Warfare: Vietnam. A Collection of Writings.* Naval History Division, Office of Chief of Naval Operations. Washington: Government Printing Office, 1972.

"Mighty Midgets in U.S. Navy." *Evening Bulletin.* 16 July 1945: 6.

Millot, Bernard. *Divine Thunder: The Life and Death of the Kamikazes.* New York: McCall, 1971.

Mooney, James L. ed. *et. al.* eds. *Dictionary of American Naval Fighting Ships Volume VI 1976.* Washington: United States Government Printing Office, 1976.

Mooney, James L. ed. *Dictionary of American Naval Fighting Ships Vol. VII.* Washington, D.C.: Naval Historical Center Department of the Navy, 1981.

Moore, Captain John RN ed. *Jane's Fighting Ships 1975-1984.* 14 Vols. New York: Franklin Watts Inc., 1975-1988.

Mordal, Jacques. *Marine Indochine [The Navy in Indochina].* trans. by Norman L. Williams and A. W. Atkinson. Paris: Le Livre Contemporain - Aimot-Dumont, 1953.

Morison, Samuel Eliot. *History of U.S. Naval Operations in WWII. Vol. 13. The Liberation of the*

Philippines: Luzon, Mindanao, The Visayas - 1944-1945. Boston: Little, Brown and Company, 1959.

Muth, Frank P. *History of the LCS(L) 9.* Undated typescript.

Naito, Hatsuho. *Thunder Gods The Kamikaze Pilots Tell Their Story.* Tokyo: Kodansha International, 1989.

Nakazato, Yanosuke. "Japanese National Traits and Kendo or Japanese Fencing," *Japan Illustrated 1934.* Tokyo, 1934. 918-920.

Navy and Marine Corps Awards Manual. Washington D.C.:Department of the Navy Headquarters, U.S. Marine Corps Bureau of Naval Personnel, 2 November, 1953.

Nichols, Major Charles S. Jr. and Henry I. Shaw, Jr. *Okinawa: Victory in the Pacific.* Washington, D.C. Historical Branch G-3 Division Headquarters U.S. Marine Corps, 1955.

Nitobe, Inazo. *Bushido The Soul of Japan.* New York: G.P. Putnam's Sons, 1905.

———. "Bushido The Moral Ideas of Japan." *The Japan Current.* April, 1908 : 21-26.

———. *The Japanese Nation.* New York: G.P. Putnam's Sons, 1912.

O'Ballance, Edgar. *The Indo-China War 1945-1954 A Study in Guerrilla Warfare.* London: Faber and Faber, 1964.

"Okinawa Invasion Balked Baka Bomb." *New York Times.* 2 July, 1945: 3.

"Okinawa Picket Line." Editorial. *New York Times.* 30 June, 1945: 16.

Ortoli, P. "La Marine Francaise en Indochine," *La Revue Maritime* (October 1952) 1497-1505.

Polmar, Norman. *Aircraft Carriers A Graphic History of Carrier Aviation and its Influence on World Events.* Garden City, N.Y.: Doubleday & Company, Inc. 1969.

Record of the Bureau of Ships (Record Group 19) 1940-47 Landing Craft Ship (L) 1-130 #5606 (Plans - LCS (L) Mark 3) Microfilm in National Archives, College Park, MD.

Reischauer, Edwin O. and John K. Fairbank. *East Asia The Great Tradition.* Boston: Houghton Mifflin Company, 1960.

Roscoe, Theodore. *United States Destroyer Operations in World War II.* Annapolis, MD: United States Naval Institute, 1953.

Sansom, George. *A History of Japan to 1334.* Stanford: Stanford University Press, 1958.

———. *Japan A Short Cultural History.* New York: Appleton-Century-Crofts, Inc., 1962.

Schnepf, Edwin A. Ed. *Hell on the Beach Landing Craft at War.* Challenge WW II Special Volume 1 Number 2, 1994. Canoga Park, CA: Challenge Publications, Inc. 1994.

Schreadley, R.L. "The Naval War in Vietnam, 1950-1970." In Uhlig, Frank, ed. *Naval Review,* 1966. Annapolis, U.S. Naval Institute. 182-209.

Sharpe, Captain Richard RN ed. *Jane's Fighting Ships 1989-1991* 2 Vols. New York: Jane's Publishing Co., 1989-1990.

———*Jane's Fighting Ships 1996-1997.* Coulsdon, Surrey: Jane's Information Group Limited, 1996.

Silverstone, Paul H. *US Warships of World War 2.* Annapolis: Naval Institute Press, 1989.

Simpich, Frederick. "As 2000 Ships are Born." *The National Geographic Magazine.* May, 1942. 551-588.

Skates, John Ray. *The Invasion of Japan Alternative to the Bomb.* Columbia, S.C.: University of South Carolina Press, 1994.

Smethurst, Richard C. *A Social Basis for Prewar Japanese Militarism.* Berkeley: University of California Press, 1974.

Smith, Stanley E. *The United States Navy in World War II.* New York: Random House, 1969.

Spector, Ronald H. *Eagle Against the Sun.* New York: The Free Press, 1985.

Steenstrup, Carl. "The Imagawa Letter; A Muromachi Warrior's Code of Conduct That Became a Tokugawa Schoolbook." *Monumenta Nipponica* XXVIII, 3 (1973) 295-316.

Strope, Walmer E. "On Japanese Naval Rearmament," *United States Naval Institute Proceedings.* June 1950, 575-584.

"5 Suicide Planes Fail to Sink Escort Ship." *New York Times.* 1 July, 1945: 3.

Summers, Harry G. Jr. *Road to the Killing Fields The Cambodian War of 1970-1975.* College Station, Texas: Texas A & M. University Press, 1997.

Taylor, Michael J.H. *Jane's Encyclopedia of Aviation.* 5 Vols. Danbury, CT: Grolier Educational Corporation, 1980.

Thomas, Charles. *Dolly Five: A Memoir of the Pacific War.* Chester, VA: Harrowgate Press, 1996.

"Tiny Submarines Destroyed in East." *New York Times.* 3 December, 1945: 2.

"Tokyo Reveals Origin of 'Human Rockets'." *New York Times.* 30 May, 1945: 3.

Toland, John. *The Rising Sun The Decline and Fall of the Japanese Empire 1936-1945.* New York: Random House, Inc., 1971.

Torisu, Kennosuke and Masataka Chihaya. "Japanese Submarine Tactics," *United States Naval Institute Proceedings.* Annapolis: United States Naval Institute, February, 1961. 78-83.

Trumbull, Robert. "U.S. Must Keep Pacific Air Bases For Peace of World, Arnold Says." *New York Times.* 25 June 1945: 1+.

Turner, Admiral Richmond K. "Kamikaze." *United States Naval Institute Proceedings.* Annapolis: United States Naval Institute, March, 1947. 329-331.

"2 U.S. Destroyers Sunk Off Okinawa." *New York Times.* 5 July, 1945: 3.

U.S.N.A.T.B. Scrapbook. Solomons, Maryland, 1944.

Vander Linde, Dean M. *Downfall: The American Plans for the Invasion of Japan in World War II.* East Lansing: Department of History, Michigan State University, 1987.

Vogel, Bertram. "Who Were the Kamikaze?" *United States Naval Institute Proceedings*. Annapolis: United States Naval Institute, July, 1947. 833-837.

Walton, Bryce. "Booby-Trapped Boat Kills 5 Americans." *The New York Times*. 3 April, 1945: 4.

Warner, Denis and Peggy Warner. *The Sacred Warriors: Japan's Suicide Legions.* Melbourne: Van Nostrand Reinhold Company, 1982.

Wells, W.C. "The Riverine Force in Action, 1966-1967." in *Riverine Warfare: Vietnam. A Collection of Writings.* Naval History Division, Office of Chief of Naval Operations. Washington: Government Printing Office, 1972.

Westcott, Alan ed. *American Sea Power Since 1775.* Chicago: J.B. Lippincott Company, 1947.

Wheeler, Keith, et. al. *The Road to Tokyo.* Alexandria, Va.: Time-Life Books, Inc. 1979.

Yamamoto, Tsunetomo. *Hagakure The Book of the Samurai.* trans. by William Scott Wilson. Tokyo: Kodansha International Ltd., 1970.

Yokoi, Rear Admiral Toshiyuki. "Kamikazes and the Okinawa Campaign." *United States Naval Institute Proceedings.* Annapolis: United States Naval Institute, May, 1954. 504-513.

Yokota, Yutaka and Joseph D. Harrington. "*Kaiten*. . .Japan's Human Torpedoes."*United States Naval Institute Proceedings*. Annapolis: United States Naval Institute, January, 1962. 54-68.

OFFICIAL REPORTS

Commander Amphibious Group Six Task Group 78.1* *Brunei Attack Group Report of Amphibious Attack on Brunei, Borneo 19 June 1945.*

Commander in Chief U.S. Pacific Fleet and Pacific Ocean Areas. *Operations in the Pacific Ocean Areas During the Month of February, 1945.* (Also March, April, May, June, 1945)

Memo for Capt. C.D. Wheelock, Head, Design Br. Shipbuilding Division BuShips, 23 May, 1944, no file, subj: LCI(L) Origin of Design.

Secret Information Bulletin No. 25. *Battle Experience Encountering Typhoons or Storms June-August 1945.* Navy Department Office of the Chief of Naval Operations.

Security Assistance Program Ships and Craft Summary. Naval Sea Systems Command, 1 October, 1992.

United States Naval Forces Vietnam Monthly Historical Summary with Supplements. 1966 through 1971.

U.S.S. LCS(L)(3) SHIP LOGS

Deck Log USS LCS(L)(3)	*1*	20Jun44 to 30Jun45
	2	19Jul44 to 30Jun45
	3	31Jul44 to 30Jun45
	4	11Aug44 to 30June45
	5	21Aug44 to 30June45

	1Jul45 to 31Dec45
6	27Aug44 to 30June45
	1Jul45 to 31Dec45
7	29Aug44 to 31Dec44
8	31Aug44 to 30Jun45
	31Aug44 to 30Jun45
9	6Sep44 to 30Jun45
11	1Jul45 to 30Jul46
12	17Sep44 to 30Jun45
14	1Jul45 to 30May46
17	30Sep44 to 30Jun45
18	1Jul45 to 3Jun46
19	7Oct44 to 30June45
20	10Oct44 to 30Jun45
22	1Jul45 to 23May46
28	8Sep44 to 30Jun45
29	12Sep44 to 30Jun45
30	16Sep44 to 30Jun45
	1Jul45 to 3Jun46
31	20Sep44 to 30Jun45
32	23Sep44 to 30Jun45
	1July45 to 31Dec45
	1Oct47 to 31Dec48
33	27Sep44 to 28Feb45
35	1Jan45 to 30Jun45
	1Jul45 to 13Aug46
36	1Jul45 to 31Jan46
	1Feb46 to 18Sep46
42	26Oct44 to 30Jun45
43	1Jan45 to 30Jun45
	1Jan46 to 28Oct46
45	1Jan46 to 28Oct46
48	26Aug44 to 30Jun45
50	11Sep44 to 30Jun45
	1Jan46 to 28Oct46
51	1July45 to 31Dec45
54	9Oct44 to 30Jun45
55	16Oct44 to 30Jun45
56	1Jul45 to 12Jun46
57	30Oct44 to 30Jun45
59	1Jul45 to 30Apr46
65	26Dec44 to 30Jun45
67	1Jul45 to 28Feb46
	1Mar46 to 20Aug46
70	1Jul45 to 31Jul46

74	26Feb45 to 30Jun45
78	1Dec45 to 8Aug 46
85	9Dec44to 30Jun45
89	27Dec44 to 30Jun45
96	24Jan45 to 30Jun45
97	1Jul45 to 7Aug46
98	2Feb45 to 30Jun45
99	5Feb45 to 30Jun45
100	1Jul45 to 31Jan46
	1Feb46 to 10Aug46
101	13Feb45 to 30Jun45
102	1Jul45 to 12Aug46
103	24Feb45 to 30Jun45
104	28Feb45 to 30Jun45
117	19Nov44 to 30Jun45
125	17Dec44 to 30Jun45
128	29Dec44 to 30Jun45
	1July45 to 1Dec45
129	31Dec44 to 30Jun45
130	3Jan45 to 30Jun45

DESTROYER AND LSM(R) SHIP LOGS

LSM(R) 189
USS Brown DD 546
USS Claxton DD 571
USS Massey DD 778
USS Van Valkenburgh DD 656
USS Saufley DD 465

INDIVIDUAL SHIP ACTION REPORTS

Action Report, Commanding Officer, *U.S.S. Hugh W. Hadley* (*DD 774*) 15 May, 1945.

Action Report - *LCS(L)(3) 19,* 12 April, 1945.

Action Report - *LCS(L)(3) 19,* 18 May, 1945.

Action Report - *LCS(L)(3) 21,* 6 May, 1945.

Action Report - *LCS(L) 29,* Manggar-Balikpapan, 2 July, 1945.

Action Report - *LCS(L) 31,* Capture and Occupation of Iwo Jima, 19 February, 8 March, 1945 - 10 March, 1945.

Action Report - *LCS(L) 32,* Capture and Occupation of Iwo Jima, 19 February - 8 March, 1945 - 10 March, 1945.

Action Report - *LCS(L) 33,* Capture and Occupation of Iwo Jima, 19 February - 8 March, 1945 - 10 March, 1945.

Action Report - *LCS(L) 36,* Capture and Occupation of Iwo Jima, 19 February - 8 March, 1945 - 10 March, 1945.

Action Report - *LCS(L)(3) 48,* Zambales, Luzon Operation, 31 January, 1945.

Action Report - *LCS(L)(3) 48,* Mariveles Harbor-Corregidor Operation, 17 February, 1945 .

Action Report - *LCS(L) 48,* Sadau and Tarakan Island, Borneo, 1 May, 1945.

Action Report - *LCS(L) 54,* Assault and Capture of Iwo Jima, 19 February - 8 March, 1945 - 14 March, 1945.

Action Report - *LCS(L) 55,* Capture and Occupation of Iwo Jima, 19 February - 8 March, 1945, - 10 March, 1945.

Action Report - *LCS(L) 60,* Miri-Lutong Operation, 21 June, 1945.

Action Report - *LCS(L) 61,* 1 April to 21 June, 1945.

Action Report - *LCS(L) 80,* Macajalar Bay Operation, 14 May, 1945.

Action Report - *LCS(L) 88,* Anti-aircraft action off Okinawa Shima, 11 May - 16 May, 1945.

Action Report - *LCS(L)(3) 90,* 1 June, 1945.

Action Report - *LCS(L)(3) 91,* 9 June, 1945.

Action Report - *LSM(R) 189,* Report of Anti-Aircraft Action by Surface Vessels. 1 May, 1945.

Action Report - *LSM(R) 190,* 18 August, 1945.

Action Report - *LSM(R) 192,* 6 May, 1945.

LCS Group Eleven Composite Action Report Okinawa Gunto 1 April, 1945 - 21.

OFFICIAL DISPATCHES, LETTERS, COMMUNIQUÉS

Aylward, T.C. Capt USN. Speedletter to the Chief of the Bureau of Ships. 26 July, 1945.

Broshele, J.J. by direction of Chief of Bureau to Chief of Naval Operations. 11 August, 1945.

Chief of Naval Operations. "George Lawley & Son Corp'n. LCI Conversion Program at." 1 August, 1945.

Chief of Naval Operations to COMSERVPAC. 30 June, 1945.

Commander in Chief U.S. Pacific Fleet and Pacific Ocean Areas. "Operations in the Pacific Ocean Areas During the Month of April 1945."

Commander LCSFlot4 Speedletter. 29 June, 1945.

Commander Task Force 31. 29 May, 1945.

Commander Task Force 31. InfoCom 3RT FLT. 29 May, 1945.

Commanding Officer *LCS(L)(3) 61.* "Letter to Commander Amphibious Forces, U.S. Pacific Fleet." 16 May, 1945.

Commanding Officer *LCS(L)(3) 61.* "Letter to Commander Amphibious Forces, U.S. Pacific Fleet. 11 July, 1945.

Commanding Officer *LCS(L)(3) 61.* "Letter to Lt. James W. Kelley U.S.N. (389715) 5 March, 1946.

Commanding Officer *USS LCS(L)(3) 94. Radar Picket Patrol, Tactical Plans for.* 20 June, 1945.

LCS 35 and *36* from Lt. Chickering 20 May, 1945.

LCS(L)(3) Group Eleven. "Letter to Lt. (jg) Mark V. Sellis. 5 September, 1945.

Sims, J.H. Officer in Charge *LSSL 67.* "Letter to Commander, Florida Group, Atlantic Reserve Fleet." 16 July, 1952.

SupShip, USN, Quincy, OinC, George Lawley & Son Corp'n. "Letter to George Lawley & Son Corp'n. LCS(L) Program - 70 Additional Vessels." 15 May, 1945.

U.S. Naval Communications Service Amphibious Forces Pacific. Communique. 23 June, 1945.

SHIP AND FLOTILLA HISTORIES

Commander LCS(L) Flotilla Three *Factual History of Commander LCS(L) Flotilla Three Staff* 21 November, 1945.

Division of Naval History, Ship's History Section, Navy Department. "History of USS LCS(L) or *LSSL 10, 16, 19, 25, 34, 38, 53, 63, 82, 118, 122*" (Most compiled in 1945 or 1955) These are individual 2-3 page reports.

Mannert L. Abele DD 733 compiled in 1952.

PERSONAL INTERVIEWS

Blyth, Robert. *LCS(L) 61.* Personal interview. 25 August, 1995.

Burgess, Harold H. *LCS(L) 61.* Personal interview. 25 August, 1995.

Davis, Franklin M., Sr. *LCS(L) 61.* Personal interview. 25 August, 1995.

Katz, Lawrence S. *LCS(L) 61.* Personal interview. 25 August, 1995.

Kaup. Harold. *LCS(L) 15.* Telephone Interview. 29 September, 1996.

Kelley, James W. Commanding Officer *LCS(L) 61.* Telephone Interview. 18 December, 1995.

McCool, Richard. Commanding Officer *LCS(L) 122.* Telephone Interview. 21 May, 1997.

Sellis, Mark V. Executive Officer *LCS(L) 61.* Personal interview. 25 August, 1995.

Staigar, Joseph. *LCS(L) 61.* Personal interview. 14 July, 1995.

MISCELLANEOUS PAPERS AND CORRESPONDENCE

Barnby, Frank L. *LCS(L) 13.* Correspondence.

Blyth, Robert. *LCS(L) 61.* Collected papers and photographs, correspondence.

Burgess, Harold H. *LCS(L) 61.* Correspondence and photographs.

Cardwell, John H. *LCS(L) 61.* Collected papers and correspondence.

Clark, James P. Communications Officer *LCS(L) 61.* Letter and photographs.

Columbus, Joe. *LCS(L) 61.* Collected papers and photographs.

Dionis, Nisi L. *LCS(L) 44.* Collected papers and photographs.

Kelley, James. Commanding Officer, *LCS(L) 61.* Collected papers and photographs.

Longhurst, Walter. *LCS(L) 61.* Collected papers and photographs.

Moulton, Franklin. *LCS(L) 25.* Collected papers, letter and photographs.

Peterson, Phillip E. *LCS(L) 23.* Collected papers, letter and photographs.

Rielly, Robert F. *LCS(L) 61.* Collected papers and photographs.

Robinson, Ed to Lester O. Willard. Letter. 10 January, 1991.

Sellis, Mark. Executive Officer *LCS(L) 61.* Collected papers and photographs.

Scrom, William J. *LCS(L) 61.* Collected papers and photographs.

Selfridge, Allen. *LCS(L) 67.* Collected papers and photographs.

Staiger, Joseph. *LCS(L) 61.* Diary and collected papers.

Strobbe, Frank L. Letter to Ray Baumler re: Flotilla Five History. 4 March, 1992.

Vu, San Huu. Deputy Chief of Staff, Vietnamese Navy Headquarters N3. Letters to the author. 24 June, 8 July, 1998, E-Mail to the author. 10 June, 27 June, 28 June, 1998.

Wackenhut, Norman H. Commanding Officer *LCS(L) 91.* Collected papers and photographs.

MAPS

Okinawa Gunto. Prepared by Objective Data Section G2 USAFPOA. 1944.

Okinawa Shima Briefing Chart. CinCPac-CinCPOA No. D-2165. December, 1944.

FILMS

Department of the Navy. *United States Navy Training Film The LCS(L)(3) Description and Employment.* 1945.

Mason, William. *The Last Battle: Okinawa.* (*circa* early 1990s).

The Saga of the LCS(L) 14. (*circa* early 1990s).

INDEX